THE
ONLY
MATH BOOK
YOU'LL EVER
NEED

THE
ONLY
MATH BOOK
YOU'LL EVER
NEED

Stanley Kogelman, Ph.D.
and
Barbara R. Heller

A DELL TRADE PAPERBACK

A DELL TRADE PAPERBACK
Published by
Dell Publishing
a division of
The Bantam Doubleday Dell Publishing Group, Inc.
1 Dag Hammarskjold Plaza
New York, New York 10017

Dell ® TM 681510, Dell Publishing Co., Inc.

ISBN: 0-440-50007-9

Reprinted by arrangement with Facts on File, Inc.
Printed in the United States of America
March 1988
10 9 8 7 6 5 4 3 2 1
MV

For my daughter, Laura,
who makes me glow with
love and pride.

S.K.

For my husband, Norman,
who taught me about the
things that really count.

B.R.H.

Contents

Preface

The first time we talked about this book was in the airport, waiting for a flight to Rochester, New York, where we were giving a workshop for college mathematics professors on how to teach math in a nonanxiety-producing way.

We had been conducting these workshops at various college campuses for several years, believing that people's dislike of mathematics stemmed largely from the way it had been taught to them—with lots of rigid rules that did not allow for creative approaches to the solution of problems—and from the fact that it dealt with seemingly irrelevant problems, like coins and "distances."

We were a good workshop team. Stan, who is extremely math competent, felt strongly that mathematics was not only an important skill, but had a logic and internal elegance that made solving problems fun. Barbara, while not exactly a math pro, works with budgets, statistics and computers everyday at work. She agreed that mathematics is a *necessary* skill but was not convinced it could be enjoyable.

Our back-and-forth discussions about math and about the way typical students learn it stimulated the teachers in the workshops to question their classroom methods and their expectations for students. As a result, all of them became more attuned to students' reactions; many changed their teaching techniques.

However, the workshps also made it clear that there were no math materials for adults. Even with new teaching strategies, teachers rarely applied them to the daily kinds of situations involving mathematics that most adults face. Which brings us to that day in the airport.

We began to talk about a book that would address the mathematics in real-life situations, and that would be written in a way that balanced Stan's facility with math with Barbara's need to study each of the underlying steps.

Some time has elapsed between our initial idea and the day that *The Only Math Book You'll Ever Need* went to press. In that time, as a result of doing the background research and of talking about the book to friends, colleagues and acquaintances, the book changed character, developing a somewhat different emphasis. It still deals with adult issues—math for finances, recreational math and the kind of math you need around the house—and it's filled with facts and ideas that we found interesting. But we played down the theory considerably. While we still showed all the mathematical steps you need to follow, we rarely explained anything general about decimals, percentages or fractions. Writing about math, just like *doing* math, requires a great amount of patience and practice—and a great amount of space. You will find many places in this book where a seemingly simple example or statement takes several pages to explain step by step.

We used the background materials to lull you into doing the math necessary to compute perimeters, calculate effective yields and figure out arithmetic means. In this way we felt you would stick with it through the computations.

We hope that after reading this book you will be more open to approaching math-based problems; more willing to attempt the math yourself and more likely to undertake a greater analysis of your own affairs, thereby gaining an added measure of control. More control is really what it's all about.

We would like to know about your experiences. Did you enjoy this book or parts of it? Were you able to adapt it to your own circumstances? Did the explanations flow logically? Were the examples realistic? Do you now have a better grasp of the underlying math? Did it raise some new questions that you'll want to research? Will you share it with a friend? Is it really the only math book you'll ever need?

Stanley Kogelman
Barbara R. Heller

Introduction

Buying this book entailed a financial transaction. It also required a mathe matical operation—subtraction—to give you the correct change, plus percentages, multiplication and addition if you live in a place that has a sales tax.

Every time you spend money, make change or use your credit card charge, you are presented with some aspect of everyday math.

The mathematics of money calls for a range of skills. There's subtraction for computing change, and percentages when you need to figure out the amount of tip or sales tax. Percentage increases (or decreases) come into play when you are dealing with inflation; exponents underlie the compound interest formula which goes into decisions about borrowing or investing money; statistics are involved in budgeting; and logarithms are a necessity in computing how long it takes to reach your investment goals.

While financial matters may make the most critical demands on your skills, spending money is not the only daily activity that involves math. Mathematics pervades things people do for fun, such as driving a sports car, traveling abroad or taking photographs. Building a fence requires an understanding of "perimeter"; the concept of "area" comes in when you carpet your den; recipes need to be doubled or halved; and sewing a round tablecloth makes use of the geometry of a circle.

Everyday math appears in the daily newspaper: in advertisers' claims as well as in business and economic news analyses, sports statistics, science reports and lottery games. And this doesn't begin to count the math that people need at work!

Many adults give up choosing the *best* alternative because they can't, or won't, tackle problems that have to do with numbers. Still others allow decisions to be made for them by a sales clerk, bank teller, spouse, waiter or friend instead of doing the arithmetic themselves. Being willing to do your own everyday math—which means being able to work comfortably with percentages and the four basic operations of addition, subtraction, multiplication and division of whole numbers, fractions and decimals—can put you back in control. Being in control:

* Makes you feel good about yourself.
* Saves you money.
* Makes you a more powerful consumer.
* Boosts your confidence.
* Lets you have more fun.
* Expands your options.
* Reassures you.

It may even make you a better cook.

The math you need to be self-reliant is the same math you were taught, and supposedly learned, in elementary school. But most of us were not taught how to apply math concepts to practical, adult life situations. Classroom math was taught—and unfortunately continues to be taught—so that children can learn *more* classroom math. It was taught, and is still being taught, by grade school teachers, many of whom have not themselves mastered math's fundamentals and thus teach it poorly, devoting little class time to it.

In 1983, the National Science Board Commission on Precollege Education and Mathematics, Science and Technology reported that:

"Many of the teachers in elementary schools are not qualified to teach math . . . for even 30 minutes a day.

"A significant fraction of . . . secondary school teachers are called upon to work in subjects for which they were never trained.

". . . there are currently severe shortages of qualified math . . . teachers in many parts of the Nation. Fewer college students are entering the teaching profession, particularly math and science teaching, and increasing numbers of experienced teachers . . . are leaving."

Since 1972 there has been a 77% decrease in the number of high school math teachers prepared for teaching, and only 55% of those who are prepared choose to teach.

The situation is becoming worse.

Largely because of inadequate training and preparation, math is being taught by means of rules and regulations that are neither correct nor helpful to the student. And it is being taught by insecure professionals who, unfortunately, introduce guilt, dislike and anxiety into the subject.

Its hardly surprising, then, that a majority of people grow up with poor skills and uneasy feelings about math. In some cases the negative feelings become so extreme that otherwise capable, intelligent adults can hardly do math at all.

It's no wonder that most young students stop taking math courses as soon as they are free to make the choice. The National Science Board Commission found that, "since the late 1960s, most students have taken fewer mathematics courses. Mathematics . . . achievement scores of 17-year-olds have dropped steadily and dramatically during the same period.

". . . 62 percent (of U.S. students) do not take Algebra II (in high school), 48 percent do not take geometry . . . Algebra I enrollments fell to 64 percent in 1981 from 76 percent in 1969."

In the First International Mathematics Survey, conducted in 1964, the achievement scores of U.S. students tended to be lowest of all the countries tested, at least for 18-year-olds. The results of the Second International Math Survey are similar.

Since coping with our world requires more math than ever, our schools should require *more* math and better trained teachers. The world abounds with statistics, calculators, computers. It has been estimated that 80% (that's eight out of 10!) of all jobs today involve computers directly or indirectly. The number of home microcomputers has already surpassed 4 million. Even the choice of a savings account, once a simple decision, now presents complex options, including variations in interest rates, compounding periods and length of time of deposit. Greater earnings are available to the person who takes the time to figure out the alternatives. And that's only one benefit to be gained from mastering basic math.

The Only Math Book You'll Ever Need helps you solve practical financial problems: balancing your checkbook, comparing investment alternatives and determining mortgage payments. It shows you how to convert foreign currency and offers aids for cooking and sewing. It fills in the gap between what you were once taught and what you need to know now.

Because we want this book to be useful, we show you *what to do,* escorting you through the mathematics so you can compute for yourself the amount of paint you need for an $8'5'' \times 12'6''$ room or how much interest you have to pay if you charge the new raincoat. And we include both timely tips, such as how to estimate when the exact amount doesn't matter, and realistic encouragement, such as "Count on your fingers if it helps you." Many of us are secret finger-counters anyway, despite the repeated admonishments of teachers and parents.

The Only Math Book You'll Ever Need is a collaborative effort of two people whose combined experience totals more than 50+ years (that's statistics for you!)

Dr. Stanley Kogelman was chairman of the Mathematics Department at the State University of New York at Purchase for five years. He spent 20 years as a classroom teacher, covering everything from remedial math for adults to math-beyond-Calculus for mathematics majors. Dr. Kogelman has taught regular mathematics courses and in special programs, working with individuals and small groups, and with students, prospective teachers and teachers-as-students. His consulting company, "Mind Over Math," and book of the same name have summarized some of his experiences with learners of all kinds and have brought him national prominence as a champion of the math-anxious person. Dr. Kogelman has been instrumental in defining how attitudes and feelings affect learning and in proposing techniques to ameliorate negative attitudes toward learning.

A Ph.D. in mathematics and the holder of an M.S.W. degree, he is also a research mathematician whose esoteric specialty—nonlinear partial differential equations (which describe such diverse phenomena as the flow of water through pipes and the motion of oil heating in a frying pan)—puts him on the frontier of mathematics.

Professor Barbara R. Heller is also an expert in the problems people have with math, although she approaches it through their difficulties in managing money and in making career decisions. Trained as an experimental psychologist, she worked on instrument panel design in single fighter jets and the deterioration in reaction time as a function of visual stimuli overload. Professor Heller has devoted the last 30 years to educational problems. For the past five years, she has been Director of Special Educational Programs at the Graduate School and University Center of the City University of New York, and she has served since 1973 as a Senior Project Director at the Center for Advanced Study in Education.

Professor Heller studies the way people learn, be they high school students, college students or adults. She designs new programs for them, often creating new courses of study and designing new materials that incorporate the new technologies. She is known throughout the country for her pioneering work in computer-assisted guidance, adult literacy, cooperative education (learning in non-classroom settings) and teacher training.

Kogelman and Heller have been working together since 1978, mostly on ways to change how mathematics is taught in high school and college classrooms. By training and re-training new generations of math teachers, they hope to increase the skills and improve the attitudes of today's students—who will become tomorrow's adults.

The Only Math Book You'll Ever Need is their expert solution for *today's* adults who want to deal effectively with the math in their lives.

Don't read it from beginning to end. Browse through it. Each topic is self-contained and has all the instructions you need. Read the section you need when you need it. Go through the steps. After a while, you'll see that everyday math really requires mastery of only a few basic ideas. This book reviews these ideas as you need them.

The bulk of the book, which focuses on the things most adults have to deal with in real life, is organized into three major divisions.

Part One is about money and the mathematics of personal finance. The chapter on earnings and taxes covers estimating earnings, finding percent increases and assessing tax brackets. The banking chapter is comprised of sections on how to balance a checkbook, compute simple and compound interest and estimate penalties for early withdrawals. Part One also covers investments, such as time deposit certificates, stocks and bonds and tax-deferred annuities and, in addition, long-term loans, such as mortgages, credit card payments and installment buying.

Part Two, Outdoor Math, has to do with such topics as eating out, markups and discounts on clothes and appliances and sales tax. A chapter on foreign travel covers the conversion of currency, temperature, measures (metrics) and electricity. Under hobbies, games and gambling, you'll find out how to adjust the f-stop on your camera and compute odds and probabilities.

Indoor Math situations are covered in Part Three. There's kitchen math, which discusses recipe conversion, timing recipes and unit pricing. Home improvement shows you how to compute area, buy paint or build a fence. "Utility" math is the math you need to read your gas or electric meter or phone bill. The section on home computers addresses the question of what they do and who needs one.

We use calculators, and *The Only Math Book You'll Ever Need* shows the key sequence for most calculations, as well as the paper-and-pencil steps. If you don't already own a small calculator, buy one. Look for a model that has some "memory," a "power" key and a square root key. Consider buying one that has a "log" button as well. A conveniently sized calculator with all these features sells for between $15 and $25—a worthwhile investment for doing all the math you'll ever need.

PART ONE

THE MATHEMATICS OF PERSONAL FINANCE

1

Earnings
and Taxes

Section 1: When Is a Lot a Little?
(Percent Increases/Decreases)

Last week at dinner, a friend announced how pleased he was with his $2,000 raise. The woman sitting next to him said that, in her opinion, $2,000 was not very special, while the third member of the party described it as "inadequate."

How can the same raise seem so vastly different to three people?

When you talk about things like raises or other increases in prices, you don't really know how much they represent until you compare them to the *base amount*—that is, the amount *before* the raise. For example, if the $2,000 increase brought your salary from $18,000 to $20,000, the *percent increase* would be considered significant by most people. However, for someone earning $10,000, an additional $2,000 would be a great boost. But it's only a so-so change for a person with a base salary of $50,000.

Here's how

Evaluating the significance of the raise requires that you be able to compute the percent increase you received. When you ask, "What is the percent increase?" you are asking, "What percent of the base amount is the increase?"

To find the percent increase, first divide the amount of the increase by the old (base) salary and then multiply by 100%:

3

Percent increase = (amount of increase ÷ base amount) × 100%

In our example, the amount of the raise was $2,000. Let's suppose that the first dinner guest's base salary is $10,000:

Percent increase = (2,000 ÷ 10,000) × 100% = 20%
By calculator:
PRESS 2,000 ⊟ 10,000 ▤ ☒ 100 ▤

In other words, the $2,000 represents a 20% salary increase to this man.

His female dinner companion earns $18,000, so that a $2,000 raise for her means a percent increase of 11.1%:

Percent increase = (2,000 ÷ 18,000) × 100% = 11.1%
By calculator:
PRESS 2,000 ⊟ 18,000 ▤ ☒ 100 ▤

(Incidentally, 11.1% is a good raise, but not nearly as good as 20%.)

The third person discussing the $2,000 raise viewed it as fairly paltry in light of the fact that her base salary is $50,000:

Percent increase = (2,000 ÷ 50,000) × 100% = 4.0%

The raise would be the equivalent of a 4.0% increase over her base salary.

So a raise of the same amount has different meanings depending on how large a portion it is of the base salary. In our little story, the significance of $2,000 depends on where you sat at dinner—or the base you started from.

Now let's consider another example of a percent increase. Suppose your rent went from $450 to $480 a month. The percent increase in your rent is:

Percent increase = (30 ÷ 450) × 100% = 6.7%

The 30 is the difference between $450 (your old rent) and $480 (your new, increased amount).

All percent increase problems are done the same way. Knowing this, let's consider what a 100% increase means. *It is when the amount of the increase is the same as the base amount.* For example, if your rent increased from $450 to $900 (which we hope won't happen to you):

Percent increase = (450 ÷ 450) × 100% = 100%

Although it may seem that prices and costs *never* decrease, there are times when this happens and you need to compute the *percent decrease.*
Here's how

PERCENT DECREASE — -$65

Because you were offered a new job in another company that has better working conditions, higher status and a brighter outlook for advancement, you are willing to consider a salary offer of $22,000, which is less than the $25,000 you are now making. This represents a reduction of $3,000.

To find the percent decrease, divide the amount of the decrease by the base amount (that is, the amount *before* the decrease) and then multiply by 100%:

Percent decrease $= (3,000 \div 25,000) \times 100\% = 12\%$
* *By calculator:*
PRESS 3,000 ÷ 25,000 ⊟ ⊠ 100 ⊨

Let's try another percent decrease problem. As a result of a move to a less expensive location, your rent dropped from $600 to $535 per month.

First, find the amount of the decrease $(600 - 535 = 65)$ and then the percent decrease:

Percent decrease $=$ (amount of decrease $\div$ base amount) $\times 100\%$
$= (65 \div 600) \times 100\% = 10.8\%$

The *process* of finding the percent increase (or decrease) is the same regardless of the context: salary raises, rent reductions, increases in the gross national product and percent markdowns on store merchandise are all instances of this type of problem.

But there's another type of related problem.

Suppose your boss tells you that you are going to be getting a 12% raise but doesn't tell you the amount of the raise. If your old salary was, let's say, $16,000, to find the new amount, you must first convert the percent to a decimal.
Here's how

CONVERTING PERCENTS TO DECIMALS 12% = .12

To convert a percent to a decimal, divide the percent by 100. (That's because the word "percent" means hundredths.) For example:

$$12\% = \frac{12}{100} = 12 \div 100 = .12$$

Similarly, 8.25% converts to the decimal .0825, like this:

$$8.25\% = \frac{8.25}{100} = 8.25 \div 100 = .0825$$

By calculator:
PRESS 8.25 ⊡ 100 ⊟

You'll notice that dividing by 100 has the effect of moving the decimal point two places to the left, so remember this rule: *to convert a percent to a decimal, move the decimal point two places to the left.*

To figure out the amount of your 12% raise and your new salary, first multiply the base salary by the decimal equivalent of the given percent:

12% of $16,000 = .12 × $16,000 = $1,920
By calculator:
PRESS .12 ⊠ 16,000 ⊟

This gives you the dollar amount of the 12% raise. So, the new salary equals $17,920 which is the old salary ($16,000) plus the raise ($1,920).

You can compute the new salary in one operation, like this:

New salary = (% raise ÷ 100) × base salary + base salary
or
New salary = (12 ÷ 100) × $16,000 + $16,000
By calculator:
PRESS 12 ⊡ 100 ⊟ ⊠ 16,000 ⊟ ⊞ 16,000 ⊟

This one-step calculation gives you the total amount of your salary with the raise, but *not* the amount of the raise.

Here's another example to consider. You read that prices have risen 11.5% during the last year because of inflation. This means that goods and services now cost 11.5% more than they did a year ago. If you paid $250 for a suit last year, what would that same item cost you today?

First, convert 11.5% to a decimal and calculate the increase:
$$11.5\% = 11.5 \div 100 = .115$$
$$.115 \times \$250 = \$28.75 \text{ (the suit will now cost \$28.75 } \textit{more)}$$

Then add the percent increase to the base amount to find the total cost today:

$$\$28.75 + \$250 = \$278.75$$

You can do it in one operation.

Total cost $= (11.5 \div 100) \times 250 + 250$
By calculator:
PRESS 11.5 ⊟ 100 ⊟ ⊠ 250 ⊟ ⊞ 250 ⊟

There's another very handy shortcut way of solving these percent increase problems, but it requires you to think about the problem somewhat differently.
Here's how

PERCENT INCREASES AS 100 + %   112%

Let's go back to the earlier example of the 12% raise (on a salary of $16,000) in which we added the amount of the raise (which we had to compute using decimals) to the old salary. In other words, the new salary is equal to the old salary *plus* the amount of the increase.

The shortcut approach is to think of the new salary as equal to 112% of the old salary; that is, the value of the old salary (100%) plus the value of the raise (12% of the old salary). To find the new salary directly with this method, all that has to be done is to compute 112% of the base salary:

New salary $= (100\% + \% \text{ increase})$ of base salary
$\qquad\quad = (100\% + 12\%)$ of $16,000
$\qquad\quad = 112\%$ of $16,000 $\left\{ \begin{array}{l} \text{Notice that the percent still must} \\ \text{be converted to a decimal.} \end{array} \right.$
$\qquad\quad = 1.12 \times \$16,000$
$\qquad\quad = \$17,920$

Now let's do the inflation rate problem by the shortcut method:

New cost = [100% (old cost) + 11.5% (inflationary increase)] of base
  amount
  = 111.5% of $250
  = 1.115 × $250
  = $278.75

It's rather fun to do percent increase problems this way. There's a certain elegance to thinking about a 7% raise as 107% of the base salary, and it's a technique almost guaranteed to impress your dinner companions.

Section 2: How Much Do I Earn?

It is always surprising—and disheartening—to look at your take-home pay after taxes and other deductions are subtracted. Your gross pay—the actual amount you earn before taxes and other payroll deductions—appears to be an almost mythical amount of money that never actually passes through your hands. And, indeed, it is mythical for all practical purposes since you can spend only "net" dollars.

When you get over the dismay of seeing how much is taken out of your salary, you may start wondering about particular deductions and why your paycheck may not be exactly the same each pay period.

Here's how

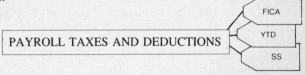

PAYROLL TAXES AND DEDUCTIONS

FICA

YTD

SS

There are at least 2, probably 3 and possibly as many as 4 different kinds of taxes charged against your salary by government.

First, there is *federal income withholding tax*, probably your single largest deduction. "Withholding" tax, first adopted in 1943, is a method by which the U.S. government collects—in advance—a large proportion of the income tax that it anticipates you will owe based on your salary. The amount of the tax withheld from your paycheck is based on your earnings and the number of dependents claimed on your W-4 withholding form. The more dependents you claim, the less is taken from your salary; the fewer the dependents, the more money is deducted.

While withheld federal taxes do not vary from pay period to pay period (unless there was a change in your gross salary or in your deductions), the *Social Security tax* deduction can change. Social Security tax, which is different from withholding tax, is also referred to as F.I.C.A. (Federal Insurance Compensation Act). In 1986, the Social Security deduction was calculated at 7.15% of wages up to a maximum taxable wage of $42,000. Every employee pays the same 7.15% of income up to $42,000. Even if you earn more than that amount, there is nothing more taken from your salary or credited to your Social Security pension account. The employer deducts Social Security and matches the deduction with a like amount. The self-employed pay a higher rate; in 1986, they paid 12.30 of their income up to $42,000.

The maximum Social Security deduction in 1986 was 7.15% of $42,000 or $3,003.00. (Since percent means hundredths, $7.15\% = 7.15 \div 100 = .0715$ and $.0715 \times 42,000 = 3,003.00$.) When your income exceeds $42,000 and nothing more is deducted, your take-home pay should increase by the amount of Social Security subtracted from previous paychecks.

Since all but seven states levy a state income tax (the ones that don't are Alaska, Florida, Nevada, South Dakota, Texas, Washington and Wyoming; Connecticut, New Hampshire, Pennsylvania and Tennessee don't tax personal and/or earned income), it is likely that state taxes may also be taken out of your gross salary. Like federal income taxes, state income taxes account for a like amount each pay period if there are no changes in claimed dependents or in wage level.

Similarly, if you live in a city that imposes a city income tax, that too may appear as a regular deduction throughout the year.

Other regular payroll deductions can include the employee's contribution to health, life and/or disability insurance premiums; savings bonds; credit union dues; union and other agency dues; savings plans and stock plans; certain kinds of loans; and the employee's portion of unemployment insurance.

Irregularly, your take-home pay may reflect charges for lost work time (penalties for lateness or absence lower your gross pay and, therefore, your net pay)—just as your gross salary may reflect extra money earned for overtime. Court liens (i.e., salary attachments or garnishments) for outstanding debts can also effect the amount of money you take home.

So, whether your paycheck is generated by computer or handwritten personally by the boss or bookkeeper, it is a good idea to do the arithmetic that will tell you whether your *net pay* is correct.

To determine your net pay, write down the amount of each deduction (checking each to be sure it applies to you). Next, add up all the deductions to arrive at a total. This total subtracted from your gross pay should equal your net pay for that pay period.

How do you find out your *gross pay* for a given pay period?

Salaries (which are invariably stated in gross amounts) are usually quoted on an annual, weekly or hourly basis. Pay periods are usually weekly, biweekly (which means every two weeks, *not* two times each week) or monthly. Given your salary for any time period, it is possible to compute your salary for any other time period.

Suppose your salary is quoted on an annual basis and you get paid weekly. You need to find your weekly salary.

Here's how

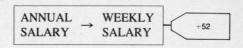

Since there are about 52 weeks in a year (there are actually 52.143 weeks in a year; 365 days ÷ 7 = 52.143), divide your annual salary by 52 to get your weekly salary.

For example, if your annual salary is $18,500:
$18,500 ÷ 52 = $355.77
By calculator:
PRESS 18,500 ⊟ 52 ⊟

If you get paid biweekly, divide your annual salary by 26 (52 weeks ÷ 2):
By calculator:
PRESS 18,500 ⊟ 26 ⊟

A good *estimate* of a weekly salary is obtained by dividing the annual salary by 50 instead of 52. Dividing by 50 is the type of calculation that can often be done in your head. In our example, the estimated weekly salary on $18,500 would be $370. (Compare this estimate to the actual $355.77 we obtained when we did the calculation based on 52 weeks.)

Now suppose your salary is given on an annual basis and you want to compute your monthly salary.

Here's how

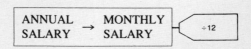

Computing a monthly salary from an annual salary is done by dividing the annual salary by 12 (since there are 12 months in a year).

For example, using our sample salary of $18,500:
$18,500 ÷ 12 = $1,541.67
By calculator:
PRESS 18,500 ÷ 12 =

If you want to compute your hourly pay when your salary is given annually, two steps are required.
Here's how

```
┌─────────────────────────────────┐
│ ANNUAL   →   HOURLY             │
│ SALARY       SALARY             │
└─────────────────────────────────┘
```

First, convert your annual salary to a weekly salary as we did above and then divide your weekly salary by the number of hours you work a week. This is your hourly wage.

Step 1 $18,500 ÷ 52 = $355.77 per week
Step 2 (if you work 35 hours a week) $355.77 ÷ 35 = $10.16 per hour
Or (if you work 40 hours a week) $355.77 ÷ 40 = $8.89 per hour

So far we have only done examples where the salary is quoted annually. It works the reverse way too.
If your salary is given on a weekly basis, you can determine how much you'll make in a year.
Here's how

```
┌────────────────────────────────────────────────┐
│ WEEKLY   →  ANNUAL  →  MONTHLY   │ ×52, ÷12
│ SALARY                 SALARY    │
└────────────────────────────────────────────────┘
```

Step 1 Multiply your weekly salary by 52 (or by 52.143 to be exact):
$355.77 × 52 = $18,500
By calculator:
PRESS 355.77 × 52 =

Now you've gotten your *yearly* total. Once you know this, you can again find your *monthly salary* by dividing by 12:

Step 2 $18,500 ÷ 12 = $1,541.67

Note that although you know the weekly salary, we do *not* advise that you try to convert directly to a monthly salary because there is not an even number of weeks in a month. (If you feel you *must* convert from a weekly to a monthly salary without stopping to compute the annual salary, use 4.3 weeks per month to do it (52.143 weeks ÷ 12 = 4.3 weeks):

$355.77 × 4.3 weeks = $1,529.81 = approximate monthly salary.

(Compare this to the actual figure of $1,541.67 we obtained before.)

By calculator:
PRESS 355.77 ⊠ 4.3 ⊟

However, if you have your weekly salary, it is easy to find your hourly salary.
Here's how

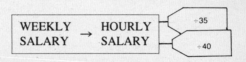

Just divide the weekly figure by the number of hours you work:

$355.77 ÷ 35 or $355.77 ÷ 40 (weekly salary divided by number of hours worked)

If you earn money on an hourly basis, then you can find how much your weekly salary is by multiplying the number of hours you work each week by the hourly amount.
Here's how

Now let's try a new example with different numbers. Let's say your hourly rate is $8.25 and you work a 40-hour week. Your weekly salary is:

$8.25 × 40 = $330 per week

From this figure you could obtain your annual salary by multiplying by 52 (or 52.143).

Now suppose you know your salary on a monthly basis and want to convert this to a weekly salary. You can get an *approximation* by dividing your monthly salary by 4.3 (the average number of weeks per month), but since this is not exact, we suggest you work through an annual salary.

Here's how

MONTHLY SALARY	→	ANNUAL	→	WEEKLY SALARY	×12, ÷52

For example, if your monthly salary is $1,200, then your annual salary is:

$1,200 × 12 = $14,400 per year

In this example, your weekly salary is:

$14,400 ÷ 52 = $276.92 per week

Sometimes salary approximations are useful. You can quickly estimate an annual salary from a weekly salary by multiplying by 50 (instead of 52). So, if a person earns $100 per week, his annual salary is about $5,000 ($100 × 50). This is a good figure to know because it means that each $100 of weekly salary is the equivalent of about $5,000 of annual salary (and vice versa—each $5,000 of annual salary equals about $100 in weekly salary).

So now you can do some quick estimates:

Table 1
Relationship of Weekly and Annual Salaries
(Approximate)

WEEKLY SALARY	ANNUAL SALARY
$ 100	$ 5,000
200	10,000
300	15,000
500	25,000
750	37,500
1,000	50,000

Sooner or later—it usually happens at a particularly boring time at work—almost everyone wonders how much they get paid each *minute*. You can compute this by dividing your hourly salary by 60 (the number of minutes in an hour). Going back to an earlier example:

$10.16 per hour ÷ 60 minutes = $.17 per minute

So, if you earn $18,500 a year for a 35-hour work week, your gross salary for each working minute is $.17! And, if you've spent 45 minutes of company time doing all these computations. . . .

Section 3: More = More (The Meaning of Tax Brackets)

"Our constitution is in actual operation, everything appears to promise that it will last; but in this world nothing can be said to be certain, except death and taxes."

While there is the truth of the inevitability of taxes, as Benjamin Franklin wrote to a friend in 1789, there are many untruths about them as well.

The untruth that we will explore here is one heard frequently: "It doesn't pay for me to earn more (or, alternatively, for my spouse to work) since that would put me into a higher tax bracket where I'd make less that I did before." This myth is the result of a misinterpretation of tax brackets.

Earning more money may indeed place you in a higher tax bracket, but only with respect to *some part of the additional income*. You may pay a higher rate on the *last dollars* earned, but because of the way the tax rate schedule is graduated, the money you made before the increase is not taxed at the higher rate. Making more money *always* means having more available after income taxes—there is no way you can end up with less.

Here's how

TAXABLE INCOME

In any discussion of income taxes, the first thing you need to remember is that taxes are not paid on your total gross income. There are adjustments to income and allowable deductions that can and should be subtracted from the total money you earn.

Allowable adjustments to income may include such things as moving expenses associated with your job, employee business expenses for which you have not been reimbursed, payments into a Keogh or IRA plan (Individual Retirement Account—we'll talk more about these tax deferred annuities in Chapter 3) and other items listed in the Internal Revenue Service (IRS) Form 1040—the booklet the IRS sends taxpayers each year.

Allowable deductions include subtractions from your income for dependents, for certain charitable contributions and medical expenses and for many other items. Your accountant or the free IRS consulting service offered in many cities (or by phone any place) can supply you with complete guidelines about income adjustments and deductions. You should also take advantage of the many books and other free literature that explain allowable deductions. One of the more helpful is the free IRS publication #17, "Your Federal Income Tax," which is available from the Forms Distribution Center in your state. Consult Form 1040 for the address. Be sure to get up-to-date editions of tax publications because tax laws change regularly and what may have been a legitimate item one year may be disallowed the next. (The reverse is also true: new allowable deductions may be added.)

The amount of income remaining after adjustments and deductions have been taken is called *taxable income*. The tax bracket you are in (and, therefore, the taxes you pay) is based on this figure. Increasing your deductions decreases your taxable income so it makes sense to carefully explore all possible deductions for which you are eligible.

Now that we have defined taxable income, we're ready to examine tax brackets—how they are constructed and what they mean. Let's start with tax rate schedules.

Here's how

TAX SCHEDULES

Included in the IRS Form 1040 booklet are several *United States Federal Income Tax Rate Schedules:* one for single taxpayers, unmarried heads of households, married taxpayers filing joint returns and qualifying widows and widowers and married taxpayers filing separate returns. These different tax schedules (another name for charts or tables) apply to different categories of people who are taxed at somewhat different rates for the same income. The first thing to do is to find the rate schedule appropriate for you.

Suppose you are a married taxpayer filing jointly and the combined taxable income for you and your spouse is $26,500. You would use Tax Schedule Y (reprinted in part as Table 1 below) to compute the amount of your tax.

To compute the taxes on the combined income of $26,500, look down column (a), the "Taxable income over" column, until you find the dollar amount *closest to but below* your taxable income. In our example, that would be $21,800—closest to but less than the $26,500 we are using as an illustration.

Next, read across the row of the table to the second column (b), "But

Table 1
1986 United States Federal Income Tax Rate Schedule Y
(for "Married Taxpayers and Qualifying Widows and Widowers")

(a) TAXABLE INCOME OVER—	(b) BUT NOT OVER—	(c) COMPUTE	(d) OF THE AMOUNT OVER—
$ 0	$ 3,670	–0–	—
3,670	5,940	11%	$ 3,670
5,940	8,200	$ 249.70 + 12%	5,940
8,200	12,840	520.90 + 14%	8,200
12,840	17,270	1,170.50 + 16%	12,840
17,270	21,800	1,879.30 + 18%	17,270
21,800	26,550	2,694.70 + 22%	21,800
26,550	32,270	3,739.70 + 25%	26,550
32,270	37,980	5,169.70 + 28%	32,270
37,980	49,420	6,768.50 + 33%	37,980

not over." In our example the amount would be $26,550. This number serves as a check for you because your $26,500 taxable income actually does fall over $21,800 but not over $26,550.

Now go on to the third column (c) and fourth column (d), which together tell you exactly how to compute your tax. In our case, the third and fourth columns say, "Compute $2,694.70 + 22% of the amount over $21,800." To figure out "the amount over" $21,800, take your income and subtract $21,800:

Your income − $21,800 = $26,500 − $21,800
= $4,700 (or the amount you'll pay 22% of)

Now your total tax according to the tax rate schedule directions is computed as follows:

Tax = $2,694.70 + 22% of $4,700
= $2,694.70 + (.22 × $4,700)
= $2,694.70 + $1,034
= $3,728.70

So the total federal tax on $26,500 is $3,728.70.

By calculator:
PRESS .22 ⊠ 4,700 ⊟ ⊞ 2,694.70 ⊟

In this calculation, we first computed 22% of $4,700, then we added $2,694.70. Note that 22% is the *highest* percent or highest tax rate you pay on an income of $26,500, but you don't pay it on the total taxable amount. The highest rate or percentage is what is meant by your *federal tax bracket.* You moved into the 22% bracket when your taxable income fell between $21,800 and $26,550. Had you earned just a little less than $21,800, the highest tax rate would have been 18%—that is the percentage in the row above in the rate schedule.

Going back to the example, though you understand what the 22% means, you may ask, where did the $2,694.70 come from? To find out, we need to go back one row in Table 1. Notice that for incomes over $17,270 but not over $21,800 the taxes are computed as "$1,879.30 + 18% of the amount over $17,270." If your taxable income was $21,800, you would have the highest permissible amount over $17,270. So the maximum "amount over" is:

$21,800 - $17,270 = $4,530

Of this amount, you next compute 18%:

18% of $4,530 = .18 × $4,530 = $815.40

Thus, the *maximum* amount of tax to be paid on incomes in the range of $17,270 to $21,800 is $1,879.30 (column [c]) + $815.40 (.18 × 4,530) = $2,694.70, which is precisely the amount in column (c) for the income range $21,800 to $26,550.

Starting at the top of Table 1, you will see that if your taxable income exceeds $3,670 (but is not over $5,940), the tax rate (for 1986) is 11%. On the next sum of money, the tax is $249.70 (the taxes you'd pay on an income of $5,940) *plus* 12% of the last dollars earned. Thus, the dollar amounts in column (c) are the total taxes on the income up to the amount in column (a), and the percentages—12%, then 14%, 16%, 18%, and so on—apply to the part of your income which is over the column (a) amount but not over the column (b) amount.

This is what a *graduated tax structure* means: each portion of your taxable income is taxed at a different and increasing amount up to a taxable income of $175,250. At this level, and thereafter, the maximum rate is 50% of the amount over $175,250 + $67,553.50 (in 1986, Schedule Y). In other words, regardless of your total taxable income, everyone pays 11% of the first $3,670 to $5,940, 12% of the amount between $5,940 and $8,200, 14% of the amount between $8,200 and $12,840—and on up to the highest rate which applies to your income. It is this highest rate which is referred to as your federal income tax bracket.*

---

*In 1987, the number of tax brackets will be sharply reduced but the concept of "tax bracket" will not change.

Now, let's examine what a raise to a new, higher income means. *Here's how*

MOVING TO A HIGHER BRACKET

In our earlier example, you were in the 22% bracket with a taxable income of $26,500. Now, let's suppose you got a $5,000 raise with no increase in deductions. This would give you a total taxable income of $31,500.

Turning back to Table 1, we find the row in which this income falls: "over $26,550 but not over $32,270." In columns (c) and (d) we see that the tax is:

$3,739.70 + 25% of the amount over $26,550.

Since $31,500 is $4,950 more than $26,550, we must compute 25% of $4,950:

Tax = $3,739.70 + 25% of $4,950
= $3,739.70 + .25 × $4,950
= $4,977.20

So, the total federal tax on an income of $31,500 is $4,977.20.

By calculator:
PRESS .25 ⊠ 4,950 ⊟ ⊞ 3,739.70 ⊟

Again notice that the highest tax rate (25%) only applies to the last $4,950 in income, even though the raise of $5,000 put you into this bracket. Thus, part of the "last dollars" you earned moved you into a new tax bracket, but the new tax rate only affects the tax you pay on the portion of *that* money and not on the money you were earning before the raise.

So, when people say that having a spouse work "isn't worth it because the additional earnings mean higher taxes," they are correct only to the extent that a higher rate is imposed on the *extra* income. What they probably mean is that what's left of this additional income after taxes have been paid does not cover the expenses incurred in going to work—travel costs, housekeeper or baby sitter, new clothes and so on. In our example, a $5,000 increase in income resulted in a tax increase of $1,248.50 ($4,977.20 − $3,728.70). This means you only got to keep $3,751.50 ($5,000 − $1,248.50). This is still a substantial increase. It's up to you to decide if the extra amount of income was worth working for.

There are tax tables in which the exact amount of tax is calculated for all taxable incomes up to $50,000, assuming a standard amount of deductions. But since the arithmetic has already been done for you, you can't determine your tax bracket from these tables.

The federal tax bracket you're in doesn't tell the whole tax story. There may be state and city income taxes as well. State and city taxable income is usually somewhat different (but not dramatically so) from your federal taxable income because of different allowable adjustments and deductions. The tax rates are built on the same kind of graduated scale, however, but state and city rates are generally quite a bit lower than federal rates. For example, for 1986 the highest federal rate was 50%, while the highest New York State income tax rate was 13.5% and the highest New York City income tax rate was 4.3%.

Since these local income taxes can add as much as 17.8% to your tax bill, your overall rate of taxes should take all taxes into account. If your state tax bracket is 10%, your city tax bracket is 3.3%, and your federal tax bracket is 22%, you are paying 35.3% (10% + 3.3% + 22%) of your "last dollar in income" in taxes.*

That's not the worst of it. Earlier in this chapter, we pointed out that Social Security tax is computed at the rate of 7.15% of your gross income up to $42,000—which means that, in addition to federal income taxes that put you in the 22% bracket and state and city taxes that raised your bill to 35.3%, you must add an additional 7.15%.

In our hypothetical example, you could easily end up paying 42.45% (35.3% + 7.15%) of your last dollar in taxes. This means you keep only about 58¢ out of a dollar—out of your last dollar. Remember, not all of your income is taxed at this rate; most is taxed at lower rates and is unaffected by any increases in income. So, the truth is, with additional income you always have some more money available—but not as much more as you would like!

---

*If state and local taxes are deductible, then the effective state and local tax rate would be lower than shown here.

2

Banking

Section 1: Checking It Out: How to Balance Your Checkbook

There are a good many people who, like our friend Arlene, don't ever balance their checkbooks. Many don't even keep records of the checks they write. Why should they bother with these recordkeeping tasks? After all, as Arlene points out, "the bank sends you a statement each month and returns your checks," and, in most cities, automatic teller machines allow you to just insert your bank card for a read-out of your balance.

There are three reasons for *carefully* recording the checks you write and *regularly* balancing your checkbook:

1. What you write in your check register (or on your check stubs) is a permanent record of your transactions. This record is absolutely essential if you want to "stop payment" on a check.
2. Banks can and do make mistakes.
3. Your running "balance forward" is the only accurate, up-to-date estimate of how much you really have in your account at a given time. The automatic teller machines tell you only what has cleared the bank.

Here's how

THE CHECKBOOK REGISTER

Every checkbook, whether for personal or business use, has space for you to write down important information pertaining to each check. Such information usually includes the number of the check, the amount, the date,

20

the name of the person or business to whom the check was drawn and the "purpose" of the check. A brief description of purpose of the check is particularly helpful in preparing tax returns since, for example, the "car registration fee" paid to the motor vehicle bureau may be a deductible expense.

A typical checkbook register looks like this:

Number	Date	Transaction	Fee	Add(+)	Subtract(−)	Balance Forward
		To:				
		For:				
		To:				
		For:				
		To:				
		For:				

Since it only takes a few moments to fill in the register *immediately after writing a check,* why don't all people do it?

All too many people have gotten into the bad habit of carrying loose checks around with them. They don't carry their personal checkbook and register or business account checkbook and register with them because it's too big or inconvenient, but they do carry loose checks "just in case." Also, joint account checkbooks are typically carried by one partner or, more likely, left at home.

There are simple solutions to these problems. If your checkbook is inconvenient to carry for one reason or another, ask your bank for a smaller one that you will keep with you. Then you can fill in the register as you go along. (But you still must remember to transfer these records to the primary checkbook register.) If you have a joint account, ask the bank for an extra checkbook and register so that both parties can carry a checkbook and record all checks as they're written.

The checkbook register enables you to record the fee for each check you write, cash withdrawals (which can be considered as checks to yourself for cash and should be handled as if they were such checks), deposits and errors. We'll come back to errors later.

Suppose your previous balance was $172.20 when you wrote a $15 check (on January 2, 1985, check #150) to the motor vehicle bureau and then paid $46.75 (on January 2, 1985, check #151) to your hairdresser. The next day you wrote a check to the electric company for $48.52 (on January 3, 1985, check #152) and made a deposit of $582.50. If your bank charges a fee of $.10 per check, your register would look like this:

Number	Date	Transaction	Fee	Add(+)	Subtract(−)	Balance Forward
		To:				
		For:				172.20
150	1/2/85	To: Department of Motor Vehicles	.10		15.00	15.00
		For: Car Registration				157.20
151	1/2/85	To: Cutting Impression	.10		46.75	46.75
		For: Perm				110.45
152	1/3/85	To: Con Edison	.10		48.52	48.52
		For: Electric Bill				61.93
	1/3/85	To: Deposit		582.50		582.50
		For:				644.43

So far, so good?

If you've kept this kind of record, you'll have all this information (not proof—the cancelled checks are proof) to help you prepare your tax returns. And, by filling in the "Balance Forward" column, you'll always have an exact record of how much money you have in your checking account.

Now we'll explain how the register was filled in. All we had to do to compute it was to add or subtract accurately.

Here's how

"BALANCE FORWARD"

From the previous pages' transactions, we started with a balance forward of $172.20. We then made two deductions, one for $15 and one for $46.75. By subtraction; the

Balance forward = $172.20 − $15.00 = $157.20
Balance forward = $157.20 − $46.75 = $110.45

After paying the electric bill, we had a running

Balance forward = $110.45 − $48.52 = $61.93

Next, we add in our deposit,

Balance forward = $61.93 + $582.50 = $644.43

so that on January 3 we have a total of $644.43 in our hypothetical account.

Notice something important! While we have recorded the check fee ($.10 per check), *we have not made it part of the running balance*. When we balance the checkbook, we'll account for these fees, but, on a daily basis, it's too confusing to do so and too easy to forget to subtract them. However, for accuracy, our account really has $.30 less in it (3 checks × $.10 per check) than the balance forward indicates.

Keeping your checkbook register filled out systematically is a necessary step in reconciling your accounting with the bank's accounting.

There are several reasons why you and the bank may not agree on how much you have in your account. Sometimes it's because either you or the bank (or both) made an error. You might have recorded the amount of a check or deposit incorrectly, or you might have subtracted or added incorrectly. The bank can also made recording errors, but you can be certain the bank did not make an arithmetic error: the operations of addition and subtraction are completely computerized and computers are perfect at these routine computations—provided they are initially fed the correct numbers.

The most common reason for a discrepancy between your balance and the bank's statement of your balance has to do with what checks and/or deposits have *cleared* the bank. Your balance forward includes *all* checks, cash withdrawals and deposits. The bank statement may not. If a person or company is slow in cashing your check, for example, the bank may not have subtracted that amount from your account and will show a bigger balance than you have. If a deposit made just before the statement was issued has not yet been recorded by the bank, the statement will show your account as smaller than it is.

The process of reconciling your checkbook with the bank statement involves accounting for bank fees, missing checks and unrecorded deposits. It also requires finding mistakes in recordkeeping and/or computation.

Here's how

BALANCING YOUR CHECKBOOK

Every month the bank sends you a statement to tell you what you have in your account according to their records. All the checks you have written that have cleared in the last month are also returned to you.

Balancing your checkbook takes several steps, and we suggest doing them in order. Follow the 10 steps as you would a recipe.

Let's start.

Step 1 *Deposits:* Go through your register and check off all deposits you made that appear on the bank's statement. After you've done this, you will have isolated any deposits you made that the bank has not yet credited to your account. (These will be the unchecked deposits in your register.) Generally, banks handle deposits promptly, but it is still possible that a recent deposit won't show up on this month's statement. If it doesn't appear on the following month's statement, contact your bank immediately. It may have been misplaced.

As you're comparing deposits, make certain that the amount of each one recorded by you and the bank agree. If they don't, go back to your original deposit slip. If the mistake was the bank's, let them know as soon as possible. (We'll tell you what to do about a mistake of yours later under "Finding Errors".)

Step 2 *Cancelled checks:* Start by arranging the returned checks in numerical order (the order you wrote them in).

Go through your check register and check off each cleared check. As you do so, make sure that the amount of the check corresponds to the amount you recorded.

Compare the amount of each cleared check with the amount the statement lists. In this way, you should be able to locate any *transposition error*, the most common type of error you or the bank is likely to make. (A transposition error consists of reversing two numbers, like this:

actual amount   10⑦⑥.54
transposed figure   10⑨⑦.54

Transposition errors are *very* hard to spot.)

At the end of Step 2, your register will have unchecked items—deposits that have not yet been credited to your account and checks that have not yet been debitted to your account (called "outstanding" checks).

Step 3 *Only if you are charged a fee for each check you write* (otherwise, go right on to Step 4): Count the number of checks that were returned to you and multiply this number by the fee you are charged for each check ($.10 in our example). The total will have to be deducted from your balance. More about this later.

Step 4 *Cash withdrawals:* If you have been considering cash withdrawals as a form of check to yourself, they should be recorded in your register.

Compare your bank statement and register, checking off cash withdrawals that appear on the statement. If you find one *you* forgot to record, you'll have to adjust for it (subtract it) later; if you find one the *bank* hasn't cleared, you'll have to add it in when balancing your account.

At this point, all the items that appear in the statement will have been checked in your register—except for fees. You probably have some outstanding checks and maybe an uncredited deposit. If you've been careful, you may have caught a recording error.

Depending on the kind of checking account you have, you may be charged a regular monthly fee, or there may be a charge for new checks or deposit slips or a penalty for returned checks that did not clear for one reason or another. These fees, like per check charges, appear on your statement and will also have to be deducted in the final steps of balancing your checkbook.

Step 5 *The Starting point:* Crucial to balancing your account is starting at the right place. *Start at the last item in your register that you checked.* Write down the balance after the last checked item. Let's suppose that the balance is $929.71.

Number	Date	Transaction		Fee	Add(+)	Subtract(−)	Balance Forward
		To:					
		For:					996.09
160	2/1/85	To: NY Telephone	✓	.10		56.38	56.38
		For: Phone Bill ✓		(last checked item)			929.71
161	2/3/85	To: Macy's				216.47	216.47
		For: lamps					713.24
		To:					
		For:					

Step 6 *Outstanding checks:* List and total all the checks that are outstanding (they should be the items with *no* check mark that come before the last checked item in your register). For example, let's suppose your outstanding checks add up to $251.55.

Step 7 *Cash withdrawals:* Now do the same thing for cash withdrawals *you forgot* to enter in your register. Suppose these total $120.

If you have a record of a cash withdrawal that has not appeared on your statement, you must note it and, in Step 9, treat it like an outstanding check.

Step 8 *Uncredited deposits:* Make a list of any deposits that were not checked off. Find the total. For our example, let's suppose this comes to $92.50.

Step 9 *Reconciling the balance:* First, add the sum of the outstanding checks (Step 6) to the starting balance (Step 5):

$251.55 + $929.71 = $1,181.26

The reason for this is that you subtracted this amount from your register balance, but the bank did not clear these checks. By adding, you are adjusting your total to better accord with the bank's total.

Then subtract the sum of the forgotten cash withdrawals (Step 7) from your balance. Again, you do this to bring your total into closer accord with the bank's total:

$1,181.26 − $120.00 = $1,061.26

Next, the sum of the deposits that were not checked off (Step 8) must be subtracted from the balance because you added this to your register, but the bank has not yet done so. By subtracting this amount, you are bringing your total even closer to the bank's:

$1,061.26 − $92.50 = $968.76

The amount of $968.76 is still not the amount that the bank shows as your closing balance this month because of check fees and service charges. Suppose these total $3.55. Subtract $3.55 as follows:

$968.76 − $3.55 = $965.21

If all has gone well, this is precisely the amount that appears as the "closing balance" on your statement. If it is, you know that you and the bank agree. The account is balanced. However, in our case, there is more to do.

Step 10 *Odds and ends:* Notice that while we considered the service charge in reconciling the account, we never actually wrote this charge down in the register as part of the running total. It's necessary to do so now so it need not be considered again when we get our next statement. Use the first empty line. Identify the period covered and subtract the amount of the service charge from your balance forward.

Also, it's good practice to make a note in the register at the point at which the account balanced—the point of the last checked item. In our example this was at $929.71.

Go back in the register and put a circle around this item to identify it as the balancing point and write something like, "OK to here." When your next bank statement comes, you'll know that any errors made occurred after this point.

Arlene says this is all well and good, but what if the account does not balance after all this work? In that case, you must try to find the source of the error.

Here's how

FINDING ERRORS

If it is a bank error, it was in *crediting or debitting* your account by an incorrect amount. If you've worked through Steps 1–4 comparing your records and the bank's, you will have located the bank's mistake. Notify them at once; some banks give you as many as 30 days to report errors, but for some the limit is 14 days (except for electronic transfers).

If the error is yours, it is most likely to be a *transposition error* which occurred when you transferred a number from one page in your register to the next. *Look for these errors first.*

The next most common type of error is *adding* a check when you meant to subtract it—or, similarly, *subtracting* a deposit that should have been added. Look carefully to be sure you added when you meant to and subtracted when that was the appropriate operation.

Arithmetic mistakes in adding or subtracting are not as frequent as you might suspect. They happen less often than the other kinds of mistakes. But if you still haven't found an error in copying or in crediting or debitting, you need to recheck all your additions and subtractions.

Finally, an error can occur because you did not account for *all outstanding checks or deposits.* You may not have gone back far enough in your checkbook register to pick up an item from several months ago, such as a check that has not yet cleared. If the item concerns a deposit, get in touch with your bank. If it's a check, you might want to contact the person or business you wrote it to to see if it was received or whether you have to stop payment and issue a replacement.

Let's assume you found an error. There are two ways to correct it. The long way involves going back and starting at the point the error was made. If it was in subtraction, you will have to make the correction in each subsequent balance. Then, of course, you will have to reconcile the account again, starting at Step 5!

A less time-consuming way to make a correction is to figure out how much you were off by—too much or too little—and add or subtract that amount using the next blank line in your register. Suppose your mistake was originally in adding a check for $100, rather than subtracting it. The result is that you gave yourself credit for $200 too much ($100 when you added it incorrectly and $100 for not subtracting it correctly). So, to compensate for this mistake, you would have to subtract $200 from your register.

In our example we have to make two corrections. The first is because we forgot to record $120 of cash withdrawals. We also forgot to subtract $3.55 in check fees.

To illustrate the first correction, if the last check you wrote was to Joe's Auto Body for $190, leaving a balance in your account of $434.19, the change would be made in your check register as follows:

Number	Date	Transaction	Fee	Add(+)	Subtract(−)	Balance Forward
		To:				
		For:				624.19
168	2/12/8	To: Joe's Auto Body	.10		190.00	190.00
		For: Car Repairs				434.19
		To:			120.00	120.00
		For: Error - Forgotten Cash withdrawal				314.19
		To:				355
		For: check fees				310.64

Arlene's checkbook is in terrible shape—she hasn't balanced it since she opened it last year. To balance it now is a horrendous, tedious task and probably an impossible one. She might as well accept the correctness of one more statement from the bank—which by now may include several errors for or against her (the ones *for* her she could probably live with)—before she resolves to take charge of her affairs.

So do what Arlene does. Forget the past and move ahead. Open a new checking account in the same bank or another one. As long as you're doing this, you might want to do some research and find a convenient bank—

located where you need it—or with lots of cash machines or extra-long hours. You might also seek a bank that has lower (or better yet, no) monthly service charges, low check charges or no required minimum balance. Look for a bank that pays you interest on your balance. Receiving no interest on a required minimum balance is tantamount to paying a fee since *the bank* is earning interest on your balance, interest that you could be earning yourself.

You can open the new account immediately, but don't close out the old one until all checks have cleared. Then you'll probably have to write one last check to yourself for the final balance, subtracting the fees that you will owe. If you're unsure, bank officers are there to help.

Section 2: A Matter of Interest (Simple and Compound Interest)

When you plan to borrow or invest money, you need to be concerned with interest. Interest rates matter because interest is a *fee*—either charged to you or earned by you as the case may be.

You are investing money with a bank and, in effect, lending the bank money and earning interest when you:

- Deposit money in a savings account
- Buy a certificate of deposit (CD) or savings certificate
- Invest in a money market fund
- Defer your income through an IRA or Keogh plan

The interest you earn is the bank's payment to you for the use of your money. It is to your advantage to get the highest rate of return on your loan.

The bank, in turn, uses your money by investing it in loans to other people and businesses. When money is *borrowed* from the bank, the borrower is charged a fee—interest—for the use of the money. As a borrower, you will be looking for the lowest interest charges.

- A mortgage, for example, is a bank loan to the potential purchaser of a house.
- A car loan (another type of mortgage) is a loan for the purchase of an automobile.
- A student loan enables the borrower to "buy" college tuition.

The mortgagee, car buyer and student each pays the bank interest for the use of money in much the same way that the bank pays *you* interest for the use of *your* money. The bank makes a profit by charging more interest on the money it loans than it pays on the money it borrows.

There are two kinds of interest: simple and compound. *Simple interest* is relatively easy to understand and compute, but it is rarely used. However, in order to understand *compound interest,* it makes sense (no pun intended) to start with an explanation of how simple interest works.

Here's how

SIMPLE INTEREST

Simple interest is usually quoted on a yearly basis; "9% simple interest" means that you would earn 9% of your investment in interest *per year*.

Let's suppose you decided to invest $500 at this rate. Your interest, after a year, would be:

$$I \text{ (for interest)} = 9\% \text{ of } \$500 \text{ for 1 year}$$
$$= .09 \times \$500 \times 1 \qquad \left\{ \begin{array}{l} \text{percent means hundredths,} \\ \text{so } 9\% = 9 \div 100 = .09 \end{array} \right.$$
$$= \$45$$

There is a formula for simple interest:

$$I = Prt$$

The Prt means $P \times r \times t$ (mathematicians are fond of leaving out the multiplication sign), where:

I means Interest
P is the Principal, or amount of money with which you started
r is the annual rate of interest
t stands for the time the money is invested at the rate of interest (r)

Let's apply the formula to the first example again, but now we'll only deposit the money for 6 months (which is $\frac{6}{12} = \frac{1}{2}$ of a year, or .50). We would then earn:

$$I = \$500 \times .09 \times .50$$
$$= \$22.50$$

A shorthand way of looking at this problem is to consider that in 6 months you would earn one-half of 9% or 4.5% of your $500 in interest:

$$I = 4.5\% \text{ of } \$500 \left\{ 4.5\% = \frac{4.5}{100} = .045 \text{ (because \% means hundredths)} \right.$$
$$= .045 \times \$500$$
$$= \$22.50$$

The next example of simple interest involves investing $1,200 at 8% for one year and 3 months. How much interest (I) would you earn? Substituting in the formula, we have:

$$I = 1,200 \times .08 \times 1.25 \left\{ \begin{array}{l} \text{Rate (r)} = 8\% = 8 \div 100 = .08 \\ \text{Time (t)} = 1 \text{ year and 3 months} \end{array} \right.$$
$$= 120 \qquad\qquad\qquad = 1\frac{1}{4} \text{ year} = 1.25$$

So you would earn $120 interest on $1,200 invested at 8% for one year and 3 months.

By calculator:
PRESS 1200 ☒ .08 ☒ 1.25 ▤

That's all there is to simple interest. But interest rates are generally compounded. *The difference between simple interest and compound interest is that with compound interest you earn interest on your interest.*
Here's how

COMPOUND INTEREST

Suppose a bank offers interest at a quoted rate of "12%, compounded monthly." This means you earn one-twelfth of 12%, or 1%, each month.

Let's start with a deposit of $500 that you leave in an account for 6 months. Each month, 1% interest is credited to your account. In each successive month, you earn 1% of the amount you have in your account at the end of the previous month. This amount will include interest that has accumulated each month. The table below shows the interest you'd earn for each of the 6 months.

Notice that each month the amount of interest increases—$5.00 for the first month, $5.05 for the second month and so on. This is because the balance (or principal) is increased each month as a result of the addition of earned interest. In other words, in the first month, 1% interest is earned on $500, but, in the second month, the interest is computed on $505. At the end of 6 months, you have $530.76 in your account.

Table 1
Compound Interest (1% Monthly)

END OF MONTH:	OLD BALANCE	INTEREST (1% OF OLD BALANCE)	NEW BALANCE (OLD BALANCE + INTEREST)
1	500.00	$.01 \times 500.00 = 5.00$	505.00
2	505.00	$.01 \times 505.00 = 5.05$	510.05
3	510.05	$.01 \times 510.05 = 5.10$	515.15
4	515.15	$.01 \times 515.15 = 5.15$	520.30
5	520.30	$.01 \times 520.30 = 5.20$	525.50
6	525.50	$.01 \times 525.50 = 5.26$	530.76

Compare this now with how much simple interest is earned on $500 for 6 months:

$$I = Prt$$
$$I = 500 \times 12 \times .50 \ \{ \ 6 \text{ months} = 6 \div 12 \text{ years} = .50 \text{ years}$$
$$I = 30$$

So, with simple interest, you would earn $30, whereas with compounding, the total interest after 6 months is $30.76. ($530.76 − $500.00). The additional $.76, the result of compounding, is the interest earned on the interest.

Big deal—$.76! Truly a small difference. But that's only because of the small amount of principal we started with and the short period of time we invested it. All other things being equal, the longer the time period, the greater the difference between the interest earned at a simple rate and that earned at a compound rate.

The computation of compound interest in the way we showed it in the chart (by doing 6 simple interest calculations) becomes more time-consuming as the number of compounding periods increases. Imagine how many calculations would have to be done if your deposit was compounded *daily* for the 6 months of your deposit!

There is a formula that allows us to calculate in one operation what the final balance would be ($530.76). The *compound interest formula* is:

$$S = P(1 + i)^n$$

It is read, "S equals P multiplied by 1 plus i to the nth power." Here's how the formula works:

S = the final amount of money (principal *plus* interest)

P = the *Principal,* or the amount we started with (in our example, P = $500) i = *the periodic interest rate divided by 100.* The periodic interest rate is the quoted interest rate divided by the number of times per year that the interest is compounded. To get i, the periodic interest rate is divided by 100. (In our example, the periodic interest rate is 12% ÷ 12 (months) = 1%, and i = 1 ÷ 100 = .01)

n = *the number of interest periods* (6 in the example because the money was deposited for 6 months and interest was credited monthly)

Let's substitute our numbers in the formula:

$$S = 500 \ (1 + .01)^6$$

First note that $(1 + .01) = (1.01)$ and that $500 \ (1.01)^6$ means $500 \times (1.01)^6$.

Raising a number to a power (6 in this case) means multiplying that number by itself *that* many ("6") times, so:

$$(1.01)^6 = 1.01 \times 1.01 \times 1.01 \times 1.01 \times 1.01 \times 1.01$$

You can do this calculation by hand or by using your calculator:

PRESS 1.01 ⊠ 1.01 ⊠ 1.01 ⊠ 1.01 ⊠ 1.01 ⊠ 1.01 ⊟

but you can easily lose count—especially as "n" gets larger (say, if the money was left on deposit for a year and n = 12, or if interest is compounded *daily* for a year and "n" becomes 365).

There is another type of calculator that does this computation faster and in one step. It's the kind that has the capacity to raise any positive number to a *power,* and it's recognizable because it has a button marked either:

Y^x	or	X^y
the positive number Y is to be raised to the "xth" power		the positive number X is to be raised to the "yth" power

This type of calculator is not very expensive (less than $20) and allows you to compute $(1.01)^6$ as follows:

PRESS 1.01 Y^x 6 ⊟ and the result 1.06152 appears.

So, to finish substituting in the formula:

$$S = 500 \times 1.06152 = 530.76$$

This amount of money (principal plus interest) is our balance at the end of 6 months.

Let's do a new example where we don't know the answer beforehand. You have $2,000 in an account that pays interest at the rate of 10%, compounded quarterly. If you leave the money on deposit for one year, how much will you have in your account?

To answer this question, we apply the compound interest formula. The first step is to identify the quantities P, i, and n. In this instance:

P = 2,000
i is obtained by first computing the periodic interest rate 10% ÷ 4 = 2.5%
   (since interest is compounded quarterly, there are 4 compounding periods per year) and then dividing 2.5 by 100. So i = 2.5 ÷ 100 = .025
n = 4, since the deposit remains in the bank for 4 interest periods

Substituting, we have:

$S = P (1 + i)^n$
$S = 2000 \times (1 + .025)^4$
$S = 2000 \times (1.025)^4$

Next, 1.025 must be raised to the 4th power:

By calculator:
PRESS 1.025 $\boxed{Y^x}$ 4 $\boxed{=}$ The result is that $(1.025)^4 = 1.1038$

Continue substituting in the formula:

$S = 2000 \times 1.1038 = 2207.60$

At the end of the year, there will be $2,207.60 in your account, which means that you earned $207.60 in interest ($2,207.60 − $2,000.00) for the year. Compare this to 10% simple interest:

$I = Prt$
$= 2000 \times .10 \times 1 = 200$

Thus, in one year, the effect of compounding is an extra $7.60 in interest.

A compound interest rate always produces more money than the same simple interest rate. All other things being equal, the more frequent the compounding, the more interest you earn. Let's test this by comparing the interest earned in one year on $100 at 10% compounded quarterly, with the interest earned on \$100 at 10% compounded monthly, and at 10% compounded daily. In the first case, compounded *quarterly*, we have:

$$S = 100 \times (1 + .025)^4 = 100 \times 1.1038 = \$110.38$$

If the interest is compounded *monthly*, we have:

$$S = 100 \times (1 + .0083333)^{12} = 100 \times 1.10471 = \$110.47$$

And if there is *daily* compounding, the result is:

$$S = 100 \times (1 + 1.000274)^{365} = 100 \times 1.1052 = \$110.52$$

With *simple* interest we would have earned \$10 for an end-of-year total of \$110.

These small differences have a way of quickly adding up. You might be surprised at how fast your investment can double. If you have a calculator that does *logarithms*, it is possible to figure this out exactly.
Here's how

DOUBLING YOUR MONEY

The following formula allows you to figure out how long it will take to double your money—any amount of money at any rate of interest—but can only be used with a calculator that has a logarithm button $\boxed{\log}$. This is the formula:

$$n = .30103 \div \log(1 + i)$$

In the formula:

n = the number of interest periods
i = the periodic interest rate divided by 100 (just as in the compound interest formula)
log (1 + i) is obtained by first entering 1 $\boxed{+}$ i $\boxed{=}$ in your calculator and then pressing the $\boxed{\log}$ button.

Logarithms are never computed by hand and we will not go into their meaning here. They are usually taught in an intermediate algebra or precalculus course. For now—if you intend to do a lot of these computations, buy a scientific calculator which will do both $\boxed{Y^x}$ and logarithms.

Let's go back to the formula and try a problem. How many *interest periods* does it take to double your money if the interest rate is 10% compounded quarterly?

Earlier in this section, we found that i = .025 when the interest rate is 10% compounded quarterly. So:

$$1 + i = 1 + .025 = 1.025.$$

Next we compute *log* (1.025)

By calculator:
PRESS 1.025 $\boxed{\text{log}}$

You'll find that log 1.025 = .01072. Substituting in the formula:

$$n = .30103 \div .01072 = 28.08$$

It takes 28.08 interest periods (quarters in this case) to double your money. That is the same as 28.08 ÷ 4 = 7 years (rounded to the nearest tenth). We divided by 4 because there are 4 quarters in a year.

We can check the answer by applying the compound interest formula, $S = P(1 + i)^n$. Suppose your principal is $1,000, the interst rate is 10% compounded quarterly, and the number of interest periods (n) is 7 × 4 or 28 quarters. Then:

$$S = 1,000 \times 1.025^{28}$$
$$S = 1,000 \times 1.9965$$
$$S = 1,996.50$$

So, in 7 years (28 quarters), we have slightly less than doubled our $1,000 investment.

The answer ($1,996.50) is not exactly doubled ($2,000.00) because we rounded off. We used n = .30103 instead of .301029995 and log 1.025 as .01072 instead of .010723865. There will always be some round-off error. In fact, even .301029995 and .010723865 are rounded-off and, therefore not exact.

The shortcut method to estimating how long it takes to double your money uses what we'll call *magic numbers*. (These numbers were derived using advanced mathematical techniques.)

Here's how

MAGIC NUMBERS

We're going to start with an example before we give you the rule of thumb.

When the interest period is quarterly, the way to determine how many years it takes to double your money is to divide the magic number 70 by the quoted interest rate. If the interest rate is 10% compounded quarterly:

$70 \div 10 = 7$ years to double your money.

That's the same answer we obtained before, using logarithms.

Here's the magic number table:

Table 2
Compound Interest Magic Numbers

IF THE QUOTED INTEREST RATE IS—

AT LEAST:	BUT LESS THAN:	COMPOUNDED:	THE MAGIC NUMBER IS:
5%	20%	Daily	69
5%	20%	Monthly	70
5%	20%	Quarterly	70
5%	20%	Semi-annually	71
5%	10%	Annually	72
10%	15%	Annually	73
15%	20%	Annually	75

What you do is look up the magic number that corresponds to both the range in which your interest rate falls and to the compounding period. Then you divide the magic number by the exact quoted interest rate and you'll have an estimate of the *number of years* it takes to double your money under those conditions. Using this shortcut magic, the answer is always in number of years.

The answer won't be exact, but in *most* instances it will be accurate to the nearest tenth of a year. In other words, if the "magic answer" is 7 years, the exact answer most probably falls between 6.9 years ($-.1$) and 7.1 years ($+.1$). If you stay within the indicated ranges in the table, you'll never be more than .2 (two-tenths) of a year off the exact amount of time it takes to double your money. (Don't forget that .2 means "two-tenths of a year" and *not* 2 months. Two-tenths of a year is about 2½ months.)

Now, suppose you were offered an interest rate of 9%, compounded daily. For this situation, and for *every* situation with daily compounding, irrespective of the rate of interest, the magic number is always 69, so divide 69 by 9. The answer is 7.7 years (that's 7 years and somewhat more than 8 months). If you figure it out with logarithms, you'd also find the answer to be 7.7 years, rounded to the nearest tenth of a year.

You *can* use the magic number table outside the indicated ranges, but be prepared for less accurate estimates. Let's try such an example. How many years would it take to double your money at 25% compounded annually? We realize that 25% is beyond the values in the table, but using the closest figure, we see the magic number is 75. Computing, $75 \div 25 = 3$ years. Compare this result with the answer of 3.1 years you'd obtain by formula $(n = .30103 \div \log[1 + i])$ and you can see that the two answers are quite close.

The magic number table is fun and provides a quick, shortcut, reasonable estimate to a tantalizing question. But it is a game to play after you've made the more serious decision about where and how to invest your money (to bring the greatest return) or where and how to borrow money (at least cost).

These decisions are *a matter of interest*. And it is *to your interest* to be able to calculate and compare opportunities.

Section 3: . . . and More about Compounding

It's really very hard for people to believe just how much money accumulates as a result of the effects of compound interest—although we saw (Section 2) how quickly money can double. Almost everyone can grasp the idea of money earned through simple interest and, because our examples tend to use small numbers and whole percentages, we can even begin to comprehend how interest compounds over one or two years.

But it is really difficult to conceive how much money you can end up with by just letting your principal and interest continue earning interest for 5 or 10 or 40 years.

Take your I.R.A. (or Keogh) account as an example of an investment where the principal and interest can remain untouched for years and years. (We'll discuss I.R.A.'s [Individual Retirement Accounts] and Keogh accounts in Chapter 3, but for now, remember you don't pay taxes on these earnings until you start making withdrawals.) Suppose you make the maximum allowable deposits for individuals of $2,000 a year for 10 years. You deposit $2,000 on December 31, 1983, $2,000 on December 31, 1984, $2,000 on December 31, 1985 and so on until December 31, 1992. The question is,

> "How much would these deposits be worth on December 31, 1993 (one year after the last deposit) if interest is allowed to accumulate and the interest rate is a steady 11% compounded monthly?"

Well, let's see.

You've deposited a total of $20,000 over the 10-year period, of which $2,000 compounded monthly for 10 years *and* another $2,000 compounded monthly for 9 years *and* another $2,000 compounded monthly for 8 years and so on . . . *plus* $2,000 that was on deposit for only one year at 11%, compounded monthly. That's . . .

But wait! There's a formula for computing the *total value* of a series of equal investments made over a span of years.

Here's how

COMPUTING TOTAL VALUE

We're going to show you the formula which can be used to compute total value exactly for any size investment, any interest rate and any number of years. Then, we'll show you a shortcut method for computing how much money you'll end up with for certain specified interest rates and time periods.

The formula for total value (TV) *one year after the last payment is made* is:

$$TV = \frac{P \times A\,(A^N - 1)}{A - 1}$$

In this formula:

P = The total amount of your payments
N = The total number of payments
A is computed according to the formula: $A = (1 + i)^k$

In addition:

k = The number of yearly compounding periods
i = The periodic interest rate expressed as a decimal. (That's the given interest rate divided by k and then divided by 100.)

In our example:

P = $2,000 (we made the maximum allowable IRA deposit)
N = 10 (10 payments—one each for 10 years)
k = 12 (since interest is compounded monthly and there are 12 months in a year)

$$i = (11 \div 12) \div 100$$
$$= .009167$$

Computing A:

$$A = (1 + i)^k$$
$$= (1 + .009167)^{12}$$
$$= 1.115723$$

To compute any number to the 12th power, use a calculator that has a $\boxed{Y^x}$ or an $\boxed{X^y}$ button:

PRESS 1.009167 $\boxed{Y^x}$ 12 $\boxed{=}$

Substituting in the formula we have:

$$TV = \frac{\$2,000 \times 1.115723 \times (1.115723^{10} - 1)}{1.115723 - 1}$$

To calculate 1.115723^{10}:

PRESS 1.115723 $\boxed{Y^x}$ 10 $\boxed{=}$

$$= \$38,358.22$$

So, the effects of compounding earned us $18,358.22 in interest ($38,358.22 less the $20,000 which we deposited) over a 10-year period.

Now we'll show you a short-cut method.

Here's how

SHORTCUT: TOTAL VALUE

Using the shortcut method to determine how much principal and interest you'll have accumulated after a given number of years of regular investments, you will need to use a "multiplier." Then you multiply your investment by this number to find total value. Table 1 presents the multipliers that are used to compute total value when interest is compounded *monthly*. Table 2 contains the multipliers to use in cases when interest is compounded or credited *once a year*. And Table 3 shows the multipliers for situations involving *daily* compounding. All three tables cover interest rates from 5% to 20% and terms from 10 to 40 years.

First, decide which table is appropriate for your situation.

Next, find the multiplier by locating the point at which the percent interest intersects the number of years you have made investments. Let's use the same example: $2,000 deposited for each of 10 years at 11%, compounded monthly.

Looking at Table 1 (interest is compounded monthly), we go down the "percent interest" column until we get to 11% and then move one column to the right to "10 years" to find the multiplier. the multiplier is 19.179.

Table 1
The Accumulation Factor ("Multiplier") for Each $1 of Regular Yearly Investment, with *Monthly* Compounding (12 Compounding Periods Per Year)

NUMBER OF YEARS OF INVESTMENT

PERCENT INTEREST	10	15	20	25	30	35	40
5	13.293	22.882	35.188	50.981	71.249	97.260	130.642
6	14.105	25.030	39.766	59.644	86.455	122.620	171.401
7	14.976	27.426	45.074	70.093	105.561	155.840	227.118
8	15.914	30.101	51.238	82.728	129.644	199.541	303.677
9	16.923	33.092	58.408	98.045	160.104	257.269	409.399
10	18.009	36.438	66.760	116.649	198.731	333.781	555.980
11	19.179	40.186	76.507	139.302	247.871	435.576	760.105
12	20.439	44.387	87.894	166.933	310.523	571.382	1,045.283
13	21.797	49.100	101.218	200.705	390.611	753.114	1,445.082
14	23.261	54.392	116.827	242.049	493.195	996.894	2,007.117
15	24.841	60.339	135.140	292.760	624.896	1,324.770	2,799.537
16	26.545	67.025	156.641	355.031	794.228	1,766.523	3,918.991
17	28.385	74.552	181.925	431.643	1,012.432	2,363.191	5,504.711
18	30.372	83.027	211.674	525.985	1,293.913	3,170.125	7,754.109
19	32.519	92.581	246.730	642.362	1,657.768	4,263.853	10,952.490
20	34.839	103.352	288.060	786.027	2,128.531	5,747.876	15,505.520

Table 2
The Accumulation Factor ("Multiplier") for Each $1 of Regular Yearly Investment, with *Annual* Compounding (1 Compounding Period Per Year)

NUMBER OF YEARS OF INVESTMENT

PERCENT INTEREST	10	15	20	25	30	35	40
5	13.207	22.657	34.719	50.113	69.761	94.836	126.839
6	13.972	24.673	38.993	58.156	83.802	118.121	164.047
7	14.784	26.888	43.865	67.677	101.073	147.914	213.610
8	15.645	29.324	49.423	78.954	122.346	186.102	279.781
9	16.560	32.003	55.765	92.324	148.575	235.125	368.292
10	17.531	34.950	63.003	108.182	180.943	298.127	486.852
11	18.561	38.190	71.265	126.999	220.913	379.164	645.827
12	19.655	41.753	80.699	149.334	270.293	483.463	859.142
13	20.814	45.672	91.470	175.850	331.315	617.749	1,145,484
14	22.045	49.980	103.768	207.333	406.737	790.673	1,529.909
15	23.349	54.717	117.810	244.712	499.957	1,013.346	2,045.954
16	24.733	59.925	133.840	289.088	615.161	1,300.025	2,738.474
17	26.200	65.649	152.139	341.763	757.503	1,668.994	3,667.388
18	27.755	71.939	173.021	404.273	933.320	2,143.652	4,912.600
19	29.404	78.850	196.848	478.431	1,150.389	2,753.919	6,580.510
20	31.150	86.442	224.026	566.377	1,418.258	3,538.009	8,812.628

Table 3
The Accumulation Factor ("Multiplier") for Each $1 of Regular Yearly Investment, with *Daily* Compounding (365 Compounding Periods Per Year)

NUMBER OF YEARS OF INVESTMENT

PERCENT INTEREST	10	15	20	25	30	35	40
5	13.301	22.901	35.227	51.053	71.373	97.464	130.962
6	14.117	25.062	39.837	59.780	86.700	123.036	172.084
7	14.994	27.476	45.188	70.322	105.987	156.597	228.415
8	15.940	30.178	51.418	83.104	130.376	200.897	306.104
9	16.954	33.186	58.638	98.546	161.121	259.238	413.084
10	18.054	36.578	67.117	117.460	200.453	337.269	562.814
11	19.238	40.381	77.024	140.531	250.596	441.352	771.954
12	20.516	44.650	88.622	168.739	314.713	580.678	1,065.265
13	21.894	49.446	102.218	203.297	396.901	767.728	1,478.006
14	23.384	54.847	118.203	245.777	502.667	1,019.952	2,061.580
15	24.987	60.902	136.916	297.796	638.293	1,358.944	2,884.179
16	26.728	67.760	159.059	362.208	814.231	1,820.019	4,057.983
17	28.610	75.491	185.154	441.674	1,041.720	2,445.328	5,728.608
18	30.646	84.221	215.969	539.953	1,336.668	3,295.886	8,113.835
19	32.848	94.080	252.370	661.571	1,719.407	4,454.048	11,523.440
20	35.224	105.182	295.262	811.720	2,214.970	6,027.685	16,387.070

Then, to compute total value, multiply your annual investment by the multiplier. In our example, we deposited $2,000 each year, so:

$$\$2,000 \times 19.179 = \$38,358$$

As you can see, the result of $38,358 is the same as the $38,358.22 we got using the total value formula if we round off to the nearest dollar. But note that the shortcut, like the elaborate formula, only works if there was a regular deposit made over a period of years. Also, both methods assume a constant rate of interest.

To show just how quickly compound interest adds up, suppose you begin making regular I.R.A. deposits at age 25 and continue doing so for 40 years. If the interest rate you obtain is 10%, compounded daily, the multiplier (from Table 3) is 562.814. This means that you will have between 500 and 600 times your annual investment at age 65. For example, depositing $1,000 each year (and that's only half of the allowable I.R.A. investment) will result in a nest egg of $562,814 at age 65. And you will have invested only $40,000 (40 × $1,000)!

If you had invested $2,000 a year for, say, 35 years, starting when you were 24 years old, and obtained a conservative annual interest rate of 9%, you would have accumulated:

$2,000 \times 235.125 = \$470,250$

That would be nearly half a million dollars by the time you were 59 years old and almost eligible to withdraw money from your I.R.A. account. Even taking inflation into consideration, that's not a bad return on an investment totalling $70,000!

Hard to believe, but true nevertheless.

3

Investments

Section 1: The Biggest Bang for Your Buck

While April may be the cruelest month, as many taxpayers know, the harshest sounding words in the language may be, "penalty for premature withdrawal." And, indeed, you are harshly penalized for taking your money out of a time deposit account before the account matures.

Some banks call them certificates of deposit (C.D.'s); others refer to them as savings certificates, while still others call them investment certificates. There are seemingly endless variations in names and conditions, but whatever the terminology, these forms of time deposits have certain elements in common. Designed primarily for the smaller investor, they all involve:

1. *A minimum dollar investment,* which can range from a low of $500 to a high of $5,000. While you cannot add money to the account during its term, you can buy another certificate at any time (provided you satisfy the minimum requirement).
2. *A fixed, predetermined time period (term) during which you have to leave your money on deposit.* The term can vary from 14 days, the shortest term we found, to 5 years: 30-day terms, 3-month, 6-month, 12-month, 18-month, and 2-year terms are most usual. Obviously, you have a wide choice.

    In selecting the term that best suits you, you are in effect entering into a *contract* with the bank (or investment house) that guarantees you a fixed rate of interest for the life of the investment. In return, you are committed to leaving your money on deposit for the specified period of time. Having fixed terms increases the bank's flexibility with respect to what it does with investors' money.
3. *Government insurance (F.D.I.C.)* typically insures your investment up to $100,000. On October 1, 1983, most government restrictions

on C.D.'s were relaxed or removed entirely: rates were no longer limited by government ceilings, compounding periods were made more generous and—most importantly—government-imposed penalties for early withdrawals were reduced.

4. *A fixed rate of interest, called the annual interest rate,* which stays in effect for the entire term, irrespective of what happens to interest rates in general. The interest rate you get varies with the term of the certificate.

5. *Penalties for early withdrawals.* Every time deposit account includes a penalty—in the form of lost interest—for early or premature withdrawal of principal from the account. Except in certain extreme instances (for example, death or adjudicated incompetency of the depositor), the principal may not be withdrawn prior to maturity, in whole or in part, without forfeiting some portion of the interest. Because of these penalties, in selecting a fixed term investment, you should consider whether or not you'll have need of your money before your investment matures.

In choosing a C.D. or savings certificate, your main concerns are the rate of interest and length of the term. If you predict interest rates are going to go up, you may not want to be locked into a long-term investment; if you expect interest rates to drop, you'll do well to lock yourself into a high rate for a longer period. But you should recognize that C.D.'s, like any other type of investment, are a gamble.

There is a bewildering array of time deposit investment opportunities. One of the primary reasons for choosing this type of investment is the rate of interest it affords—generally, quite a bit higher than the interest you'd earn in a savings account or a N.O.W. account (a form of interest-bearing checking account). Banks are competing for your business. They offer different interest rates, compounding periods and terms, all of which make it virtually impossible for the consumer to *easily* figure out the most profitable alternative. But they also help the investor by publishing the "annual effective yield" along with the fixed or annual interest rate.

"What," you ask, "is the annual effective yield? How is it computed?"

Here's how

ANNUAL EFFECTIVE YIELD

The annual effective yield is the actual interest rate you would realize on $100 invested for one year at the quoted compound interest rate. Compounding enables you to earn interest on your interest. So the actual interest you earn (the annual effective yield) is always higher than the quoted interest rate. The formula for computing annual effective yield takes into account both the quoted interest rate and the compounding period. Thus, the annual effective yield enables you to compare the earnings from investments with different quoted compound interest rates. In this respect, it is an indispensable tool.

Let's backtrack. When putting money in a savings account, C.D., I.R.A., Keogh or any other savings-investment plan, you are faced with different rates and different compounding periods (as well as different terms). That makes it difficult to compare one option with another.

We already saw that, all other things being equal, compounding increases your earnings. So, if you had to choose between 9.1% simple interest and 9.1%, compounded quarterly, you'd select the quarterly compounding. And if the decision was between 9.1%, compounded quarterly, and 9.1%, compounded daily, you'd know the daily compounding was the better deal.

But, in this real world, the options are rarely that simple. More likely, you will be faced with a lower rate that is compounded more frequently than the higher rate: for example, 9.25% compounded quarterly, as contrasted with 9.1% compounded daily. Is the effect of compounding enough to make 9.1% compounded daily a more attractive investment than 9.25% compounded quarterly? That's the type of question the annual effective yield helps you to answer.

As stated in the beginning of this section, the annual effective yield is the interest you'd earn on $100 if the $100 was left in an account at the quoted interest rate for a period of one year. The formula is:

Annual effective yield $= 100 \ (1+i)^k - 100$

This formula is quite similar to the compound interest formula (page 32), where:

k = *the number of times per year* that interest is compounded
i = the *periodic interest rate divided by 100* (the periodic interest rate is the quoted interest rate divided by K)

The first part of the formula computes the total interest and principal you would have after one year, based on a principal of $100. By subtracting 100 (the last step in the formula), we remove the principal, leaving the interest earned on $100.

Now, let's compute the annual effective yield on 9.25% compounded quarterly:

k = 4 because interest is compounded quarterly and there are 4 quarters in a year

Periodic interest rate = 9.25% ÷ 4 = 2.3125%, so

i = 2.3125 ÷ 100 = .023125

Substituting in the formula, we have:

$$\text{Annual effective yield} = 100 \, (1 + .023125)^4 - 100$$
$$= 100 \times (1.023125)^4 - 100$$

The quantity $(1.023125)^4$ is read, "1.023125 to the 4th power." That means that 1.023125 is multiplied by itself 4 times.

$$1.023125 \times 1.023125 \times 1.023125 \times 1.023125 =$$

While this multiplication can be done by hand or on your regular calculator, it is best done (faster, without losing your place, and without forgetting the decimal point) on a calculator that computes "powers" directly. Such a calculator, as we described earlier, has a button marked:

$\boxed{Y^x}$ or $\boxed{X^y}$

On *that* calculator, to compute $(1.023125)^4$

PRESS 1.023124 $\boxed{Y^x}$ 4 $\boxed{=}$

The result is 1.0958. This completes the information we need for the formula:

$$\text{Annual effective yield} = 100 \times 1.0958 - 100$$
$$= 109.58 - 100$$
$$= 9.58$$

The result of 9.58 is actually the percentage interest (9.58%) you earn if you invest your money at 9.25% compounded quarterly for a one-year period. The interest earned is exactly the same as it would be if you had deposited your money at 9.58% compounded annually for one year.

Now let's compare the annual effective yield on 9.25% compounded *quarterly* with the annual effective yield on 9.1% compounded *daily*. To do this, we also need to figure out the annual effective yield on 9.1% with daily compounding:

Assuming 365 days per year:

k = 365
Periodic interest rate = 9.1% ÷ 365 = .02493% , so
i = .02493 ÷ 100 = .0002493

In addition:

Annual effective yield = $100 \times (1 + .0002493)^{365} - 100$
$= 100 \times (1.0002493)^{365} - 100$

Yes, you *could* multiply 1.0002493 by itself 365 times—but it's almost impossible to do so without error. It's also time-consuming and extraordinarily boring. Instead, use a calculator that does "powers":

PRESS 1.0002493 $\boxed{Y^x}$ 365 $\boxed{=}$ 1.0953

To finish substituting:

Annual effective yield = $100 \times 1.0953 - 100$
$= 109.53 - 100$
$= 9.53$

Thus, 9.1% compounded daily is the same as 9.53% compounded annually.

This result, 9.53%, is slightly less than the yield of 9.58% obtained on 9.25% compounded quarterly. Therefore, 9.25% compounded quarterly represents a slightly better investment—all other things being equal.

But, as we've seen over and over again, all other things aren't equal. There's wide variability in terms and equally far-ranging differences in the

PENALTY FOR EARLY WITHDRAWAL

Banks are not kidding when they talk about the severe penalties you can incur. Penalties for withdrawing your money from a time deposit account before the date of maturity are always *forfeitures of interest:*

• One typical bank extracts a 3-month interest penalty on time deposits of 6 months or less; it penalizes you 6 months' worth of interest on accounts of more than a 6-month fixed period.
• Another bank requires that you give up 30 days' interest on one year (or shorter) C.D.'s. It has a 90-day interest penalty on time accounts of from 2 to 5 years.

In most (but not necessarily all) cases, the interest penalty is calculated on the basis of simple interest at the quoted rate. We've made up some examples to show you how this is done. To start, let's see what some penalties would amount to on a $500 investment.

In the first example, we have a 12-month C.D. with a quoted interest rate of 9.1% compounded daily. There is a 6-month interest penalty on early withdrawals. Assuming we took out our money after 11 months (330 days), how much is the penalty?

To answer this question, we use the *formula for simple interest* to find out how much interest is earned in 6 months. (Compounding is ignored at this point since we are assuming that penalties are calculated on the basis of simple interest at the quoted rate.)

The formula is:

$$I = Prt$$

Substituting, we have:

$$I = 500 \times .091 \times .5 \quad \left\{ \begin{array}{l} 9.1\% = 9.1 \div 100 = .091 \\ 6 \text{ months equal six-twelfths of a year,} \\ \text{or } 6 \div 12 = .5 \end{array} \right.$$
$$= 22.75$$

In other words, you have to pay a penalty of $22.75. But your $500 was on deposit for 330 days (about 11 months) at 9.1% compounded daily; applying the compound interest formula, and doing the calculations, you earned $42.87 in interest. You have to subtract the penalty of $22.75 from the earned interest ($42.87 − $22.75), which means that in 11 months you earned a total of $22.10 on your $500. This would be equivalent to 4.4% compounded daily, which has an annual effective yield of 4.5%—a mighty poor return on your money. (You'll have to trust us on the calculation of the annual effective yield which calls for more math than you may want to know.)

Now, let's do another problem. What is a 30-day penalty on $500 invested in a 6-month C.D. at 9.25% compounded monthly? To obtain the penalty, we need to figure out the simple interest for a 30-day period:

$$I = 500 \times .0925 \times .082 \quad \left\{ 30 \div 365 = .082 \right.$$
$$= 3.79$$

The penalty is $3.79. Suppose the $500 was on deposit for 5 months, during which time it earned 9.25% interest, compounded monthly. Applying the compound interest formula, $S = P(1 + i)^n$, you can calculate your earnings to be $19.57, from which you must forfeit $3.79. So over the course of 5 months, you actually made $15.78 in interest, which comes out to be the equivalent of 7.48% compounded monthly—or an annual effective yield of 7.74% (again, please trust us on this computation.)

As you can see from these examples, the penalties for early withdrawal of money from time deposits involve substantial percentages. Though the actual dollar amounts in our examples are relatively small, they are not necessarily without meaning. After all, for $22.75 two people can go out to dinner, while $3.79 is the price of a shrimp Newburg frozen dinner. Remember, however, that the actual dollar amount of the penalty is proportional to the size of the original investment. If you had invested $5,000 instead of $500, for example, the dollar penalty under the conditions just described would be $10 \times \$3.79 = \$37.90$. That's the price of shrimp Newburg for two in a good restaurant!

Typically, people withdraw principal from investment certificates before the date of maturity because they need the use of the money for other things or because they have a chance to make a better investment. In the first case, if you need your $500 to pay an unanticipated bill, you probably don't have much choice in the matter and you'll just have to accept the loss of interest. If you want to re-invest the principal, however, you will want to know whether the higher rate of return on the new investment will make up for the interest you forfeited. After all, the whole point of investing is getting a bigger bang for your buck.

Section 2: The Bulls and the Bears (Stocks and Bonds)

We are *not* investment gurus.

Like you, we are still searching for the one perfect investment which is:

- Completely *secure* (never worth less than what you paid).
- *Liquid* (can be turned back into cash at any time).
- *Appreciates* in value (becomes worth more than its original price).
- Offers a *high yield* (rate of interest).

Unfortunately, investing always involves risks. The more certain you are in one area, such as liquidity, the more you trade-off in another, such as appreciation.

Consider real estate. Real estate investments offer possibilities of appreciating but tend not to be liquid. It generally takes *time* to turn property back into cash and, if you should need cash immediately, you might have to sell at a loss.

Stocks rate high in liquidity but vary widely with respect to security and appreciation. For example, highly secure stocks that also offer a good yield tend to appreciate very slowly. In contrast, the more speculative stocks may show very rapid appreciation—or equally rapid and dramatic drops in value—but are likely to have zero yield (that is, pay no dividends). Even a well-established corporation can fail to pay expected dividends if its profit status is poor. Happily, a company can also declare an unexpected dividend increase when it is doing well.

Typically, bonds produce higher yields than stocks. However, bonds that have the highest quality ratings, signifying greatest security, according to Standard & Poor's and Moody's, for example, generally have lower yields than bonds which are rated less highly. But no bond is totally secure. In fact, if the corporation, utility or federal, state or city agency that issues the bond runs into financial trouble and cannot pay its debts (defaults), the bond may not be redeemed at all, or it may be redeemed for less than its face value at maturity.

The security factor (whether or not you'll get at least your original investment back) is based largely on the anticipated financial health of the economy and the issuing corporation, agency or government body. The security of some investments—savings accounts and certificates of deposit—is *insured* by the F.D.I.C. Some of these investments offer good yields as well, but they do not appreciate. Those with the highest yields (C.D.'s, for example) may also carry a penalty for early withdrawal.

Liquidity is the most intuitively obvious aspect of investments. It pertains to how readily an investment can be turned back into dollars. You can usually sell a stock in one business day, although not necessarily for the price you originally paid for it. Not so with real estate (or art, for example, or antiques).

Appreciation tends to be even more speculative since it primarily reflects future occurrences. However, the lure of getting more than your original investment back is one of the major attractions of investing.

The yield on stocks and bonds is essentially the rate of interest you earn on your original investment.

Here's how

YIELD ON STOCKS

is computed.

On time deposit investments, for example, savings accounts, the annual effective yield is the rate of interest you'd realize if you left your money on deposit for a one-year period at the quoted interest rate (see Chapter 3, Section 1).

Stocks are a little different. The yield on stocks is the *amount of money you earn in dividends expressed as a percentage of the price you paid per share of the stock*. Let's consider the Hilton Corporation stock as an illustration.

In February 1984, Hilton Corporation stock was paying a yearly dividend of $1.80 per share. If you owned 100 shares of Hilton, you would earn a dividend of:

$1.80 × 100 = $180 each year.

And if you owned 500 shares of this stock, your dividends would amount to:

$1.80 × 500 = $900 a year.

The total amount of dividends you receive is *independent* of what you paid for the stock. It reflects only the *total number of shares you own*. Everyone who owns shares of this stock receives the same per-share dividend. By contrast, the yield on your investment *is* based on the price you paid for each share of stock. It is independent of the number of shares you own. Let's consider your yield to see why this is so. Suppose you bought Hilton on January 23, 1984 at the closing price of $55.50 per share. The dividend of $1.80 per share (per year) is like earned interest. Finding the yield means finding the interest rate:

Percent yield = (dividend ÷ price) × 100%

For the shares of Hilton you purchased in January:

Percent yield = (1.80 ÷ 55.50) × 100%
           = .0324 × 100%
           = 3.24%

If your friend had bought the stock for less money, say $40.25 per share, her yield would be higher because the amount of the dividend remains the same:

Percent yield = (1.80 ÷ 40.25) × 100%
           = .0447 × 100%
           = 4.47%

But if another colleague had paid more for the stock than you did, his yield would be smaller than yours. If he bought Hilton at $60.25 per share, the yield for him would be:

Percent yield = (1.80 ÷ 60.25) × 100%
        = .0299 × 100%
        = 2.99%

Thus, since the yield on stocks is a percentage based on the dividend and price paid per share, people who buy the same stock at different prices actually earn different yields (just as people who invest in certificates of deposit at different times and through different banks or investment houses can earn different rates of interest).

That's why it's important to distinguish between your yield and the current price of the stock. If a few weeks after you bought Hilton at $55.50 per share, it went up to $60.25 per share, it wouldn't affect your yield. For no matter what the current price of the stock is, the fact remains that you invested $55.50 per share, and you earn $1.80 per year on that amount. That's a yield of 3.24% per year during the time you keep the stock, assuming that dividends are paid as promised.

A yield of 3.24% may not seem particularly high. Your money would probably earn a higher rate of interest in a C.D. and it would also be guaranteed secure. But you bought Hilton stock anticipating that, in addition to providing a respectable yield, the price would rise. Let's suppose you bought shares at $55.50 and, one year later, the stock rose to $59.90 per share. This is an increase of $4.40 per share (a percent increase of 7.93%—see Chapter 1, Section 2.) If you sell the stock at the $59.90 price, you will have realized an annual return of 11.17% (11.17% = the 7.93% price appreciation + the 3.24% dividend yield.)

If you sell the stock for more than you paid for it, you have a *capital gain* of $4.40 per share. However, if you bought it at $55.50 per share and sold it at $40.25 (a loss of $15.25 a share), you would have a *capital loss* resulting from the price decrease. Irrespective of appreciation (capital gain) or depreciation (capital loss), the yield does not change during the time you own the stock. But the annual return varies up or down with capital gains or losses.

To compare different investments, for example stocks and C.D.'s, look at the *annual return* and *annual effective yield*. In the previous example, the stock was sold after one year, so computing the annual yield was relatively straightforward. In real life, however, it wouldn't be as simple because you probably won't sell the stock in exactly one year. If you don't, the computation of annual return (called "internal rate of return") becomes very complex, well beyond the scope of this book. You'll need to use a business calculator, such as the Hewlett-Packard 12C, that has the internal programming to compute it automatically.

Yields on bonds are computed in much the same way as yields on stocks.

Here's how

YIELDS ON BONDS

Bonds are issued with a maturity date (the date they are redeemable for the dollar value printed on the bond—the face or par value). Generally, the smallest bond you can buy is for $1,000. Each bond pays a specified rate of simple interest based upon the face value. Your interest payments are often obtained by clipping coupons and cashing them in at regular intervals.

Suppose the interest rate is 9½% on the bond you own. Applying the simple interest formula (see Chapter 2, Section 2), this means that you earn $9.50 for each $100 of face value:

$$\text{Interest} = 9\frac{1}{2}\% \text{ of } \$100$$
$$= 9.5\% \text{ of } 100$$
$$= .095 \times 100$$
$$= \$9.50$$

Since the face value of your bond is $1,000, your annual interest would amount to $95 ($.095 × $1,000).

Let's try another example.

On January 25, 1984, Pacific Gas & Electric issued bonds at 12% with a maturity date of 2016. If you bought a $1,000 bond and paid $1,000 for it (that is, paid its full face value), you would earn $120 per year in interest. Your yield would be the quoted 12% interest.

But you rarely pay the face value when you buy a bond. Bonds such as Pacific Gas & Electric change hands innumerable times before the year 2016 when they can be redeemed at their face value (provided the issuing agency is in sound financial condition). In the interim transactions (and even at the time of issue), bonds are usually traded or sold for more or less than their face value. The selling price depends on general market conditions, the soundness of the issuing agency and competing interest rates.

As with stocks, *your yield on bonds depends on the price you pay for each $100 of face value,* even though the quoted interest rate remains unchanged. If you paid a *premium* of more than $100 (per $100 of face value), your yield on Pacific Gas & Electric would be less than 12%. If you bought the bond at a *discount* (less than $100 per $100 of face value) your yield would be higher than the quoted interest rate.

Yields on bonds are computed as follows:

$$\text{Current Yield} = \frac{\text{Quoted interest rate}}{\text{Price paid per \$100 of face value}} \times 100\%$$

So if you paid the premium price of $105 for Pacific Gas & Electric:

$$\text{Current Yield} = \frac{12}{105} \times 100\%$$
$$= \frac{12}{105} \times \frac{100}{1}\%$$
$$= \frac{1200}{105}\%$$
$$= 11.4\%$$

This result (yield) is less than the quoted 12% interest.

On the other hand, if you bought this bond at the discounted rate of $93 (per $100 of face value), the yield would be:

$$\text{Current Yield} = \frac{12}{93} \times 100\%$$
$$= \frac{1200}{93}\%$$
$$= 12.9\%$$

This yield is nine-tenths of a percent more than the specified rate of interest. The selling price of bonds is, in large part, dependent upon prevailing interest rates in the marketplace. A bond issued at a low rate of interest, in terms of current standards, is likely to sell at a considerable discount, thereby boosting the yield to a level that is more in line with other interest rates.

For example, on January 25, 1984, an AT&T bond, maturing in 2003, sold for $63.25 with a quoted interest rate of 7⅛%. In this case:

$$\text{Current Yield} = \frac{7\frac{1}{8}}{63.25} \times 100\%$$
$$= \frac{7.125}{63.25} \times 100\%$$
$$= \frac{712.5}{63.25}\%$$
$$= 11.3\%$$

The yield of 11.3% was thus substantially higher than the quoted interest rate.

On the same day, an earlier issue of an AT&T bond (maturing in 1991) sold for $104.83. It had a quoted interest rate of 13¼%, but the fact that it was selling at a premium lowered the yield to 12.6% as you can see:

$$\text{Current Yield} = \frac{13\frac{1}{4}}{104.83} \times 100\%$$
$$= \frac{13.25}{104.83} \times 100\%$$
$$= \frac{1325}{104.83}\%$$
$$= 12.6\%$$

Like the yield on stocks, the yield on bonds is independent of what the bond sells for before or after *you* buy it. The yield only reflects the price *you* paid and the rate of interest quoted. However, if you sell the bond before maturity, you may experience a capital gain or loss which would affect your total return, just as it did on stocks.

People buy bonds because:

• They tend to be a reasonably secure investment.
• They are redeemable at maturity for their full face value (if the issuer is then financially healthy enough to meet the debt).
• Their yield is relatively high.

Moreover, unlike stocks, some bonds offer additional tax advantages because the earned interest may not be subject to federal or state tax. This is generally true of municipal bonds.

But like any investment, neither stocks nor bonds come ''up to par'' on every factor that needs to be considered. So, whether you choose to invest in bonds, certificates of deposit, stocks, real estate or savings accounts, examine your personal needs and weigh the importance of the factors of yield, security, appreciation and liquidity against one another. Remember, there's no such thing as a perfect investment; investing always involves some gamble. If this wasn't the case, there would be lots more millionaires!

Section 3: On Golden Pond (Tax-Deferred Annuities)

Just as a regular schedule of exercise and good eating habits have immediate health benefits as well as payoffs in later years, so too does investing in such tax-deferred annuities as I.R.A.'s, Keogh's, and other tax-deferred basic retirement plans.

The advantages of these plans are that they:

• Save you taxes now.
• Offer you a wide choice of investment options.
• Earn tax-free interest until withdrawal.
• Guarantee you retirement income.

It used to be that tax shelters were mainly for the very rich. Now, with government approved I.R.A. (Individual Retirement Accounts) and profit-sharing retirement plans and money purchase pension plans, they are available to everyone.

Here's how

WHO QUALIFIES?*

Everyone who is employed—whether you work for someone else or are self-employed—can open an Individual Retirement Account, irrespective of whether or not you also participate in an employee pension plan.

Through 1986, you may contribute up to $2,000 to your I.R.A., or 100% of your *earned* income, whichever is less. If you are the only wage earner with a non-working spouse, you may shelter an additional $250 in separate I.R.A.'s (for an annual total of $2,250). However, if both you and your spouse are employed, each of you can open an I.R.A., so that a working couple's annual contribution can be as much as $4,000. And it doesn't matter whether you file a joint return!

The amount of money you contribute to an I.R.A., of course, is up to you. But it is in your best interest to try to invest the maximum each year. In any case, it's better to invest something than nothing and many banks and investment institutions will allow you to open some type of I.R.A. with an initial deposit of as little as $50. They also permit subsequent contributions of as little as $10.

You can start a new I.R.A. every year (or contribute to an already established one) and have a wide choice of investment vehicles and institutions. In fact, in any one year you may open as many different I.R.A.'s as you like so long as your total investment for the year does not exceed the $2,000 maximum. And you have until April 15 to open an I.R.A. for the previous calendar year—and to make your contributions to it. (Note that if

---

*The Tax Reform Act of 1986 dramatically changes the categories of people eligible to make a (tax) *deductible* I.R.A. contribution beginning in the 1987 tax year.

you file on a fiscal year basis, your deadline will be different. Check it with an accountant.)

Everyone can have an Individual Retirement Account. New tax laws also allow you to invest in other types of retirement programs, such as the Profit Sharing Retirement Plan or Money Purchase Pension Plan. We advise you to talk to an accountant and to your employer to determine whether you're eligible to participate in these. Contributing to an I.R.A. and to another tax-deferred retirement plan is doubly advantageous.

The deadline for opening a *first* tax-deferred basic retirement plan is December 31. Once opened (even with a small investment—say, $100), however, you can keep investing each year's contribution (up to the maximum) until April 15 of the following year.

Since you defer paying income taxes on the money you contribute to these retirement plans, you save real dollars now.

Here's how

TAX DEDUCTIONS

The amount you invest in I.R.A. or Keogh each year is deducted from your taxable (net earned) income for the year, even if you don't itemize your deductions. This means that you pay less income tax for the years you make investments.*

Let's suppose you are a married taxpayer filing a joint return and your taxable income this year is $34,500. Using the 1986 Federal Tax Rate Schedule Y (reprinted in part in Chapter 1, Section 3 [Table 1] and discussed there), we see that this income puts you in the 28% tax bracket. This means that according to Schedule Y you would owe in federal taxes:

$5,169.70 + 28% of ($34,500 − $32,270) $\left\{ \begin{array}{l} \text{\% means hundredths, so} \\ 28\% = 28 \div 100 = .28; \\ \text{"of" means "times"} \end{array} \right.$
= $5,169.70 + .28 × $2,230
= $5,169.70 + $624.40
= $5,794.10

By calculator:
PRESS .28 ⊠ 2,230 ⊟ ⊞ 5,169.70 ⊟

A $2,000 I.R.A. contribution reduces your taxable income from $34,500 to $32,500. Recomputing your taxes, you will obtain:

$5,169.70 + 28% of ($32,500 − $32,270)
= $5,169.70 + .28 × $230
= $5,169.70 + 64.40
= $5,234.10

---

*The new tax laws limit the deductibility of I.R.A. contributions to four categories of people, although everyone can still contribute to an I.R.A. Check with your accountant to see if you qualify and if it is a worthwhile investment for you.

$$= \$4,790 + \$196$$
$$= \$4,986$$

We find that your tax bill is now $5,234.10—a savings of $560 in taxes ($5,794.10 minus $5,234.10) because of your I.R.A. contribution. (Since you are in the 28% tax bracket, you could have computed your tax savings directly as 28% of $2,000. That's $.28 \times \$2,000 = \$560$.)

Had you invested *less* than the maximum in an I.R.A., you would still realize tax savings amounting to 28% of your contribution as long as your total income fell into this same tax bracket. What happens if your I.R.A. contribution places you in a *lower* tax bracket? Let's answer that question with another example.

Suppose your taxable income was $32,600 before you made the maximum I.R.A. investment. That means you were in the 28% tax bracket, according to Schedule Y. You would owe $5,262.10 in taxes [$5,169.70 + 28% of ($32,600 − $32,270) = $5,169.70 + .28 × $330 = $5,169.70 + $92.40 = $5,262.10]. Your full I.R.A. contribution lowers your taxable income to $30,600, which moves you into the 25% bracket. On this income, the total taxes are:

$$\$3,739.70 + 25\% \text{ of } (\$30,600 - \$26,550)$$
$$= \$3,739.70 + .25 \times \$4,050$$
$$= \$3,739.70 + \$1,012.50$$
$$= \$4,752.20$$

So you saved $509.90 in taxes. If you want to estimate your savings on your $2,000 I.R.A. contribution in one step, look at where the bulk of the last $2,000 fell in the tax table. Most of it was in the 25% range: 25% of $2,000 = $500, which is close to $509.90.

Now let's look at what the tax savings would be if your taxable income totalled $32,600 but was made up of $28,000 in wages and $4,600 that you earned free-lancing.

Current regulations (they change rapidly, so keep up-to-date) permit you to contribute $2,000 to an I.R.A. and 15% of $4,600 or $690 (15% × $4,600 = .15 × $4,600 = $690) to a Profit Sharing Retirement plan. As a result of these contributions, your taxable income of $32,600 has been reduced to $29,910.

The taxes on $32,600 we computed before come to $5,262.10. The taxes on $29,910 are:

$$\$3,739.70 + 25\% \text{ of } (\$29,910 - \$26,550)$$
$$= \$3,739.70 + .25\% \times \$3,360$$
$$= \$3,739.70 + \$840$$
$$= \$4,579.70$$

By contributing a total of $2,690 to your I.R.A. and another tax-deferred retirement plan, you saved $682.40 in taxes.

Exactly *what* do you contribute *to* when you contribute to an Individual Retirement Account or one of the other tax-deferred retirement plans? You have several options, and your contributions can be invested in many ways. *Here's how*

INVESTMENT OPTIONS

To begin with, you are not limited to investing through a bank or savings institution. As with any investment, you can also invest through a mutual fund, insurance company or brokerage firm. You can also select the type of investment you prefer: bank certificates of deposit, stocks, bonds, money market mutual funds or certain real estate investments. We found the book, *How to Buy Stocks,* by Engel and Boyd (7th Ed.), Bantam Books, 1983 to be a particularly helpful introductory guide.

Not all types of institutions necessarily offer the full range of investment opportunities. In deciding which type of investment you want and which institution you want to manage your money, you need to consider yields, growth and appreciation, (see Chapter 3, Section 2) as well as fees and commissions.

Banks and savings institutions typically offer money market or time deposit I.R.A.'s. Those that have other government-approved tax-deferred retirement plans offer these vehicles as well as equity investments (common stocks) and fixed income investments (intermediate and long-range bonds). Banks and savings institutions generally don't charge a fee for opening a retirement plan. However, they may impose some annual maintenance charges (which can range from $5 to $20 per year), and some banks have fees for transferring your account, for closing it out or for distributing the funds to you when you retire. Almost all banks and savings institutions charge a fee (of about $25) for early withdrawals from a time deposit investment like a C.D., in addition to the interest penalty they levy.

In general, mutual fund institutions, insurance companies and brokerage firms charge fees and/or commissions for every transaction. There may be a start-up fee, an annual fee, an administrative fee, a commission on each year's contribution and/or a commission on securities bought and sold. Since fees and commissions can mount up substantially and thus cut into the interest you earn, it's a good idea to consider the fee structure when you are comparing investment options—as well as the factors of security, liquidity and appreciation.

Because most I.R.A. accounts and a large proportion of other tax-deferred retirement plans are handled by banks, let's examine their most common investment offerings: time deposits. We already described some of the important features of time deposits—lengths of term, yields and the penalties for early withdrawals—when we covered certificates of deposit in Section 1 of this Chapter. Now, we will discuss variable and fixed interest rates.

Banks offer both short- and long-term growth accounts, typically of 6 months to 5 years duration. Each has either a fixed or variable rate of interest.

A *fixed rate* account guarantees a specific rate of interest for the entire term. The fixed rate in one representative bank reflects the most current 52-week yield on U.S. Treasury Notes. If you think interest rates have peaked and will be going down, or if you just feel more comfortable knowing *exactly* by how much your money will grow, the fixed rate option is right for you. So, lock in that current market rate for 6 months, 18 months, 30 months or 5 years!

Variable interest rates change, usually monthly. The interest you earn keeps pace with fluctuating market conditions and is typically based on the latest 3-month average of the yields of one-year U.S. Treasury Bills. Variable rate time deposit accounts are for investors who believe interest rates are going up. (They can, of course, go down.)

You can split your contribution, placing a portion in a fixed rate account and the remainder in a variable rate one, or splitting it between time deposits and mutual funds—which lets you hedge your bet. But remember, you can always transfer your I.R.A. to a new type of investment or to a new trustee, and, if you do so within 60 days of closing an account, you don't lose your tax-deferred advantage. Nor do you lose your tax-free interest. (Remember, if you move a C.D. before it matures, you still have to pay an early withdrawal penalty.)

Here's how

TAX-FREE INVESTMENT

The interest on your investment in a tax-deferred retirement plan is tax-free as long as you leave it in the plan or transfer it speedily into a new plan. Thus sheltered, your account grows rapidly as the interest compounds over time.

To show just how quickly it can grow, let's look at a simple example of an I.R.A. account that earns a constant 10% interest rate, compounded annually.

In the beginning of the first year, you make an I.R.A. contribution of $2,000. By the end of the year, you earned $200 interest (10% of $2,000—see Chapter 2), so that you have a total of $2,200.

By the end of the second year, you earn 10% interest on the first year's contribution (that's 10% of $2,200 or $220). You also earn another $200 on the second year's contribution of $2,000 (which you made at the beginning of the second year).

By the end of the second year, you have earned:

$220 interest on $2,200 (the first year's investment plus one year of interest), and

$200 interest on $2,000 (the second year's investment).

Adding principal and interest together, your I.R.A. funds now total $4,620.

At the beginning of the third year (which is the same as the end of the second year), you deposit an additional $2,000. For the third year you earn 10% interest on $6,620 ($4,620 + $2,000). That's $662 in interest, so at the end of the third year, you have $6,620 + $662 or $7,282.

If you continued contributing $2,000 for each of 10 years (that's $20,000) at a fixed 10% compounded annually, the principal and accumulated interest would amount to $35,062—not one penny of which has been taxed! (A shortcut way of doing this computation will be explained in the next chapter.)

If you had bought certificates of deposit at the rate of $2,000 a year, your net earnings would have been much less (unless, of course, the interest rate was astronomical), because you would be taxed on the interest earned. Also, by contributing to a tax-deferred retirement plan, you saved in taxes by reducing your taxable income each year for 10 years. So there's really a dual advantage to this method of saving.

Can you really get away with *never* paying taxes on this money? The answer is "no," but the retirement plans were designed so that you generally pay a lower tax rate on the money when you do pay taxes.

Here's how

RETIREMENT INCOME

Let's suppose that you withdraw the $35,062 in one lump sum as soon as you are able to without penalty (at age 59½—more about this later). If you were still working and reporting a taxable income of $10,000 at that time, the addition of $35,062 gives you a taxable income of $45,062, immediately moving you up into the 33% tax bracket. Your federal income taxes for the year (again using the 1986 Schedule Y) would be $9,105.56:

$$= \$6,768.50 + 33\% \text{ of } (\$45,062 - \$37,980)$$
$$= \$6,768.50 + .33 \times \$7,082$$
$$= \$6,768.50 + \$2,337.06$$
$$= \$9,105.56$$

However, let's assume that at age 59½ you withdraw the whole $35,062, but you have no other taxable income. You are, in effect, retired. The $35,062 places you in the 28% tax bracket, and your retirement income is taxed at a lower rate.

But you can still earn an income *and* reduce the taxes that you will have to pay on your retirement income because:

- You don't have to withdraw your money in one lump sum.
- Nor do you have to do it beginning at age 59½.

You *may* begin to receive distributions from your I.R.A. as early as age 59½ (even if you are still working). You *must* begin to make withdrawals by the end of the calendar year in which you reach 70½. (Isn't there something slightly incongruous about half-birthdays after your fifth or sixth one?)

You can opt for a lump sum payout or withdraw your money *in installments*. The size of the installment payment is determined by dividing the total amount of money in the plan by the number of years of remaining life expectancy of you or your spouse, according to actuarial tables.

Taxes are paid *only* on the amount of money you withdraw, and you continue to earn tax-free interest on the balance remaining in the account. Withdrawals from an I.R.A. account are taxed immediately as if they had been earned during one tax year.

In fact, I.R.A.s and the other tax-deferred plans are *retirement plans*. The assumption is that when you make withdrawals you will pay less tax on the money because your annual income is less than it was during the years when you were making your contributions to the plan. When your income is less, you are in a lower tax bracket and your taxes are less.

You may choose to withdraw all or part of your retirement account funds at any time before age 59½. But, if you do so for reasons other than disability, you may have to pay a *penalty tax* (which can be as much as 10% on the amount withdrawn)—in addition to income taxes, of course. And, if you withdraw from a time deposit investment that has not yet matured, you will also incur an early withdrawal penalty and may have to pay an early withdrawal fee.

There are many good reasons for opening an I.R.A. account and other tax-deferred retirement plans if you are eligible and for trying to make the maximum annual contribution, if possible. Among the more compelling reasons are that such plans can en*rich* your later years and make them truly *gold*en.

4

Long-term
Loans

Section 1: Home Mortgages, Automobile Loans and Present Value

A home mortgage is probably the largest loan you'll ever have, and the next largest is a car loan; these are generally a family's biggest lifetime purchases. But any type of loan where you pay back part of the principal and interest in *periodic installments* over time (or have this paid out to you, as with a pension) works much the same way.

Until the introduction of adjustable-rate mortgages (complex home loan mortgage plans where the interest is adjusted periodically, typically reflecting U.S. Treasury bill yields), all mortgages operated at a fixed rate of interest. This meant that the interest rate did not fluctuate and, consequently, the amount of the payment remained constant over the life of the loan.

The amount of the payment is based on the total amount of the loan, the length of the loan (its *term*), the rate of interest and the frequency of payments. It also involves the concept of *present value,* which we will be discussing later. Did you ever wonder how the bank figures it out given all the different combinations?

Here's how

COMPUTING LOAN PAYMENTS

There is a remarkable formula for computing the exact amount of your mortgage payment or the payment on an auto loan or on any other long-term, fixed-rate loan. (There are also tables that list the exact payment for different size loans at different rates of interest.) The formula is remarkable for two reasons: first, because it can be used for computing payments on loans of any amount, at any fixed interest rate and for any term; second, because, although it looks imposing,

$$\text{Payment} = \text{Amount of loan} \times \frac{i \times (1 + i)^n}{(1 + i)^n - 1}$$

it has only two unknowns, n and i, and is very similar to the compound interest formula with which we worked in Chapter 2.

In this formula:

$i = $ *The periodic interest rate divided by 100.* (The periodic interest rate is the quoted interest rate divided by the number of times per year that interest is compounded.)

$n = $ *The total number of payments to be made.*

Let's use the formula to figure out the mortgage payments on a house you're thinking of buying. Suppose the house costs $80,000, and you make a $10,000 down payment. This means you must borrow $70,000, so you shop around and find a 30-year mortgage at 12% interest with monthly payments. (When loans are paid off monthly, the quoted interest rate is usually understood to be compounded monthly.) The question is, "how much is each monthly payment?"

The first step in using the formula is to figure out the unknowns:

n, the total number of payments to be made, is 30 (years) $\times$ 12 (months per year) = 360;

The *periodic interest rate* is 12% $\div$ 12 = 1%,

So i, the periodic interest rate divided by 100, is 1.00 $\div$ 100 = .01

And the quantity $(1 + i)^n$ is

$$(1 + i)^n = (1 + .01)^{360}$$
$$= (1.01)^{360}$$

To compute this quantity, you must have a calculator that computes powers. If you don't have one, you'll have to buy one because it's the only way to do the arithmetic needed for finding exact mortgage payments (and for figuring out compound interest in Chapter 2). Look for a calculator that has a $\boxed{Y^x}$ or $\boxed{X^y}$ key. Then, to compute $(1.01)^{360}$ on this calculator,

PRESS 1.01 $\boxed{Y^x}$ 360 $\boxed{=}$

(The answer will take a moment to appear; it takes the calculator a few seconds to complete this computation.)

$$(1 + i)^n = (1.01)^{360} = 35.9496$$

Now we can substitute in the formula:

$$\text{Payment} = \$70,000 \times \frac{.01 \times 35.9496}{35.9496 - 1}$$
$$= \$70,000 \times \frac{.359496}{34.9496}$$
$$= \$720.03$$

This means that your mortgage payment would be $720.03 a month, every month for 30 years.

Now let's see what happens to the monthly payment on a $70,000 *20-year* mortgage at 12%. (We've changed the term of the mortgage, but left the other variables the same.)

Going back to the formula:

n now equals 20 (years) × 12 (months per year) = 240;
$i = (12\% \div 12) \div 100 = .01$;
$(1 + i)^n = (1 + .01)^{240} = (1.01)^{240}$

PRESS 1.01 $\boxed{Y^x}$ 240 $\boxed{=}$ 10.8926

Substituting in the formula, we have:

$$\text{Payment} = \$70,000 \times \frac{.01 \times 10.8926}{10.8926 - 1}$$
$$= \$70,000 \times \frac{.108926}{9.8926}$$
$$= \$770.76$$

Thus, the effect of a shorter term (all other factors being unchanged) is to *increase* the amount of each payment.

To figure out payments on a car loan we use exactly the same formula. Here is an example. You are going to buy a new car which costs $10,000 by paying $2,000 and borrowing the remainder ($8,000). The quoted rate is 13%, and you are to make equal monthly payments for 3 years. How much will your monthly car payments be?

Looking at the payment formula, we find the amount of the loan to be $8,000. The number of payments, n, is 36; i, the periodic interest rate is $(13\% \div 12) \div 100 = .010833$. And $(1 + .010833)^{36} = (1.010833)^{36}$.

PRESS 1.010833 $\boxed{Y^x}$ 36 $\boxed{=}$ 1.4739

So:

$(1 + i)^n = 1.4739$

Substituting in the formula, we have:

$$\text{Payment} = \$8,000 \times \frac{.010833 \times 1.4739}{1.4739 - 1}$$
$$= \$8,000 \times \frac{.01597}{.4739}$$
$$= \$269.59$$

Keep as many decimal places as possible. Keeping only a limited number of decimal positions results in slight inaccuracies in your answers compared with the answers the bank would obtain. In this case, for example, the bank would have computed the payment to be $269.55.

This is the exact amount of your monthly installment.

You can always compute the exact payment on any fixed-rate loan by using the formula. But it is also possible to *estimate* the payment and to be within 2% of the exact amount.

Here's how

ESTIMATING LOAN PAYMENTS

We're going to show you a new technique for approximating payments on long-term loans. The technique *assumes monthly payments* (and monthly compounding of interest). You can do it on a regular calculator.

In estimating payments you will be working with a formula that has two numbers for you to compute. The *approximation formula* is:

Approximate payment = (Amount of loan) × (*i*) × (Multiplier)

In this formula:

i = the periodic interest rate divided by 100. (In this case, the periodic interest rate is the quoted interest rate divided by 12 because interest is compounded monthly.)

The *multiplier* is found according to the value of N in the following table:

Table 1
Estimated Loan Payment Multipliers

N
(YEARS OF LOAN ×
QUOTED INTEREST RATE)

		MULTIPLIER
Over 400	$\longrightarrow$	1
300–400	$\longrightarrow$	1.03
250–299	$\longrightarrow$	1.08
200–249	$\longrightarrow$	1.12
175–199	$\longrightarrow$	1.17

As an illustration, a 25-year mortgage at 12% has a multiplier of 1.03 because 25×12 (years of loan × interest rate) = 300 and the multiplier for the 300–400 range is given as 1.03.

Let's do an example. You are interested in a $150,000 20-year mortgage at an interest rate of 11%. What is the approximate monthly payment?

$$i = (11\% \div 12) \div 100 = .009166667$$

Again, when computing i, keep as many decimal places as appear on your calculator display. Rounding off can lead to serious over- or under-approximations when you multiply i by a very large number (the value of the mortgage).

N = 20 (years of loan) × 11 (the quoted interest rate) = 220
From Table 1, 220→Multiplier of 1.12

Substituting, we have:

Approximate payment = $150,000 × .009166667 × 1.12 = $1,540

(The exact payment is $1,548.)

PROBLEM 1:
What is the approximate monthly payment on a $90,000 mortgage at 13.4% for 25 years?

$i = (13.4 \div 12) \div 100 = .01166667$
$N = 25 \times 13.4 = 335 \rightarrow$ Multiplier (from Table 1) of 1.03
Approximate payment = $90,000 \times .01166667 \times 1.03 = $1035

(The exact payment is $1,042.)

PROBLEM 2:
You borrowed $120,000 for 30 years at an interest rate (compounded monthly) of 14.5%. About how much will this loan cost you a month?

$i = (14.5 \div 12) \div 100 = .012083333$
$N = 30 \times 14.5 = 435 \rightarrow$ Multiplier = 1
Approximate payment = $120,000 \times .012083333 \times 1 = $1,450

(The exact payment is $1,468.)

PROBLEM 3:
Our friends, the Wests, have a $60,000 mortgage which they got some time ago at 7% interest. If they have 30 years to pay off the loan, about how much is their monthly payment?

$i = (7 \div 12) \div 100 = .005833333$
$N = 30 \times 7 = 210 \rightarrow$ Multiplier = 1.12
Approximate payment = $60,000 \times .005833333 \times 1.12 = $392

(The exact payment is $399.)

In talking about mortgages and other long-term loans we are talking about payments spread over a period of time. However, a payment made today is *worth more* to the bank than next month's payment because the bank can re-invest today's payment and begin to earn interest on it immediately. The exact payment formula (and also the approximate one) for mortgages takes the concept of *present value* (''worth'') into account.
Here's how

PRESENT VALUE: WORTH

Let's spend a little time exploring how banks, financial institutions and many, many people think about the *value of money*. Consider what happens first to a small and then to a large amount of money in a relatively short period of time. Start with $1,000 and a going rate of interest of 12% compounded monthly. (If you haven't done so, please read the section about compound interest in Chapter 2; it will help you better understand the concept of present value.)

Twelve percent compounded monthly is 1% per month ($12\% \div 12 = 1\% = .01$). Therefore, the interest earned on $1,000 in one month is:

$$.01 \times \$1000 = \$10$$

So, if you had invested your $1,000 for a month, you would have earned $10. But if instead you kept the money under the proverbial pillow or in a no-interest checking account for one month, you'd "lose" $10 in the sense that you *could have* earned that $10 had you invested your money at that interest rate.

Would not having the $10 disturb you very much? Maybe yes or maybe no, depending on various factors. In fact, it might be worth $10 to you to have the convenience and joy of sleeping with $1,000 under your pillow for a month!

But $1,000 is a small sum of money in comparison to the $3,000,000 you just won in the lottery. Here, one month's interest earns:

$$.01 \times \$3,000,000 = \$30,000$$

This is more than most people make in a year. You certainly won't want to lose a month's interest on $3,000,000 for the fun of having it in bed!

To emphasize the impact of interest on large sums of money, let's change the interest rate to 10% compounded daily. This means:

The daily interest rate $= 10\% \div 365$
$= .0274\%$ { % means hundredths, so
$= .000274$ { $.0274\% = .0274 \div 100 = .000274$

O.K., what does this daily interest rate yield on $1,000?

.000274 × $1,000 = .274

That's about 27¢ per day. But on $3,000,000?

.000274 × $3,000,000 = $822

That's $822 a day!

And on one billion dollars (that's $1,000,000,000), 10%, compounded daily, yields:

.000274 × $1,000,000,000 = $274,000

That's more than one-quarter million dollars each day!

Banks have millions or possibly even billions to invest each day. With such large sums involved it is understandable that a bank would never want to leave its money idle (that is, uninvested)—not even for a single day. So, when a bank gives you a loan for a house, or car, or anything else, it must consider the *time* each payment is made. A payment made today is worth more to the bank than a payment made next month because the bank can re-invest today's payment immediately.

Thus, a payment made to the bank far into the future is worth much less than the payment made today. *The present worth (that is, the worth today) of a payment made in the future is called present value.*

Let's start with an example of 10% simple interest. If you start out investing $100 today at 10% simple interest, you will have $110 in your account at the end of one year. In other words, given a 10% simple interest rate, $110 a year from today has a *value* of $100 today. To put it still another way, the *present value* of $110 a year from today is $100 (at the quoted interest rate).

Now, let's do an example involving compound interest. Suppose you deposit $500 in an account paying 12% compounded monthly. That means you earn 1% (.01) interest each month. At the end of the first month you will have 1% interest credited to your account:

.01 × $500 = $5 interest credited to your account,
            for a total of $505

(The present value of $505 one month from today at 12% compounded monthly is $500.)

Since for the second month and each month following you'd be earning interest on the principal and on the previous month's interest, you'd want to employ the compound interest formula to compute, for example, how much money you'd have at the end of six months. Repeating the compound interest formula, $S = P (1 + i)^n$ where:

P = the principal or amount with which you start
  (In the example, P = $500.)
i = the periodic interest rate divided by 100
  (The periodic interest is the quoted interest rate divided by the number of times per year that interest is compounded. In our example, it is $12\% \div 12 = 1\%$, and $i = 1 \div 100 = .01$.)
n = the number of interest periods
  (There are 6 interest periods in our example because interest is credited monthly for 6 months.)
S = the final amount of money, including both principal and interest

To finish the problem, substituting in the formula:

$$S = \$500 \ (1 + .01)^6$$
$$= \$500 \ (1.01)^6$$
$$= \$500 \times 1.0165$$
$$= \$530.75$$

So, at the end of 6 months, you'd have $530.75 in your account.

Another way of saying this is, given 12% interest compounded monthly, $530.75 6 months from today has a present value of $500 (is worth $500 today).

Up to now, we have actually been taking an amount of money and determining its *future value* and then restating the example in present value terms. But we can also answer the question, "At the quoted interest rate, how much money do I need to deposit today to pay a $400 bill due 3 months from now?" Answering this type of question involves *discounting*, which is finding the present value of a future amount.

Here's how

DISCOUNTING

The essence of a problem in discounting is that the final amount is known (that's S, the interest plus principal in the compound interest formula), and you wish to find the original amount (P, or principal in the compound interest formula). By way of illustration, suppose you know that the first year of your son's college tuition will be $2,500. That bill must be paid 2 years from now. If the interest rate is now 8% compounded monthly, how much money will you need to put into a bank account today to insure that you have $2,500 in 2 years? In this example, the $2,500 is like a payment made in the future, and the amount you'd need to deposit today (equivalent to the principal in the formula) is like the present value of that payment.

Now, the compound interest formula can be restated as:

$$S \text{ (future value)} = P \text{ (present value of payment)} \times (1+i)^n$$

If the future value or payment is a known quantity, say our $2,500 tuition, the question being asked by this formula is, ''What amount deposited today (PV) will yield, with accumulated interest, the given future value (FV) of $2,500 after n (24 in this case because it must be paid in 2 years or 24 months) interest periods?'' The equation above can be solved for present value (PV) by dividing both sides of the equation by the quantity $(1+i)^n$. This results in the formula for present value:

$$PV = \frac{FV}{(1+i)^n}$$

In our example, we have:

$$PV = \frac{\$2,500}{(1+.00667)^{24}} \quad \begin{cases} 8\% \text{ compounded monthly gives a periodic in-} \\ \text{terest of } (8 \div 12) \div 100 = .00667 \end{cases}$$
$$= \$2,500 \div (1.00667)^{24}$$
$$= \$2,500 \div 1.1729$$
$$= \$2,131.47$$

The present value of $2,500 2 years (24 months) from today, given an interest rate of 8%, compounded monthly, is $2,131.47.

Let's try another example. Suppose that in settlement of an old debt you are promised $1,000 three years from now. If the going rate of interest is 12%, compounded quarterly, how much should you be willing to accept today as an equivalent payment of the debt?

In the problem just posed, the future payment is $1,000; i is $(12\% \div 4) \div 100 = .03$; and n = 12 (3 years × 4 quarters per year). Using your calculator, you will find that:

$$(1+i)^n = (1+.03)^{12}$$
$$= 1.4258$$

Therefore:

PV = $1000 ÷ 1.4258 = $701.36

Therefore, $701.36 today is worth $1,000 three years from now if the interest rate is 12% compounded quarterly.

We can double check the answer by applying the usual compound interest formula:

$$S = P (1 + i)^n$$

We just found that, if the interest rate is 12%, compounded quarterly, and $n = 12$, then $(1 + i)^n = 1.4258$. With $P = 701.36, we have:

$$S = $701.36 \times 1.4258 = $1,000.00$$

Knowing how discounting works lets you do advance planning to meet future obligations. We just saw that an obligation of $1,000 three years from now is equivalent to an out-of-pocket expense of just over $700 today (assuming the interest is 12% compounded quarterly.) With larger obligations and longer time spans, the difference between present and future value is even more dramatic. For example, a tuition bill of $20,000 due in 15 years only requires a deposit of $4,788 today if the interest rate is 10% annually. Long-range planning and an understanding of present value can ease the burden of future obligations.

Section 2: It's Real Interesting: Determining Your Interest

In negotiating long-term loans and especially "easy payment" installment plans, you may at times receive information that actually disguises the true interest rate you will be paying.

Here's an example of what we mean. When buying a car, you may be told that your loan for $8,000 has been approved and that you'll be paying it off in 36 equal monthly payments of $270, with interest amounting to $1,720.

36 × $270 = $9,720 (in total payments)
    − $8,000 (the amount of the original loan)
    = $1,720 (in interest)

On the surface, it looks as if you'll be paying an interest rate of about 7.3%, figured like this:

($1,720 ÷ $8,000) ÷ 3 years = 7.33% per year

But *that's the wrong way to compute the rate of interest!* Surprisingly, when you do it correctly, you'll find you're actually paying 14%.
Here's how

ESTIMATING INTEREST RATES

In our discussion of home and automobile mortgages (Chapter 4, Section 1), we explained the concept of present value—today's worth of a payment made in the future. You will recall from that discussion that as far as the bank or lending institution is concerned, since each payment is made at a different time, it is worth a different amount. Given the number of payments, the amount of each payment and the amount of the loan, it is possible to compute the interest rate on a long-term loan. But it is not possible to come up with an exact formula. However, advanced mathematics makes it possible to develop computer programs that will compute interest rates to any desired degree of accuracy.

And that's what we did in this Section.

By writing a computer program, we developed a table of payment factors that lets you look up your *annual effective interest rate* (the actual yearly interest rate you are paying, as we showed in Chapter 3, Section 1) to the nearest whole percent. For all practical purposes, this close approximation is all you need to be sure you're not being charged a usurious rate of interest. (By definition, a usurious rate is a rate greater than that allowed by law.)

The technique we devised shows you a new way of determining your annual effective interest rate, given the amount of the loan, the size of the equal monthly payments and the total number of payments. This technique, published here for the first time, involves first applying a very easy formula, then looking the answer up in the table that ends this section. That's all there is to it.

Let's start.

In order to estimate the rate of interest you are paying, you must know the amount of the loan, the monthly payment (assuming the loan is paid off in equal monthly installments) and the total number of payments.

Step 1 Compute the *Payment Factor* (PF):
$$PF = \frac{\text{Amount of loan}}{\text{Monthly payment}}$$

In the example above:

$$PF = \frac{8,000}{270}$$
$$= 29.63$$

Step 2 Knowing the total number of payments (36 in the example), locate this number in the left column of Table 1. (This column lists the number of monthly payments, in 6-month intervals, ranging from 12 [one year] to 360 [30 years]. If the exact number of payments you are required to make is not given, use the nearest number, but remember that your resulting estimate will be somewhat less precise.)

Step 3 After you've located the total number of payments, look across that row horizontally from left to right to find the column where the PF closest to the one you have computed appears.

Notice that the PFs decrease as you go across the row and that the last number in this row on the first page of the table is 30.37. So, go on to the second page of the table and continue moving across the row that corresponds to 36 payments.

You will find the number 29.98 followed by 29.60, which is as close to our example PF of 29.63 as we can get using these tables. Now, look up to the top of the column in which 29.60 appears, and you'll see the heading corresponds to an interest rate of 14%. Since 29.60 isn't exactly 29.63, the interest rate you'll be paying is not exactly 14% but close to it. That's considerably less than the original estimate of 7.3% we thought we'd be paying when we did the obvious, but incorrect, calculations at the beginning.

To check, let's go back to one of the examples we used in the previous section, even though we know the interest rate. There, we were buying an $80,000 house with a $10,000 down payment. We borrowed $70,000 on a 30-year mortgage at 12% compounded monthly (this is an annual effective rate of 12.7%). In that section, we learned to compute the monthly payment, which amounted to $720 ($720.03).

The *incorrect* way of determining interest rates would be:

$720 × 360 (that's 12 payments/year × 30 years)
= $259,200 (total interest and principal to be paid)
− $70,000 (in principal)
$189,200 (in interest)

Dividing 189,200 by 70,000 and then by 30 years results in an (incorrect) interest rate of 7.51%.

Estimating *correctly,* we find the PF to be:

$$\frac{\$70,000}{\$720} = 97.22$$

Going down the left column to 360, we look across the row to the PF closest to 97.22. Looking up this column to the heading at the top, we see 13%—fairly close to the 13% (effective rate) we know we are paying.

Installment loans on a complete 7-piece bedroom set costing $3,400 that, say, call for $30 down and 24 equal payments of $179 are much less common than they used to be. This "bargain" ends up costing you $4,326, of which $926 is interest. According to the method we used here, this is equivalent to a 27% annual effective rate of interest!

Truth in Lending Laws make it easier to find out the rate of interest you are actually paying, if you bother to read the whole contract. The table in this Section provides you with a fast way of double-checking annual effective interest rates under the condition of equal monthly payments. . . . It's in your interest to do this check.

Table 1
Table of Payment Factors

TOTAL NUMBER OF PAYMENTS	7%	8%	9%	10%	11%
		ANNUAL EFFECTIVE INTEREST RATES (%)			
6	5.88	5.87	5.85	5.84	5.81
12	11.57	11.51	11.46	11.40	11.29
18	17.07	16.95	16.82	16.71	16.48
24	22.38	22.17	21.97	21.76	21.37
30	27.52	27.20	26.89	26.59	26.00
36	32.49	32.04	31.61	31.19	30.37
42	37.29	36.70	36.13	35.57	34.51
48	41.93	41.18	40.46	39.75	38.41
54	46.42	45.49	44.60	43.74	42.10
60	50.76	49.64	48.57	47.54	45.59
66	54.96	53.64	52.37	51.16	48.88
72	59.01	57.48	56.02	54.62	51.99
78	62.93	61.18	59.51	57.91	54.94
84	66.72	64.74	62.85	61.05	57.72
90	70.38	68.16	66.05	64.05	60.34
96	73.93	71.45	69.12	66.90	62.82
102	77.35	74.62	72.05	69.63	65.17
108	80.66	77.67	74.86	72.22	67.38
114	83.86	80.61	77.56	74.70	69.48
120	86.95	83.43	80.14	77.06	71.46
126	89.94	86.15	82.61	79.31	73.32

Table of Payment Factors *(continued)*

TOTAL NUMBER OF PAYMENTS	\multicolumn{5}{c}{ANNUAL EFFECTIVE INTEREST RATES (%)}
	7%	8%	9%	10%	11%
132	92.84	88.76	84.98	81.45	75.09
138	95.63	91.28	87.25	83.50	76.76
144	98.33	93.70	89.42	85.45	78.34
150	100.95	96.03	91.58	87.31	79.83
156	103.47	98.27	93.49	89.08	81.24
162	105.91	100.43	95.40	90.77	82.57
168	108.27	102.51	97.22	92.38	83.82
174	110.55	104.50	98.98	93.92	85.01
180	112.76	106.43	100.66	95.38	86.13
186	114.89	108.28	102.26	96.78	87.19
192	116.95	110.06	103.80	98.11	88.20
198	118.95	111.77	105.28	99.38	89.14
204	120.87	113.42	106.69	100.59	90.04
210	122.73	115.00	108.04	101.75	90.88
216	124.53	116.53	109.33	102.85	91.68
222	126.28	118.00	110.58	103.90	92.44
228	127.96	119.41	111.76	104.90	93.15
234	129.58	120.77	112.90	105.85	93.83
240	131.16	122.08	113.99	106.76	94.46
246	132.68	123.34	115.04	107.63	95.06
252	134.15	124.55	116.04	108.46	95.63
258	135.57	125.71	116.99	109.25	96.17
264	136.94	126.83	117.91	110.00	96.68
270	138.27	127.91	118.79	110.72	97.16
276	139.55	128.95	119.63	111.40	97.61
282	140.79	129.95	120.44	112.05	98.04
288	141.99	130.91	121.21	112.67	98.44
294	143.15	131.84	121.95	113.27	98.83
300	144.28	132.73	122.66	113.83	99.19
306	145.36	133.58	123.34	114.37	99.53
312	146.41	134.41	123.99	114.88	99.85
318	147.42	135.20	124.61	115.37	100.16
324	148.40	135.97	125.21	115.84	100.45
330	149.35	136.70	125.78	116.28	100.72
336	150.26	137.41	126.32	116.71	100.97
342	151.15	138.09	126.85	117.11	101.22
348	152.00	138.74	127.35	117.50	101.45
354	152.83	139.37	127.83	117.87	101.66
360	153.63	139.98	128.29	118.22	101.87
	12%	13%	14%	15%	16%
6	5.81	5.79	5.78	5.76	5.73
12	11.29	11.24	11.19	11.13	11.03

Table of Payment Factors *(continued)*

TOTAL NUMBER OF PAYMENTS	ANNUAL EFFECTIVE INTEREST RATE (%)				
	12%	13%	14%	15%	16%
18	16.48	16.36	16.25	16.14	15.93
24	21.37	21.18	21.00	20.82	20.46
30	26.00	25.72	25.44	25.17	24.65
36	30.37	29.98	29.60	29.23	28.52
42	34.51	34.00	33.50	33.02	32.10
48	38.41	37.77	37.16	36.56	35.41
54	42.10	41.32	40.57	39.85	38.47
60	45.59	44.67	43.78	42.92	41.30
66	48.88	47.81	46.78	45.79	43.91
72	51.99	50.77	49.59	48.46	46.33
78	54.94	53.55	52.22	50.95	48.57
84	57.72	56.16	54.68	53.27	50.63
90	60.34	58.63	56.99	55.44	52.54
96	62.82	60.94	59.15	57.46	54.31
102	65.17	63.12	61.18	59.34	55.94
108	67.38	65.17	63.08	61.10	57.45
114	69.48	67.10	64.85	62.73	58.85
120	71.46	68.91	66.51	64.26	60.14
126	73.32	70.61	68.07	65.69	61.33
132	75.09	72.22	69.53	67.01	62.43
138	76.76	73.73	70.90	68.25	63.45
144	78.34	75.15	72.18	69.41	64.39
150	79.83	76.49	73.38	70.48	65.26
156	81.24	77.74	74.50	71.49	66.07
162	82.57	78.92	75.55	72.42	66.81
168	83.82	80.04	76.54	73.30	67.50
174	85.01	81.08	77.46	74.11	68.14
180	86.13	82.07	78.32	74.87	68.73
186	87.19	82.99	79.13	75.58	69.27
192	88.20	83.86	79.89	76.24	69.77
198	89.14	84.68	80.60	76.85	70.24
204	90.04	85.45	81.27	77.43	70.67
210	90.88	86.18	81.89	77.96	71.07
216	91.68	86.86	82.47	78.46	71.43
222	92.44	87.50	83.02	78.93	71.77
228	93.15	88.11	83.53	79.36	72.09
234	93.83	88.67	84.01	79.77	72.38
240	94.46	89.21	84.46	80.15	72.65
246	95.06	89.71	84.88	80.50	72.89
252	95.63	90.18	85.27	80.83	73.12
258	96.17	90.63	85.64	81.13	73.34
264	96.68	91.05	85.98	81.42	73.53
270	97.16	91.44	86.31	81.68	73.71
276	97.61	91.81	86.61	81.93	73.88
282	98.04	92.16	86.89	82.16	74.04

Table of Payment Factors *(continued)*

TOTAL NUMBER OF PAYMENTS	ANNUAL EFFECTIVE INTEREST RATE (%)				
	12%	13%	14%	15%	16%
288	98.44	92.49	87.16	82.38	74 18
294	98.83	92.80	87.41	82.58	74.31
300	99.19	93.08	87.64	82.77	74 43
306	99.53	93.36	87.86	82.94	74.55
312	99.85	93.61	88.07	83.11	74.65
318	100.16	93.86	88.26	83.26	74.75
324	100.45	94.08	88.44	83.40	74.84
330	100.72	94.30	88.60	83.53	74.92
336	100.97	94.50	88.76	83.66	75.00
342	101.22	94.69	88.91	83.77	75.07
348	101.45	94.86	89.05	83.88	75.13
354	101.66	95.03	89.18	83.98	75.19
360	101.87	95.19	89.30	84.07	75.25

	17%	18%	19%	20%	21%
6	5.73	5.72	5.70	5.69	5.66
12	11.03	10.98	10.93	10.89	10.79
18	15.93	15.83	15.73	15.63	15.44
24	20.46	20.29	20.12	19.96	19.64
30	24.65	24.40	24.15	23.91	23.44
36	28.52	28.18	27.84	27.52	26.89
42	32.10	31.66	31.23	30.81	30.01
48	35.41	34.86	34.33	33.82	32.83
54	38.47	37.81	37.18	36.56	35.39
60	41.30	40.53	39.79	39.07	37.70
66	43.91	43.03	42.18	41.36	39.80
72	46.33	45.33	44.37	43.44	41.70
78	48.57	47.45	46.38	45.35	43.42
84	50.63	49.40	48.22	47.09	44.97
90	52.54	51.19	49.91	48.68	46.38
96	54.31	52.85	51.45	50.13	47.65
102	55.94	54.37	52.87	51.45	48.81
108	57.45	55.77	54.17	52.66	49.85
114	58.85	57.06	55.37	53.76	50.80
120	60.14	58.25	56.46	54.77	51.65
126	61.33	59.34	57.46	55.69	52.43
132	62.43	60.34	58.38	56.53	53.13
138	63.45	61.27	59.22	57.29	53.77
144	64.39	62.12	59.99	57.99	54.34
150	65.26	62.91	60.70	58.63	54.86
156	66.07	63.63	61.35	59.21	55.34
162	66.81	64.29	61.94	59.75	55.76
168	67.50	64.91	62.49	60.23	56.15
174	68.14	65.47	62.99	60.67	56.50

Table of Payment Factors *(continued)*

TOTAL NUMBER OF PAYMENTS	ANNUAL EFFECTIVE INTEREST RATES (%)				
	17%	18%	19%	20%	21%
180	68.73	65.99	63.45	61.08	56.82
186	69.27	66.47	63.87	61.45	57.10
192	69.77	66.91	64.25	61.79	57.36
198	70.24	67.31	64.60	62.09	57.60
204	70.67	67.68	64.93	62.37	57.81
210	71.07	68.03	65.22	62.63	58.00
216	71.43	68.34	65.49	62.87	58.18
222	71.77	68.63	65.74	63.08	58.34
228	72.09	68.90	65.97	63.27	58.48
234	72.38	69.15	66.18	63.45	58.61
240	72.65	69.37	66.37	63.62	58.73
246	72.89	69.58	66.55	63.76	58.83
252	73.12	69.77	66.71	63.90	58.93
258	73.34	69.95	66.86	64.02	59.02
264	73.53	70.11	66.99	64.14	59.09
270	73.71	70.26	67.12	64.24	59.17
276	73.88	70.40	67.23	64.33	59.23
282	74.04	70.53	67.34	64.42	59.29
288	74.18	70.65	67.43	64.50	59.34
294	74.31	70.75	67.52	64.57	59.39
300	74.43	70.85	67.60	64.63	59.43
306	74.55	70.94	67.67	64.69	59.47
312	74.65	71.03	67.74	64.75	59.51
318	74.75	71.11	67.80	64.80	59.54
324	74.84	71.18	67.86	64.84	59.57
330	74.92	71.24	67.91	64.89	59.60
336	75.00	71.30	67.96	64.92	59.62
342	75.07	71.36	68.00	64.96	59.64
348	75.13	71.41	68.04	64.99	59.66
354	75.19	71.46	68.08	65.02	59.68
360	75.25	71.50	68.11	65.04	59.69
	22%	23%	24%	25%	26%
3	2.90	2.90	2.89	2.89	2.89
6	5.66	5.65	5.64	5.62	5.61
9	8.29	8.26	8.24	8.21	8.18
12	10.79	10.75	10.70	10.66	10.61
15	13.17	13.10	13.04	12.97	12.90
18	15.44	15.34	15.25	15.16	15.07
21	17.59	17.47	17.34	17.22	17.11
24	19.64	19.48	19.33	19.18	19.03
27	21.59	21.40	21.21	21.03	20.85
30	23.44	23.22	23.00	22.78	22.56

Table of Payment Factors *(continued)*

TOTAL NUMBER OF PAYMENTS	ANNUAL EFFECTIVE INTEREST RATES (%)				
	22%	23%	24%	25%	26%
33	25.21	24.95	24.69	24.43	24.18
36	26.89	26.59	26.29	26.00	25.72
	27%	28%	29%	30%	31%
3	2.88	2.88	2.88	2.87	2.86
6	5.60	5.59	5.57	5.56	5.54
9	8.16	8.13	8.11	8.08	8.03
12	10.57	10.52	10.48	10.44	10.36
15	12.84	12.77	12.71	12.65	12.53
18	14.98	14.89	14.80	14.72	14.55
21	16.99	16.88	16.77	16.66	16.44
24	18.89	18.75	18.61	18.47	18.20
27	20.68	20.50	20.34	20.17	19.85
30	22.36	22.16	21.96	21.76	21.38
33	23.95	23.71	23.48	23.25	22.81
36	25.44	25.17	24.91	24.65	24.15

Section 3: *It's in the Cards: Credit Card Interest*

When you buy by credit card, such as VISA or MASTERCARD, or a department store charge, you are, in effect, borrowing money. Just as in any other situation that involves loans, you, as the borrower, must pay interest.

Not all credit card interest is the same. Different companies (banks, stores) charge different rates, and they compute the balance on which the interest is paid in different ways, with considerable variation from one to another. So, shopping for a credit card makes as much sense as trying to get the best price on any deal. Since all cards require you to make payments each month when there is a balance due, getting the "best" card—the one with terms most advantageous to you—will result in a saving every month.

The credit card company's terms are usually stated in small print in an out-of-the-way place on the bottom or on the back of your monthly statement. Here's a typical example:

We figure the finance charges [a fancy phrase for interest] on your account as follows: On purchases, by adding together the outstanding purchase balance at the end of each day in the billing cycle, including unpaid finance charges and giving effect to a purchase from the later of the date the purchase is made or the first day of the billing cycle, dividing that sum by the number of days in the billing cycle and applying to that balance the periodic rate.

This 77-word sentence is confusing, to say the least. Notice that the rate of interest is referred to in the last three words—"the periodic rate." The rest of this long sentence describes how the company computes the balance on which the interest is applied. In trying to understand what you will be paying in finance charges, you need to consider two factors: first, the *annual effective interest rate* and second, the *average daily balance*.

What is *not* important is to spend any time checking the bank's monthly calculations since these are done by computer. It's safe to assume that all the arithmetic is correct. You should, however, check to make certain that there were no errors in recording the individual charges and cash advances— by matching the amount shown on your statement with the amount on your (the "customer's") copy of each charge slip.

The rest of this section is about how finance charges work. Let's start with the rate of interest you actually pay.

Here's how

ANNUAL EFFECTIVE INTEREST RATE

The annual effective rate of interest is based on the quoted rate of interest (also given on each monthly statement) and is the actual interest rate you pay per year for the use of the credit card.

To understand the annual effective rate, think of the bank, store or credit card company as earning interest—from you. Interest can be charged on new purchases and on old balances. If you waited until the end of the year to pay your bill, you would be adding *additional interest* on the interest, purchases and balance. In effect, you would be paying interest on the interest.

This is what happens with many, but not all, credit cards. Because some time elapses by the time you get your statement that includes any previous balance owed, plus new purchases, plus interest, you may be billed for interest on the interest you owe from the time of the previous period until the time your payment is received.

Interest paid on interest, the situation we just described, is exactly the same as the concept of compound interest (which we talked about in Chapter 2, Section 2). This concept also underlies the idea of *annual effective yield*, or annual effective *rate*. If you're uncertain about the relationship between annual effective yield (or annual effective rate) and the quoted interest rate, rereading Chapter 3, Section 1 will help.

The formula for annual effective rate is:

Annual effective rate $= 100 \, (1+i)^k - 100$

In this formula:

> $k =$ the number of *times per year* that interest is paid;
> $i =$ *the periodic interest rate divided by 100*. (The periodic interest rate is the quoted interest rate divided by k.)

Notice that now we need to know more about the periodic interest rate and the quoted interest rate.

The Sonesta Bank's interest charges on its MASTERCARD purchases are given as follows (this information appears on the monthly statements):

> Annual percentage rate 18.90%
> Monthly periodic rate 1.575%

The *monthly periodic rate* is determined by dividing the annual percentage rate (or quoted interest rate) of 18.90 by 12 months, as follows:

$$\frac{18.90}{12}$$
$$= 1.575\% \text{ per month}$$

This is the rate of interest you pay every month on your average daily balance. (This rate is what was referred to in the long sentence we quoted at the beginning of this section.)

Going back to the formula for annual effective rate, let's first finish computing i:

$$i = \frac{1.575}{100} = .01575$$

And $k = 12$.
Therefore, substituting in the formula we have:

$$\text{Annual effective rate} = 100 \times (1 + .01575)^{12} - 100$$
$$= 100 \times (1.01575)^{12} - 100$$

Computation of 1.01575^{12} must be done on a calculator that has a $\boxed{Y^x}$ or an $\boxed{X^y}$ button. To do this computation:

PRESS 1.01575 $\boxed{Y^x}$ 12 $\boxed{=}$

The result is 1.2063, so:

Annual effective rate $= 100 \times 1.2063 - 100$
$= 120.63 - 100$
$= 20.63\%$

This means that the quoted annual percentage rate of 18.90% results in your paying interest at the rate of 20.63% per year!

In some sense, that was the easy part. Now let's consider how the Sonesta Bank figures your average daily balance.

Here's how

AVERAGE DAILY BALANCE

We'll show you two different methods for computing the average daily balance and we'll compare them. Before we start, remember that the *average daily balance* is not calculated in the same way by all banks or credit card companies. Some companies exclude finance charges if you pay your balance on the required date, while others include them. Some do not add interest charges on to new purchases *if* those purchases are paid for on time. There are credit cards that require you to pay interest from the date the purchase is made (the date of the transaction), while other cards begin computing interest from the *posting date* (the day the company or bank received the bill from the establishment where the purchase was made).

As you can begin to see, the possibilities and combinations are so varied that we couldn't cover them all here. Rather, we present two typical examples of different methods of computing the average daily balance on a real bill we just received from the Sonesta Bank.

Method 1

This is a reproduction of our current, December/January monthly statement:

POSTING DATE	DATE AND DESCRIPTION OF TRANSACTION		$ AMOUNT
12/14	12/07	New England Store	28.88
12/27	12/17	Dynasty Szechuan	29.70
01/07	12/21	Sunshine Records	19.20
01/07	12/27	Razzi Restaurant	29.16
01/09		Payment—Thank you	200.00

Here's some additional information we collected from this bill and from the previous month's statement:

Closing Date:	1/11/85 (from current bill)
Previous Closing Date:	12/11/84 (from previous bill)
Previous Balance (including interest due):	$1,291.47 (from current bill)
Prior Month's Interest Charge:	$ 20.48 (from previous bill)
Monthly Periodic Rate:	1.575% (from both bills)

Method 1 of calculating the average daily balance is the simplest method and also the one with the terms that are most advantageous to you. It *excludes* both interest payments and new purchases but takes into account the fact that your payment (of $200) wasn't received until 01/09. It also takes into consideration that $1,291.47 (the previous balance including $20.48 in interest) was due on 12/11. Method 1 is most likely to be used by credit card companies that want you to pay your full balance each month.

Three steps are involved in computing the average daily balance.

Step 1 Compute the number of days in the billing cycle that runs from 12/11/84 to 01/11/85:

From 12/11/84 to 12/31/84 there are:	20 days
From 12/31/84 to 01/11/85 there are:	11 days
TOTAL	31 days

Step 2 Subtract the interest due from both the previous balance and the payment (Method 1 excludes interest payments):

net previous balance due = $1,291.47 − $20.48 = $1,270.99
net payment made   = $ 200.00 − $20.48 = $ 179.52

Step 3 Find the average daily balance:

(a.) Count the net previous balance due (from Step 2) 31 times (there are 31 days in the billing cycle):
1,270.99 × 31 = 39,400.69

(b.) Count the net payment made (from Step 2) 3 times (since the payment was "present" during only 3 days of the billing cycle—i.e., the payment was made on 01/09 and the closing date is 01/11 = 3 days)
179.52 × 3 = 538.56

(c.) Subtract the amount calculated in (b.) from amount calculated in (a.) and divide by 31
(39,400.69 − 538.56) ÷ 31 = 1,253.62

This ($1,253.62) is the average daily balance using Method 1.

To compute *current interest due* charges, multiply the average daily balance by the specified monthly periodic rate:

Current interest due $= 1.575\% \times \$1{,}253.62$
$\qquad\qquad\qquad = 0.01575 \times \$1{,}253.62$
$\qquad\qquad\qquad = \$19.74$

To compute the *total you owe* on your Sonesta Bank credit card this month, add the previous balance due (including previous interest due), the current interest due, the total of all new purchases (which are $\$28.88 + \$29.70 + \$19.20 + \$29.16 = \$106.94$) and subtract the amount paid:

Total due $= \$1{,}291.47 + \$19.74 + \$106.94 - 200.00$
$\qquad\qquad = \$1{,}218.15$

According to this Method, our total amount due is $1,218.15.

We'll now figure out what we would owe using another common method of computing the average daily balance, a method which is more costly to you.

Method 2

Method 2 for computing the average daily balance tends to be favored by stores and banks that encourage you to carry forward a balance by requiring only a token minimal payment each month. As you might expect, Method 2 includes interest charges and new purchases in the computation of the average daily balance.

Method 2 was somewhat cryptically described in the 77-word sentence that started this Section. New purchases will be counted from the *transaction date* unless that date is earlier than the beginning of the current billing cycle. If that is the case, the new purchase will be considered to have occurred on the first day of the billing cycle. (This situation can arise if the establishment where the purchase was made did not submit its bills to the credit card company quickly.)

Now let's go through the five steps of Method 2 using the same monthly statement we used earlier.

Step 1 Compute the number of days in the billing cycle. This is done exactly as in Method A, Step 1. The result, as before, is 31 days.

Step 2 Count the previous amount due, *including interest*, 31 times. (There are 31 days in the billing cycle.) (Notice that in Step 2 of Method 1, interest was excluded.)

$$1{,}291.47 \times 31 = 40{,}035.57$$

Step 3 (This is the step that accounts for new purchases.) Count the appropriate number of days for each purchase and multiply the amount of the new purchase by that number of days.

(a.) The first purchase of $28.88 was made at the New England store on 12/07/84 (the transaction date). Since the closing date of the last billing cycle was 12/10/84, the date of this transaction is taken to be the first day of the current billing cycle, which is 12/11/84; thus this purchase is counted 31 times.

$$28.88 \times 31 = 895.28$$

(b.) The purchase of $29.70 was made on 12/17/84. To compute the number of days, note that:

From 12/17/84 to 12/31/84 there are	15 days
(counting 12/17 as one of those days)	
From 01/01/85 to 01/11/85 there are	11 days
TOTAL	26 days

$$29.70 \times 26 = 772.20$$

(c.) The purchase of $19.20 was made on 12/21/84.

From 12/21/84 to 12/31/84 there are	11 days
(counting 12/21 as one of those days)	
From 01/01/85 to 01/11/85 there are	11 days
TOTAL	22 days

$$19.20 \times 22 = 422.40$$

(d.) The purchase of $29.16 was made on 12/27/84

From 12/27/84 to 12/31/84 there arc	5 days
From 01/01/85 to 01/11/85 there are	11 days
TOTAL	16 days

$$29.16 \times 16 = 466.56$$

Step 4 Count the full payment made ($200.00) 3 times since it was "present" during only 3 days of the billing cycle

$$200.00 \times 3 = 600.00$$

Step 5 Compute the average daily balance. Find the sum of the items in Steps 2 and 3, subtract the result in Step 4, and then divide by the number of days in the billing cycle (Step 1).

$$\text{Average Daily Balance} = \frac{(\text{Step 2}) + (\text{Step 3}) - (\text{Step 4})}{\text{Step 1}} =$$

$$\frac{(40,035.57 + 895.28 + 772.20 + 422.40 + 466.56 - 600.00)}{31}$$

$$= \$1,354.58$$

Using Method 2, the average daily balance is $1,354.58, substantially different from the result we got with Method 1 ($1,253.62). The difference is $100.96.

We next have to calculate the interest charges (1.575%) on the average daily balance:

Current interest due $= 1.575\% \times \$1,354.58$
$\qquad\qquad\quad = .01575 \times \$1,354.58$
$\qquad\qquad\quad = \$21.33$

The total amount you owe the credit card company is the sum of the previous balance due, the current interest due, the total of all new purchases ($\$28.88 + \$29.70 + \$19.20 + \$29.16 = \$106.94$), less the amount paid:

Total due $= \$1,291.47 + \$21.33 + \$106.94 - \$200.00$
$\qquad\qquad = \$1,219.74$

According to Method 2, we owe $\$1,219.74$ on this credit card.

The difference between the total amount due in Methods 1 and 2 is $\$1.59$ and is the result of the way the average daily balance was computed. It reflects the difference in the amount of interest due (Method $1 = \$19.74$; Method $2 = \$21.33$).

Is $\$1.59$ significant? No one can answer that question for you. The significance of *any* sum of money depends on many factors. One factor is what it can buy. For $\$1.59$ you can probably have a "breakfast special" in your neighborhood luncheonette, a glossy magazine, 3 daisies, 4 cups of coffee. . . .

But when it comes to credit cards, keep in mind that there will be a difference between Methods 1 and 2 every month. So if you kept to the identical purchasing and payment patterns, the yearly difference would be

$12 \times \$1.59 = \$19.08$ per year

This more than pays for the yearly cost of most credit cards, and, if you increase the amount of your purchases, the difference would be still greater. The difference would be even more if you wait a little longer to make a payment.

Sometimes the method of computing the average daily balance is more significant than the variability in interest rates.

Here's how

SUPERCARD VS. CLASSYCARD

Let's suppose that SUPERCARD computes the average daily balance by Method 2 and charges an *annual percentage rate* of 18.00%. CLASSYCARD uses Method 1 to figure out the average daily balance, but has a 19.00% annual percentage charge. Which card offers you the most advantageous terms?

SUPERCARD
The monthly interest rate is $18\% \div 12 = 1.5000\%$.
The average daily balance on the bill used in the example, computed
    by Method 2 = $1,354.58.
The interest charge is $.015000 \times \$1,354.58 = \$20.32$.

CLASSYCARD
The monthly interest rate is $19\% \div 12 = 1.5833\%$.
The average daily balance (Method 1) = $1,253.62.
The interest charge is $.015833 \times \$1,253.62 = \$19.85$.

In this example, CLASSYCARD turns out to be less expensive to you even though it charges a higher rate of interest.

Clearly, the most advantageous credit card will be the one that both charges the lowest interest and computes the average daily balance by a method that comes close to Method 1. If you are using a credit card that computes the average daily balance by Method 2, try to pay your bill as quickly as possible so that you don't pay more interest on your interest.

It is never necessary for you to go through any of the computations we showed you in this section. You can be quite certain that the credit card company's computers are doing it correctly.

It is important for you to read the

small print

Take careful note of which items are included in the average daily balance. In particular, check each of your credit cards contracts to see if they include interest and new purchases; if so, this is disadvantageous to you. Also, see if new purchases are being considered from the posting date (better) or transaction date (worse for you). *Try to use the credit card that gives you the best deal* even if it may mean you have to pay the entire balance each month. As we've explained before, it's all in the cards.

PART TWO

OUTDOOR MATH

5

Restaurants
and Boutiques

Section 1: Eating Out: Don't be a Soft Touch (Estimating and Tipping)

Handling the bill and computing a tip in a restaurant can be a source of anxiety for many people. While the origins of tipping are obscure, it's a practice with a long history. And, although you may sometimes want to curse the first person who gave someone a coin for performing a task, the fact is that tipping is a well-established custom, and you just have to learn to cope with it. We'll start with some general guidelines for estimating your bill.

Here's how

ESTIMATING YOUR BILL

There are times when you need to be able to approximate the amount of a bill even though you don't require an exact total. One such time is an unplanned trip to the market when you might like to know whether you're carrying enough money to pay for your purchases *before* you get to the checkout counter. Another time is when you're standing outside a restaurant examining the menu and trying to decide if you like the place and the selections *and* if you can afford to eat there.

Let's start with a walk through the supermarket. You have $10 when you stop at the market to pick up a few items. (With today's prices, even without estimating, you know that you can't get more than a few!) You want a container of milk (79¢), furniture polish ($1.99), 2 cucumbers (43¢), cheese ($1.19), a box of strawberries on special (89¢), dog food (4 cans for $2.57) and a 2-liter bottle of soda ($1.29). Do you have enough money to pay for all this?

Whenever you estimate in these types of situations, it's better to err on the high side—that is, to overestimate. This leaves you with a cushion—and few surprises. So, as a general rule, *round prices up.* The second trick to remember is that since you'll be doing mental addition, round prices to numbers that are easy to work with, such as whole dollars, half dollars, quarters . . .

In this way:

ACTUAL PRICE		ROUNDED PRICE	CUMMULATIVE ADDITION
.79	⟶	1.00	1.00
1.99	⟶	2.00	3.00
.43	⟶	.50	3.50
1.19	⟶	1.25	4.75
.89	⟶	1.00	5.75
2.57	⟶	2.50	8.25
1.29	⟶	1.25	
$9.15, actual			$9.50, estimated

Estimating prices in this way leaves you enough to pay the tax on the furniture polish and still buy a newspaper on the way home.

Let's now try another example where you'll want to estimate probable costs in whole dollars. The Coral Inn Restaurant lists the following prices on the menu in the window: entrees ranging from $9.95 to $12.95; appetizers from $1.75 to $4.95; and desserts from $2.00 to $3.95. There are also salads ($1.75 to $3.00), soups ($1.50, $2.50) and beverages (from $1.00 for coffee to $1.50 for espresso). Assuming the two of you will each have a glass of wine, about how much will dinner for two cost?

To estimate, you must first try to figure out how hungry you are. Will you have a full dinner? An entree and dessert and coffee? How about salad, an entree, dessert and coffee for one; an appetizer, entree, salad and coffee for the other. Be generous. This is one situation where your eyes should be bigger than your stomach—so your stomach isn't bigger than your pocketbook!

Use whole dollars and, again, estimate costs on the high side:

Salad, $3; entree, $13→$16; +dessert, $3→$19; +coffee, $1→$20 (for one person); *plus:*
Appetizer, $4→$24; +entree, $13→$37; +salad, $3→$40; +coffee, $1→$41.

Add wine ($2.50/glass × 2 = $5), tax and the tip and eating at the Coral Inn can easily amount to $55 or $60. Of course, you can probably eat for a lot less by eating a lot less—which is what some people do when they want to try a restaurant slightly out of their price range.

Now that you know the basics, let's move inside the restaurant. You've had your meal, the bill arrives and you're faced with an important choice: whether or not to estimate the accuracy of the bill or to calculate it exactly. We frequently estimate, but that's because *we are willing to be wrong* by a small amount, especially on a large check. By estimating the accuracy of the total rather than checking it exactly, you are, in effect, saying that you don't care if there's an error in the other party's favor—that you are willing to pay as much as a couple of dollars extra for the *luxury* of not adding the bill.

Here's what we do when we want to know if a check is *approximately* correct. First, we make sure that only items we ordered are included on the bill. Then we check to see that the charge for each item is the same as the charge listed on the menu (or on the price tag). In most restaurants these days the arithmetic part (the adding and the computation of taxes) is done by computerized cash register, so most errors are inadvertent charges for items you didn't order or ordered and never received. It is also common for the price of the item to be wrong. Therefore, whether you're estimating the accuracy of the total bill or calculating it exactly, always go through these steps.

Now you're ready to round the dollar amounts to numbers that are easy to add in your head—whole dollars, halves, quarters—and add up the items cumulatively as you go down the column of figures. On a $30 bill, your estimated total and actual total should agree within a couple of dollars.

Going down the check you come to a subtotal, then to the tax. To understand how the sales tax (and tip) is computed, you'll need to understand percentages.

Here's how

COMPUTING THE TAX EXACTLY

In many places in the United States there is a state and/or city sales tax on restaurant meals; maybe on the nonfood items in your grocery basket as well, such as furniture polish, soap and so on; and perhaps on other purchases like clothes or appliances. These taxes can range from as low as 1% or 2% to as high as the 8.25% in New York City. Taxes are generally applied to your total restaurant bill: food and bar beverages.

Calculating the amount of sales tax involves two computations:

Step 1 Convert the sales tax percentage to a decimal by dividing it by 100. (To divide by 100, move the decimal point 2 places to the left.)

Step 2 Multiply the price of the item(s) by this decimal. The result is the sales tax.

That's all there is to it, although you might want to find the total cost, including tax, by adding the sales tax to the original price.

EXAMPLE 1: Dinner for two comes to $33.75. Local state and city sales tax is 6%. Find the dollar amount of the tax and the total amount of the bill, including tax.

SOLUTION:
(1) Convert 6% to a decimal:
 $6\% = 6/100 = .06$
(2) Multiply by the decimal to find the tax:
 $.06 \times \$33.75 = \$2.03 = \text{Tax}$
(3) Add the tax and the cost to find the total bill:
 $\$2.03 + \$33.75 = \$35.78 = \text{Total Cost}$

EXAMPLE 2: In New York City the sales tax is 8¼%. If a new car is $7,870, how much will the car cost us and how much of this will we be paying in tax?

SOLUTION: Step 1 involves converting the percent to a decimal. Converting 8¼% requires first converting ¼ to a decimal. If you don't recognize that ¼ = .25, you can obtain this result by dividing 1 by 4. (All fractions can be converted to decimals by dividing the numerator by the denominator.) Thus, 8¼% = 8.25%. Now:
 $8.25\% = 8.25 \div 100 = .0825$
 $\text{Tax} = .0825 \times \$7,870 = \$649.28$
 $\text{Total Cost} = \$649.28 + \$7,870 = \$8,519.28$

Helpful hint: There's one good thing about having a 8¼% sales tax—it's easy to figure out a tip by just doubling the tax. This works because the tax is almost always shown separately on a bill and twice 8¼% is 16½%. That's slightly more than the traditional 15% tip, so all you have to do is leave a little bit less. (You might now want to read the rest of this section for a more complete picture of tipping.)

With paper and pencil, or better yet with a pocket calculator, it's always possible to figure out the tax *exactly,* but in a restaurant you may be satisfied with an approximation.

Here's how

ESTIMATING THE TAX

Approximating the tax involves mental arithmetic and three steps:

Step 1 Round off the bill to the *nearest* whole dollar.

Step 2 Multiply the whole dollar amount by the tax, forgetting about the decimal point. (Multiply by 4 for 4%, 3 for 3%, etc.)

Step 3 Now consider the decimal and in your answer move the decimal point two places to the left.

EXAMPLE: What is the approximate tax on $17.27 at an 8.25% rate?
SOLUTION:
  Step 1 $17.27 → 17
  Step 2 17×8 (we're simplifying 8.25)
        = 136
  Step 3 136 = 1.36

The approximate tax on $17.27 is $1.36, which is pretty close to the exact tax of $1.42. We're slightly off because we rounded (down) both the dollar total and the tax rate so that we would have numbers that were easier to work with.

It may happen that the only number that appears on a bill is the *total* price, including tax. (Let's call this the *gross price*.) In such cases, it may be desirable to be able to figure out the *net price* (the price before the tax was added) and the amount of the tax itself. This kind of problem commonly occurs in retail businesses, for example, when the cashier fails to list the tax separately. Knowing only the gross receipts, the manager/owner must determine the net receipts and tax in order to know how much he owes to the local government.

Here's how

COMPUTING NET PRICE AND TAX

To find the amount of tax when you only know the tax rate and gross price (and not the net cost) requires using two formulas. First, to compute the net price, substitute:

$$\text{Net price (receipts)} = \frac{\text{Gross price (receipts)}}{1+(P/100)}$$

where P is the tax percentage.*

Then to find the amount of tax, subtract the net price from the gross price as follows:

Tax = Gross price (receipts) − Net price (receipts)

As an illustration, suppose that a restauranteur finds that the gross receipts for December 12 totaled $876.84. She needs to determine how much of that amount is sales tax, knowing that the local tax rate is 5%.

To solve this problem, calculate the net receipts according to the formula given above:

$$\text{Net receipts} = \frac{\text{Gross receipts}}{1+(P/100)}$$
$$= \frac{\$876.24}{1+(5/100)}$$
$$= \frac{\$876.24}{1+.05}$$
$$= \$876.24/1.05$$
$$= \$834.51$$

Now, to find the tax:

Tax = Gross receipts − Net receipts
     = $876.24 − $834.51
     = $41.73

The only thing we haven't considered is the tip and how it's computed. *Here's how*

---

*N = Net price; G = Gross price
N + (P/100)N = G
[1 + (P/100)]N = G
N + G/[1 + (P/100)]

CALCULATING THE TIP

A tip, of whatever size you care to leave, should be computed on the total check before the tax is added on.

There are exact ways to calculate tips of any size and estimates that you might care to use. Estimating a tip, like estimating anything else, involves some deviation above or below the exact amount, but you can easily compensate for this by subtracting or adding a little.

Except in certain situations, like coat checks and baggage handling, where tips are usually figured on a per piece basis, tips are expressed in percentages. These percentages must be converted to decimals as we did with the tax. Let's consider a tip of 15%, which has become an accepted standard for good food and good and amicable service. Remember:

$$15\% = \frac{15}{100} = .15$$

Suppose your check came to $6.72 before taxes. To calculate a 15% tip exactly:

$$.15 \times 6.72 = 1.01$$

In practice, you wouldn't worry about leaving exactly $1.01. In fact, computing 15% of an amount like $6.72 is pretty difficult to do in your head. To make it easier, remember that:

$$15\% = 10\% + 5\%$$

So an easy way to figure out what 15% is is to calculate 10% and then add to it half of that amount (5%).

First, compute 10% of 6.72:

$$10\% \times 6.72 = .67 \text{ (Multiplying by 10\% is the same as merely moving the decimal point one place to the left)}$$

Since 10% is .67, half of that is .335 or .34. So the 15% tip is:

$$.67 + .34 = \$1.01$$

This is precisely what we got when we computed it the other way.

To calculate 15% of $6.72 in your head, you might want to round off the dollar amount to $7. Then $7 × 10% = $.70 + half of that = $.35. $.70 + $.35 = $1.05, which is a little higher than the exact calculation because we rounded up.

Let's do another example both ways. What is a 15% tip on a check of $27.75?

SOLUTION (exact):
   (1) Calculate 10% of 27.75   = 2.78
   (2) Take ½ of that amount (5%) = 1.39
   (3) Add the 10% and the 5%   = 4.17

SOLUTION (approximate):
   (1) Round $27.75 to $28
   (2) Calculate 10% of 28   = 2.80
   (3) Take ½ of that amount   = 1.40
   (4) Add the 10% to the 5%   = 4.20

There are other quick tricks to approximate a 15% tip. In New York City the sales tax is 8.25%. By doubling the amount of the tax, you get 16.50% which is pretty close to 15%. So, you simply double the tax and subtract a little bit.

You can also do this if the tax where you live is 7%. Double it and you have 14%. Add a little to the total to come close to 15%. If your sales tax is 5%, multiply the tax shown by 3 to get 15%. Similarly, if your sales tax is 3%, multiplying the amount shown by 5 will result in 15%.

Tips were once an expression of appreciation for *extra* services. Today, tips are expected, and many jobs are dependent on them. A 15% tip has become the unwritten standard for reasonable service, while 20% rewards truly outstanding service. A small tip, say 5%, or no tip at all is your way of saying you were dissatisfied. In that case, however, it's doubly effective if you also describe the problems you encountered to the waiter or manager.

While we may believe that the quality of service and social custom actually determine the size of the tip, an article in the April 4, 1985 edition of the New York *Daily News* makes it clear that other factors can also play a part. The *News* reported that a psychology professor carried out a study on ways to increase the tip. In the study as the customers were given their change, they were either touched lightly on the hand, touched on the shoulder or not touched at all. Customers who were touched on the shoulder tipped an average of 14.4%; those who were touched on the hand tipped 16.7%; and those who weren't touched at all tipped 12.2% on average. We think the moral might be "don't be a soft touch!"

Section 2: What a Buy! Discounts and Markups

Since we are redecorating, we are particularly interested in the following ad that appeared in this morning's paper—

ORIENTAL RUG SUPER BUYS!
SAVE 35% TO 65%
4 DAYS ONLY

—which illustrates one of the problems of discounting, that of determining the price you pay for an item after the discount is taken. This is the sale price and we'll show you two ways to compute it.

Method 1

This method is for situations where you know the original price of the item and the percent discount, and you want to find the sale price. It allows you to figure out both how much money you'll be saving (the dollar amount of the discount) *and* the price of the item after the discount is subtracted. This method involves three steps:

Step 1 First convert the percent discount to a decimal by dividing by 100. (This is the same as moving the decimal point 2 places to the left.)

Step 2 Then multiply the original price by the decimal number found in Step 1. This is the amount of money you save—the discounted amount.

Step 3 Finally, subtract the amount of the discount from the original price to find the sale price.

Let's do an example. Suppose the original price of the oriental rug was $450 and it is on sale at 35% off. To find the sale price:

(1) $35\% = 35 \div 100 = .35$
(2) 35% of $\$450 = .35 \times \$450 = \$157.50$
(3) $\$450 - \$157.50 = \$292.50$

In this example, the discount equals $157.50 (the amount in Step 2) and the rug on sale costs $292.50 (Step 3).

There is another way to compute the sale price that is more direct, saves some work and eliminates one source of arithmetic error. To understand it requires a little more insight into the discounting process.

Method 2

We just showed how to find the amount of the discount (the amount saved) and then subtracted it from the original price to arrive at the sale price. However, it's really not necessary to calculate the discount in order to obtain the sale price.

Follow this line of reasoning. Think about the original price as being 100% of itself. The discount is 35% of the original price. After subtracting the discount percentage from 100%, you are left with 65% of the original price ($100\% - 35\% = 65\%$). This remainder is the sale price.

Therefore, to find the sale price using Method 2:

> **Step 1** Subtract the discount percentage from 100%. Let's call the answer the "sale price percentage."
> **Step 2** Convert the sale price percentage to a decimal by dividing by 100; or move the decimal point 2 places to the left.
> **Step 3** Multiply the original price by the decimal (from Step 2). The result is the sale price.

Let's use the same illustration of a rug costing $450 originally and being on sale at 35% off. Again, we want to find the sale price. To solve the problem using Method 2:

(1) $100\% - 35\% = 65\%$
(2) $65\% = 65 \div 100 = .65$
(3) $.65 \times \$450 = \$292.50$

As we would hope, Methods 1 and 2 give the same result. But this second method has several advantages. By eliminating the need to subtract the calculated discount amount from the original price (Step 3, Method 1), we reduce the chance of making an error and save some computing time. Method 2 is also easier to do in your head. In fact, if you need to figure out the sale price of an item, it's a lot easier to do just one mental multiplication than it is to do both a multiplication and a subtraction.

We're now ready to turn to the second problem associated with discounting, which is computing the *percent discount*.

Here's how

COMPUTING THE % DISCOUNT

Another ad for an oriental rug quoted the sale price of a 6 foot by 9 foot rust and blue antique rug as $999. The ad also described its value as $2,500, making the sale price sound like a really good bargain. How good a buy becomes more clear when we figure out the percent discount. Again, this involves three steps, as follows:

Step 1 Find the difference between the original price and the sale price.
Step 2 Divide the difference by the original price.
Step 3 Convert the result of Step 2 to a percent by dividing by 100.

These operations can be summarized by a formula:

$$\text{Percent discount} = \frac{\text{Original price} - \text{Sale price}}{\text{Original price}} \times 100\%$$

Let's do an example from the last ad that gave the rug's sale price as $999 and the original value as $2,500. What we want to do is to find the percent discount, assuming that the quoted value was the original price. Substituting in the formula:

$$\text{Percent discount} = \frac{\$2,500 - \$999}{\$2,500} \times 100\%$$

$$= \frac{\$1,501}{\$2,500} \times 100\%$$

$$= .6004 \times 100\%$$
$$= 60.04\%$$

Sixty percent is really an excellent discount—*if* the rug was really worth $2,500. Unfortunately, many such supposed "values" or list prices are often inflated so that the discount will sound bigger. This makes people feel like they are getting a better bargain.

The opposite of discounts are *markups*. Business people "mark up" the cost of an item over what they paid for it to arrive at the price they will charge. The markup is also known as the *margin* (the retail food business operates on a "small margin") or *gross profit,* which is the "profit" before costs, including overhead, are subtracted. The relationship between cost, markup and retail or selling price can be summarized this way:

Cost + Markup = Selling price

A markup is quoted as either a percentage of the cost price or of the selling price of the item depending on accepted practices of the particular type of business or industry. We'll show you ways both types of markups are computed.

Here's how

Method 1

There are two methods for computing the selling price when the markup is based on cost. They are very similar to the ways we showed you of calculating the sale price when the percent discount is known. As was the case there, Method 1 involves three steps:

Step 1 Convert the markup percentage to a decimal by dividing by 100. (Move the decimal point 2 places to the left.)

Step 2 Multiply the cost of the item by this decimal to find the dollar amount of the markup.

Step 3 Add the markup to the cost of the item to obtain the selling price.

EXAMPLE: Toodles department store buys suits for $225. The store marks the suit up 80% based on its cost. Find the selling price.

SOLUTION:

(1) 80% = 80 ÷ 100 = .80

(2) Markup = .80 × $225 = $180

(3) Selling price = $225 + $180 = $405

The other way to compute the selling price when the percent markup is based on known cost avoids the last step of addition.

Method 2

This method considers the cost as 100% of itself. In this case, follow the 3 steps below to calculate the selling price.

Step 1 Add the given percent markup to 100%.

Step 2 Convert the total percent obtained in Step 1 to a decimal by dividing by 100.

Step 3 Multiply the cost of the item by the decimal (from Step 2). The result is the selling price.

Let's redo the same example that we used to illustrate the first method, where a suit cost a department store $225, and the store's markup is 80% of cost. To find the selling price using Method 2:

(1) 100% + 80% = 180%
(2) 180% = 180 ÷ 100 = 1.8
(3) Selling price = 1.8 × $225 = $405

By eliminating the last step of Method 1 (which requires adding the amount of the markup to the cost to arrive at the selling price), Method 2 enables you to determine the selling price faster and in a way that has less possibility for arithmetic errors.

How can we compute the selling price when the markup is based on the selling price? At first glance it may seem impossible to do, except maybe by guessing. However, while it is not impossible, it does require some fairly involved algebra. Here, we'll leave out the algebraic manipulations and just show you how to do the computations. If they seem mysterious, remember that we're only showing you the end result.

Here's how

% MARKUP BASED ON SELLING PRICE

When the markup percentage (P) is known to be based on the selling price, we can figure out the selling price according to the following formula—provided we also know the cost*:

$$\text{Selling price} = \frac{\text{Cost}}{1 - (P/100)}$$

Suppose the suit in the previous example still costs Toodles $225 but the store's markup is computed as 80% of the *selling price*. To find the selling price, substitute in the formula:

---

*C = Cost; S = Selling price
 C + (P/100)S = S
 C = S[1 − (P/100)]
 S = C/[1 − (P/100)]

$$\text{Selling price} = \frac{\$225}{1 - (80 \div 100)}$$

Then carry through the calculations:

$$= \frac{\$225}{1 - .80}$$
$$= \frac{\$225}{.20}$$
$$= \$1,125$$

That's quite a price for a suit! We didn't make a mistake, but rather chose this example to illustrate the effect of computing markups as a percentage of selling price. For any given percent markup, the markup is always higher when it is computed on the basis of selling price than when it is figured as a percent of cost. This is because the selling price is always higher than the cost. The best way to find out whether the markup is based on cost or on selling price is to ask!

Markups based on selling price are not generally used in the clothing industry but are typical, for example, of the way cosmetics are priced.

If the selling price and the cost are known, you can compute the markup percentage that is based on cost.

Here's how

FINDING THE MARKUP % BASED ON COST

There's a formula for use in situations in which you want to find the markup percentage, and you know it's based on cost; you also know the cost and the selling price. This is the formula:

$$\% \text{ Markup} = \frac{\text{Selling price} - \text{Cost}}{\text{Cost}} \times 100\%$$

EXAMPLE: If a suit is selling for $270 and it cost the store $190, what is the percent markup based on cost?
SOLUTION:

$$\% \text{ Markup} = \frac{\$270 - \$190}{\$190} \times 100\%$$
$$= \frac{\$80}{\$190} \times 100\%$$

$$= .421 \times 100\%$$
$$= 42.1\%$$

If the selling price and cost are known, you can also compute the markup percentage that is based on selling price.

Here's how

FINDING THE MARKUP % BASED ON SELLING PRICE

If you know the markup percentage is based on selling price and if you also know the selling price and cost, use this formula to find the markup percent:

$$\% \text{ Markup} = \frac{\text{Selling price} - \text{Cost}}{\text{Selling price}} \times 100\%$$

(Please take note of the fact that the only difference in the formulas for computing percent markup based on selling price and percent markup based on cost is that, in the former case, you divide by the selling price while, in the latter case, you divide by the cost.)

Let's find the percent markup based on the selling price of a suit selling for $270 that cost Toodles department store $190.

SOLUTION:

$$\% \text{ Markup} = \frac{\$270 - \$190}{\$270} \times 100\%$$
$$= \frac{\$80}{\$270} \times 100\%$$
$$= .296 \times 100\%$$
$$= 29.6\%$$

Notice that the same dollar markup of $80 is a smaller percentage of the selling price than of the cost price because the selling price is higher than the cost.

Now let's find the *cost* when the percent markup is based on cost.

Here's how

FINDING COST: % MARKUP BASED ON COST

If you happen to know the percent markup (P) and the selling price, you can always figure out the dealer's cost. This is the formula*:

$$\text{Cost} = \frac{\text{Selling price}}{1 + (P/100)}$$

A VCR sells for \$325 at Mad Louie's. It's well-known that Mad Louie operates on an 8% markup. What is Mad Louie's cost?

To answer this question, substitute in the formula and carry through the calculations:

$$\text{Cost} = \frac{\$325}{1 + (8/100)}$$
$$= \frac{\$325}{1 + .08}$$
$$= \frac{\$325}{1.08}$$
$$= \$300.93$$

This VCR costs Mad Louis \$300.93. You can always find the dealer's cost if you know the selling and the percent markup.

You can also find the cost when the markup is based on the selling price.

Here's how

FINDING COST: % MARKUP BASED ON SELLING PRICE

In this type of markup situation, you calculate the cost by finding the dollar amount of the given markup percentage of the selling price (P) and subtracting that from the selling price. (You can also do this computation in one step.) The simple formula is as follows:

---

*S = Selling price; C = Cost
C + (P/100)C = S
C[1 + (P/100)] = S
C = S/[1 + (P/100)]

Cost = $[1 - (P/100)] \times$ Selling price

As an example, at Friendly Phyllis', makeup is generally marked up 40% based on selling price. If Rose Creme sells for $8.99, what is Friendly Phyllis' cost?

SOLUTION:
Cost = $[1 - (40/100)] \times \$8.99$
$= (1 - .40) \times \$8.99$
$= .60 \times \$8.99$
$= \$5.39$

Friendly Phyllis buys Rose Creme for $5.39.

Understanding how discounts are computed lets you assess how much of a savings you can realize from sale items, especially if you buy from reputable dealers and wait for seasonal sales, such as summer rug, furniture and bedding sales and mid-February coat sales.

Being able to figure out markups, costs and selling prices gives you an advantage in negotiating realistically since you have a feel for dealers' costs. Familiarity with the concepts of discounts and markups, and facility in computing them, increases your power as a consumer.

6

Foreign Travel

Section 1: An American Abroad: Dromedaries, Drachmas and Dollars (Currency Conversion)

So you're going to travel out of the country . . .

Once you've plotted your itinerary and planned your wardrobe, the remaining nagging worry is coping with the foreign country's currency—those multi-colored, over- and under-sized bills and funny-shaped coins that will buy an expensive memento—or cheap souvenir—if you could only figure it out!

Unless you can translate foreign currency amounts into your own currency—American dollars—you'll be playing with monopoly money, never certain whether you've paid for "Boardwalk" or "Mediterranean Avenue."

In dealing with foreign currency, you should first decide whether you want to know *exactly* how much is entailed in American dollars or whether a *reasonable dollar approximation* will suffice. Since approximation always involves some error—up or down—your budget and the price tag will be the determining factors.

For small purchases (or extremely costly ones where being a few dollars off won't make that much difference), most travelers are generally content with knowing the approximate dollar amount. In choosing a restaurant, for example, it is important to know if dinner will cost $8 or $80, but it may not matter if you estimate and figure on $6 (when the bill actually will come to $7.50) or $83 (when the meal will end up costing $90).

If the exact amount matters (and toward the end of a trip, the dollars and cents you gained or lost because of estimating do have a way of adding up), you can always do an exact conversion—by hand with paper and pencil—or, preferably, by calculator.

Your pocket calculator is the most precise, efficient and fastest way of converting drachmas into dollars. Small calculators are so much in evidence in the streets, at market stalls and in shops and restaurants that using one won't label you any more "foreign" than a camera, walking shoes or large carry-all.

Whether you decide to be exact or approximate, however, your goal is the same: to determine the price in dollars. To do this, *you need to know the value in dollars of one unit of the foreign currency.* In other words, how much is *one* drachma (or one franc, one mark, one pound or one lire) worth an American dollars?

Here's how

FINDING THE EXACT VALUE IN DOLLARS
OF ONE UNIT OF FOREIGN CURRENCY

| 1 drachma = ?$

You can find the exact value in dollars of a unit of foreign currency by looking it up in a newspaper or checking at a bank or exchange bureau for the current rate.

Foreign exchange rates, which change every banking day but usually by very small amounts, appear daily in the business sections of *The New York Times* and other major newspapers.

On December 27, 1985, the exchange rate was:
one Italian lire = $.00060
one Dutch guilder = $.36
one English pound = $1.45

Some U.S. listings only express the exchange rate as the number of units of foreign currency you can get for one dollar. These listings would look like this:

$1 = 1680.00 Italian lire
$1 = 2.77 Dutch guilders
$1 = .69 English pounds

In this case, you must convert to get the value in dollars of one unit of foreign currency.

The value in $ of one unit of $= 1 \div$ The number of units of for-
foreign currency   eign currency per dollar

So, on December 27, 1985:
   one Italian lire = 1 ÷ 1680.00 = $.00060 (rounded off)
   one Dutch guilder = 1 ÷ 2.77 = $0.36
   one English pound = 1 ÷ .69 = $1.45
By calculator (for lire):
PRESS 1 ÷ 1680 =

Once you have calculated the value in dollars of one unit (irrespective of whether you looked it up or computed it), you are now ready to find the dollar amount of *any number* of units of the foreign currency. At this point, you can either estimate or do an exact conversion as the particular situation arises. Let's do it exactly first.
Here's how

FINDING THE EXACT DOLLAR VALUE OF ANY NUMBER OF UNITS OF FOREIGN CURRENCY

78 guilders = ?$

Let's say you're shopping in Amsterdam and you find a shirt that costs 78 Dutch guilders. To determine whether you want to buy it, you need to know its equivalent in dollars.

Remember, in our example, the Dutch guilder = $.36:

The $ value of the foreign currency	=	The $ value of one unit of the foreign currency	×	The number of units of the foreign currency

So, the dollar value of:
   78 guilders = $.36 × 78 = $28.08
   54850 lire = $.00060 × 54850 = $32.91
   46 pounds = $1.45 × 46 = $66.70
By calculator (for guilders):
PRESS .36 × 78 =

There are times when you may need to reverse the process: to convert dollars into foreign currency amounts.
Here's how

**FINDING THE EXACT FOREIGN CURRENCY VALUE OF
ANY NUMBER OF AMERICAN DOLLARS**

$500
= ?guilders

You'll probably need this conversion most often when you are buying foreign currency and you want to know how many of "them" you'll get for any specified number of dollars. How many guilders (or pounds or lire) will you get for $500?

| The foreign currency value of a given number of dollars | = | The number of dollars | ÷ | Value in dollars of one unit of foreign currency |

Therefore:

$500 ÷ $1.45/pound = 344.83 pounds
$500 ÷ $.36/guilder = 1388.89 guilders
$500 ÷ $.00060/lire = 833,333.33 lire

By calculator (for pounds):

PRESS 500 ÷ 1.45 =

This is the same type of conversion the bank or exchange bureau does when selling you foreign currency. The actual amount you receive, however, is always somewhat less than you have computed, because they charge a commission (fee) for the transaction. The fee is equal to the difference between the amount of money you get and the amount you figured you would receive, according to the conversion formula.

We're now ready to estimate.

Here's how

**ESTIMATING THE DOLLAR VALUE OF
FOREIGN CURRENCY**

drachmas
= ? about$

You may well ask: why bother estimating when the exact conversion of foreign currency is so streamlined by calculator? Take the dollar value of one guilder, multiply by the number of guilders and, *voilá,* you have a precise dollar and cents answer.

But sometimes it is necessary to estimate: you forgot your calculator, the battery died, you left your reading glasses on the night table and can't see the display.

Also, some people find it fun to approximate the dollar cost of items. It gives them a sense, not only of mastery, but also of belonging. They have a good feeling about themselves when they can approximate speedily, while achieving reasonable accuracy.

Estimating is done in your head and involves little tricks, such as rounding numbers so they are easier to work with. The more you practice, the easier it becomes to think of little shortcuts that simplify the mental arithmetic. But even the best schemes always involve an error factor—the dollar amounts you arrive at are, at best, close. They are rarely exact. So, every time you want to convert foreign currency into American dollars, you should first decide whether you want a close or precise answer. (Exact numbers require a calculator.)

To do either, however, you must know the value in dollars of one unit of foreign currency. Find this out before you start your trip.

The strategy we are presenting for estimating the dollar value of any number of units of foreign currency can be applied to any and all of the world's currencies: that's why the conversion on the next page looks complicated. It, and the other steps, cover *all* currencies. However, you're only interested in one currency conversion at a time, so all you have to do is:

- Pick the case that describes the exchange rate of the currency you're interested in (Cases B and C require some preliminary steps).
- Find the line in the conversion table that shows the shortcut multiplications and/or divisions.
- Do the one or 2 steps in your head.

Don't be put off by the steps and the different cases. Remember, you're only going to be dealing with one foreign currency at a time. If you do a few practice examples with that currency, the approximate conversion will soon become second nature.

Ready?

SELECTING THE CASE THAT FITS THE DOLLAR VALUE
OF ONE UNIT OF FOREIGN CURRENCY

You know the dollar value of one unit of the currency of the country you're interested in: one Italian lire = $.00060; one Dutch guilder = $.36; one English pound = $1.45.

First, select the case that best describes this dollar value.

Case A The $ value of a unit of foreign currency is between $.10 and $.99 (example, one Dutch guilder).

Case B The $ value of a unit of foreign currency is less than $.10 (this covers any amount that has one or more zeros to the right of the decimal; example, one Italian lire).

Case C The dollar value of a unit of foreign currency is $1 or more (example, one English pound).

(Remember, you only do this one time for each different foreign currency.) Now, turn to the appropriate case.

CASE A: ESTIMATING THE DOLLAR AMOUNT OF FOREIGN CURRENCY WITH A $ VALUE PER UNIT OF BETWEEN $.10 and $.99

This case describes most European currencies and is also the one involving the fewest steps.

A shirt costs 73 guilders; what is its approximate dollar amount?

Step 1 Find the number in the conversion table that is closest to the dollar value of one guilder. Given that one guilder = $.36, the closest number is .33.

Step 2 Follow the directions for .33 in column III of the table, which says, "Divide by 3". 73 ÷ 3 is about $24 (since 73 is about 75, you can also do 75 ÷ 3, or $25).

For comparison, the exact value is .36 × 73 = $26.28.

SAMPLE PROBLEM: Given that one Canadian dollar = $.82, convert 35 Canadian dollars to American dollars.

SOLUTION: In Table 1, .82 is closest to .80. The shortcut direction is to first multiply by 8, then move the decimal point one place to the left.

Multiplying 35 × 8 gives 280 and moving the decimal point one place to the left gives $28. For comparison, the exact value is .82 × 35 = $28.70.

Table 1
Conversion Table Directions

I CLOSEST DECIMAL NUMBER	II APPROXIMATE (OR EXACT) FRACTIONAL EQUIVALENT	III DIRECTIONS FOR SHORT-CUT MULTIPLICATION
.10	$\frac{1}{10}$	Move the decimal one place to the left
.13	$\frac{1}{8}$	Divide by 8
.17	$\frac{1}{6}$	Divide by 6
.20	$\frac{2}{10}=\frac{1}{5}$	Multiply by 2 and move the decimal point one place to the left
.25	$\frac{1}{4}$	Divide by 4
.30	$\frac{3}{10}$	Multiply by 3 and move the decimal point one place to the left
.33	$\frac{1}{3}$	Divide by 3
.40	$\frac{4}{10}=\frac{2}{5}$	Multiply by 4 and move the decimal point one place to the left
.50	$\frac{1}{2}$	Divide by 2
.60	$\frac{6}{10}=\frac{3}{5}$	Multiply by 6 and move the decimal point one place to the left
.67	$\frac{2}{3}$	Divide by 3, then multiply by 2
.70	$\frac{7}{10}$	Multiply by 7, then move the decimal point one place to the left
.75	$\frac{3}{4}$	Divide by 4, then multiply by 3
.80	$\frac{8}{10}=\frac{4}{5}$	Multiply by 8 and move the decimal point one place to the left
.90	$\frac{9}{10}$	Multiply by 9 and move the decimal point one place to the left
.95+	1	Nothing to do (just multiply by 1)

CASE B: ESTIMATING THE DOLLAR AMOUNT OF FOREIGN CURRENCY WITH A $ VALUE PER UNIT OF LESS THAN $.10

When the dollar value of a unit of foreign currency is less than $.10, there are more than 10 units to the dollar. (We saw earlier that there were actually 1,680 lire to a dollar.) In this situation, the shortcut conversion requires moving decimal points (to get rid of zeros) and making the numbers you are working with smaller (so you can do the arithmetic in your head).
Here's how

A sweater costs 27,500 lire; approximately how much is this in dollars?

Step 1 First, look up the dollar value of a unit of foreign currency. Then, move the decimal point (to the right) until it is just to the left of the first non-zero digit. (Count how many places you moved.) Now you can find the number in the table that is closest to your new number.
Given that one lire = $.00060, moving the decimal point 3 places to the right gives you .60.

Step 2 To convert the total amount of foreign currency on the price tag, move the decimal point in the price as many places to the *left* as you moved it to the right in Step 1.
Thus 27,500 lire becomes 27.500 or about 28. (If by doing this you have no numbers remaining before the decimal, the item costs less than $1. If the item was tagged at 275 lire, for example, moving the decimal 3 places to the left would give .275—which is $.17, much less than $1.)

Step 3 Follow the directions in the Table 1 for the number you looked up, applying them to the foreign currency amount remaining after you moved the decimal place.
In our example, "Multiply by 6 and move the decimal point one place to the left." (28, which is about 30, or 30×6 is 180. and moving the decimal point gives you $18.)
For comparison, the exact value is $.00060 \times 27,500 = \$16.50$.

Did this seem a little complicated? Don't worry, it will get easier with just a little practice because Step 1 is only done one time for each different currency.

SAMPLE PROBLEM: Convert 5620 lire to dollars.
SOLUTION: We have already done Step 1 for lire at $.00060, moving the decimal 3 places right and finding .60 on the conversion chart.

Now, taking the 5,620 lire, we move the decimal point 3 places to the left to get 5.620. Multiply by 6 to get 36 (5.620 × 6 is about 6 × 6 = 36), and move the decimal point one place to the left to get $3.60.

For comparison, the exact value is .00060 × 5,620 = $3.31.

CASE C: ESTIMATING THE DOLLAR AMOUNT OF FOREIGN CURRENCY WITH A $ VALUE PER UNIT OF $1 OR MORE

Currencies that fit this situation include English pounds (at the present rate of exchange) and currencies from some other British Commonwealth nations. In all Case C instances, your answer will be a "larger" number than that on the price tag.

The shortcut conversion has 3 steps.

A hat costs 15 English pounds. About how many dollars is this?

Step 1 Multiply the price tag amount by the *dollar portion* of the dollar value of one unit of foreign currency.

The dollar value of one pound is $1.45. Of this amount, "1" is the dollar portion. Thus, we multiply 15 × 1 = 15.

Step 2 Find the number in the conversion table closest to the *decimal* portion of the dollar value and follow the directions in Column III.

The closest number to .45 is .50 (or .40—but .50 is easier to work with). The directions for .50 tell you to divide 15 by 2, so 15 ÷ 2 = 7.50.

Step 3 Add the resulting numbers together.

In our example this would be: 15 + 7.50 = $22.50.

For comparison, the exact value is $1.45 × 15 = $21.75.

SAMPLE PROBLEM: Given that one dinar (Kuwait) = $3.4317, convert 25 dinars to American dollars.

SOLUTION: Multiply 25 by 3 (25 × 3) to give 75. Look up .43 in Table 1 (the closest number is .40) and "multiply by 4" (25 × 4 = 100), "then move the decimal point 1 place to the left" (100 becomes 10) and "add the two numbers together" (75 + 10 = $85).

For comparison, the exact value is 3.43 × 25 = $85.75.

If you read through all 3 cases without working through each step, you should do so now to convince yourself that estimating is fast and fairly accurate.

Keep in mind that much of the "work" involved in estimating is done once and only once for each foreign currency and can be done *before* you even board the plane.

Wherever you're going, find out in advance the dollar value of one unit of foreign currency. This piece of information tells you whether you have a Case A, B, or C conversion situation; it also tells you the arithmetic directions for the shortcut conversion.

So, if you're going to Amsterdam, leave the U.S. knowing that the guilder is $.36. This is a Case A currency situation, so all you have to do is "divide by 3" (the directions in the conversion chart for .33). In Holland, then, all prices are divided by 3 to give you the approximate dollar value.

If you're off to Italy (where the lire = $.00060, a Case B conversion), you have memorized moving the decimal 3 places to the right and the directions for .60. To estimate the dollar amount of an item, what you do is first move the decimal 3 places to the left (to give you a handier number to work with), multiply by 6 and finally, move the decimal point one more place to the left.

Before you start out for London, you've learned the dollar value of one English pound and the conversion directions for the number nearest the decimal portion of this value. If the pound = $1.45, estimating the dollar value then entails only doing the "division by 2" and adding this answer to the number of pounds (since pounds were multiplied by one).

That's really all there is to it.

Section 2: Going International: Temperature Conversion

If you've grown up in the United States and have done little traveling abroad, you've probably seldom given much thought to the fact that temperature is measured in degrees *Fahrenheit (°F)* in this country. This scale was named after the German physicist, Gabriel Daniel Fahrenheit (1686–1736), who devised it and also improved the thermometer by substituting mercury for other materials.

Like other temperature scales (such as Celsius, Kelvin or absolute), the Fahrenheit scale has two fixed points: the melting point of ice (or the freezing point of water) and the boiling point of water. Fahrenheit set 32 as the designation for the freezing point of water and equally arbitrarily designated 212 as its boiling point. The Fahrenheit scale thus divides the interval from 32 to 212 into 180 equal parts called degrees (denoted with the symbol °).

Few of us worry about the arbitrariness of this scale, especially if we are accustomed to it. Over the course of years we have learned to translate scale readings into "feel"; we automatically know the "feel" of various temperatures. We know, for example, that temperatures between 68°F and

72°F are comfortable indoor temperatures; 80°F is quite warm, but most welcome following a long winter; a temperature of 100°F is *hot;* a 50°F reading requires a light outer garment; and a temperature of 98.6°F is the average normal body temperature.

But the United States is one of the few countries in the world that measures temperature in degrees Fahrenheit. Other countries that do so include Great Britain, Australia, New Zealand and Ireland—clearly, Britain exported this scale along with the English language to her colonies. In continental Europe and the rest of the world, however, temperature is measured in *degrees Celsius* or *centrigrade (°C)*. The Celsius temperature scale was also named after its creator, the Swedish astronomer, Anders Celsius (1701– 1744), who invented it in 1742 (about 28 years after Fahrenheit had devised his scale).

The freezing point of water was set at *0* on the Celsius scale and the boiling point of water was set at *100* so that there could be 100 equal subdivisions (called degrees Celsius) between them. The convenience of one hundred subdivisions made this scale ideal for scientific uses, and it has long been the standard scale of scientific temperature measurement. For a long time in English-speaking countries the Celsius scale was called the centigrade scale ("cent" meaning 100 divisions or parts), but in 1948, the Ninth General Conference on Weights and Measures decided to abandon the name centigrade and use only "Celsius," in part to honor its creator.

If you've grown up using the Celsius scale, you probably think as little about its nature as those who have grown up with Fahrenheit think about their scale. Instead, you know what the temperature readings feel like: 20°C is quite comfortable, 37°C is normal body temperature and −5°C (which is read as "minus five degrees Celsius") would be the reading on a cold, but not unusually bitter winter day.

Here are some reference points tying the Fahrenheit and Celsius scales together:

$$98.6°F = 37°C$$
$$68°F = 20°C$$
$$23°F = -5°C$$

It's as difficult for a European to picture Fahrenheit degrees as it is for an American to get the feel of Celsius. But, when we convert to metrics, we'll all have to make the change to Celsius. Even now, more and more temperature readings in the United States are reported in degrees Celsius, and this is certainly true if you're going abroad.

There are formulas that can be used to convert *exactly* any Fahrenheit temperature to a Celsius temperature. (There's also a formula for doing the exact conversion from Celsius to Fahrenheit.)

Here's how

$$\boxed{\text{FAHRENHEIT} \rightarrow \text{CELSIUS}} \quad \text{EXACT}$$

The exact conversion formula is:

$$C = \frac{5}{9}(F - 32)$$

In this formula:

C stands for degrees Celsius.
F stands for degrees Fahrenheit.
The parentheses tells us to complete this operation first, and the multiplication sign is implicit.

If we wanted to convert 75°F to Celsius, we would *first* substitute 75 for F in the formula, like this:

$$C = \frac{5}{9}(75 - 32)$$
$$= \frac{5}{9} \times \frac{43}{1}$$

75 minus 32 = 43. Next we made 43 a fraction by dividing it by one which does not change its quantity $(43 = \frac{43}{1})$.

Then we inserted the multiplication sign.

The final step involves carrying out the multiplication:

$$= \frac{5}{9} \times \frac{43}{1}$$
$$= \frac{215}{9}$$
$$= 23.9$$

So, 75°F is equivalent to 23.9°C, or approximately 24°C.

A Fahrenheit degree is smaller than a Celsius degree. It takes precisely 1.8 Fahrenheit degrees to make one Celsius degree. This is because there are 180 Fahrenheit degrees between freezing and boiling $(212 - 32 = 180)$, as compared with 100 Celsius degrees between the same two points $(100 - 0 = 100)$. This gives a ratio of 180 to 100, which is:

$$\frac{180}{100} = \frac{18}{10} = \frac{9}{5} = 1.8$$

But for *approximation* purposes, when the exact conversion is not important, we'll use 2 Fahrenheit degrees to make one Celsius degree (1.8 is very close to 2.)

Here's how

FAHRENHEIT → CELSIUS — APPROXIMATE

If a Fahrenheit degree is smaller than a Celsius degree, it follows that a Celsius degree is "larger" (there are fewer of them to account for the distance between the freezing and boiling points of water.) One-half of a Celsius degree is about one Fahrenheit degree. Actually, the exact ratio, the inverse of the ratio above, is:

$$\frac{100}{180} = \frac{5}{9} = .55$$

So, the *exact* relationship is .55 Celsius degree to each one Fahrenheit degree, but .50 or ½ is close enough for approximation. (Incidentally, we can substitute .55 for 5/9 in the exact conversion formula and do the computations without involving fractions at all.)

Now, look back at the example used in the conversion formula where 75°F = 23.9°C. The result of 23.9°C makes sense since 68°F was already given to be equivalent to 20°C, and an increase of 7°F (from 68°F to 75°F) is equivalent to a rise of about 3.5 degrees Celsius (½ of 7). So, 20 ÷ 3.5 = 23.5, or about 24°C.

Let's do an example.
EXAMPLE: Find the approximate Celsius temperature of 50°F.
SOLUTION:
Step 1 Remember that 50°F is 18° above freezing (50 − 32 = 18).
Step 2 Eighteen Fahrenheit degrees are roughly equivalent to about 9 Celsius degrees (½ of 18). So, in Celsius measurement, the temperature is approximately 9° above freezing.
Step 3 Freezing is 0°C. Therefore, 0°C + 9°C = 9°C, equivalent to about 50°F.

The exact Celsius equivalent is 10° $\left[\frac{5}{9} (50 - 32) \right]$ but, practically, the approximation is close enough.

Another way of obtaining a rough estimate is to first subtract 30 from the Fahrenheit reading and then divide the answer in half. Like this:

$$50°F - 30 = 20°F$$
$$20°F \div 2 \ = 10°C$$

(We subtract 30 rather than the 32 that appears in the exact conversion formula because 30 is an easier number to work with mentally. Dividing the answer in half is done because, as we explained, there are about 2 Fahrenheit degrees to every Celsius degree.)

EXAMPLE: Find the approximate Celsius temperature of 25°F.
SOLUTION:
Step 1 Subtract 30° from 25° = −5°F.
Step 2 Divide −5°F by 2 (divide in half) = −2.5°C or −3°C. (The exact Celsius equivalent is −3.89° or −4°C.)

Let us next practice converting from Celsius to Fahrenheit, which is what we'd be doing in most travels outside the country.
Here's how

The exact conversion formula is:

$$F = \left(\frac{9}{5}\right)C + 32$$

$$F = 1.8C + 32$$

If you want to solve the problem of converting 15°C to Fahrenheit, first substitute in the formula:

$$F = (1.8 \times 15) + 32$$

Then complete the calculations:

$$= 27 + 32$$
$$= 59$$

So, 15°C = 59°F.
Now let's see what result we get by approximation.
Here's how

CELSIUS → FAHRENHEIT ⟨APPROXIMATE⟩

In converting 15°C to Fahrenheit, recall that one of the reference points given was 20°C = 68°F. In approximating the conversion, we'll use the 20°C reference point because it is fairly close to the value (15°) we are considering.

Step 1 Note that 15°C is 5°C below 20°C.

Step 2 The 5 Celsius degrees are equivalent to about 10 Fahrenheit degrees. (There are about 2 Fahrenheit degrees to each Celsius degree, as you remember).

Step 3 Since we are 5°C below 20°C, we should be about 10°F below 68°F. Thus, 20°C is about 58°F.

This certainly compares very well indeed to the exact value of 59°F.

Another fast way of estimating Fahrenheit degrees given a Celsius reading is to double the Celsius figure and then add 30. (Again, we use 30 because it's somewhat easier to work with than 32; and we *double* the Celsius reading because each Celsius degree is equivalent to about one half (.55) of a Fahrenheit degree.)

EXAMPLE: Convert 34°C to Fahrenheit.
SOLUTION:
  (1) Double the Celsius reading (34 × 2 = 68).
  (2) Add 30 (68 + 30 = 98).

Thus 34°C is about 98°F. Actually, the *exact* conversion is 93.2°F. This quick-and-dirty technique for estimating can produce a fairly substantial error. However, 93°F is as much of a beach day as 98°F would be!

Obviously, temperature conversion formulas are requisite if you need to have an exact temperature equivalent. However, aside perhaps from body temperature, this is generally not necessary in everyday life, and approximations will do just fine. To do approximations, you'll need to have handy some reference points, such as:

  20°C = 68°F
  0°C = 32°F

You'll also need one or 2 facts:

One Celsius degree is about 2 Fahrenheit degrees.
One Fahrenheit degree is about one-half Celsius degree.

With this information firmly in mind, you can happily take off for China knowing you'll need to take along a jacket for temperatures that range from 15°C to 18°C.

Section 3: Let's Go Metric: Measurement Conversion

The U.S. system of weights and measures is an adaptation of the British system. For example, our inches, ounces and pounds are directly inherited from the British, while our gallon is only about ⅚ of the British Imperial gallon.

Most other countries, especially those outside the British sphere of influence, use *metric measurements,* which is also the measurement system of choice for scientific purposes throughout the world. As more and more goods are manufactured for worldwide consumption, eventually everyone will be on metrics. Breaking with hundreds of years of tradition, Canada is in the process of totally converting to metrics and, sooner or later, and probably with great resistance, the United States will go metric as well.

We are used to the British (or American) system of measurement. We have the same "feeling" for the distance represented by a "mile" that we have for temperatures expressed in degrees Fahrenheit. Nevertheless, metrics are a more *rational* system. In metrics, all measures of length, weight and liquid volume are built on the *decimal* system. *All quantities are expressed in 10's or multiples of 10*. This makes computations and comparisons relatively easy.

In this section we will show you how to convert to and from metrics and, importantly, also give you a "feel" for metric units in much the same way that we did with "degrees Celsius."

Here are some things you need to know. In metrics:

Milli means one-thousandth (¹⁄₁₀₀₀).
Centi means one-hundredth (¹⁄₁₀₀).
Deci means one-tenth (¹⁄₁₀).
Kilo means one thousand (1000).
One kilometer – ⅝ (.625) mile.
One meter = 39.37 inches.
One inch = 2.54 centimeters.
One mile = ⅝ (1.6) kilometers (approximately).

The language of the metric system provides hints for doing the conversions *within* the metric system. For example, since "centi" means one-hundredth (¹⁄₁₀₀), one centimeter equals ¹⁄₁₀₀ meter, and 250 centimeters equals ²⁵⁰⁄₁₀₀ meters (which is equivalent to 2.5).

As another illustration, consider milligrams. One milligram equals ¹⁄₁₀₀₀ gram, so 325 milligrams equals .325 grams. (You arrive at this by dividing 325 by 1000.)

The conversion of kilograms to grams also flows from the language of metrics. Since one kilogram equals one thousand (1000) grams, 2.5 kilograms (2.5 thousand grams) equals 2500 grams (2.5×1000).

Now, let's convert grams to kilograms. Because one kilogram equals 1000 grams, 350 grams is equal to ³⁵⁰⁄₁₀₀₀ kilograms or .35 kilograms.

The examples we just did focus on conversions within the metric system. In the rest of this section, we will convert between the metric and British system.

Here's how

MEASURING LENGTH

"How tall are you, Antoine?"

"Oh, I'm about 180 centimeters."

"That's what I thought—about average. It's your brother, Pierre, who's really tall . . . I'd guess about 2 meters."

This conversion makes perfect sense to a Parisian, although it may not to you. Yet, if you had to guess at Antoine's height from the little hints, you might say that his "about average" height of 180 centimeters is about 5 feet 10 inches, the average height of a man in the United States. Similarly, you'd probably consider 6 feet 6 inches "really tall."

Converting from centimeters and meters to inches and feet (and vice versa) requires a few definitions and facts. The actual conversion process takes only a few moments.

To Convert Centimeters or Meters to Inches Exactly:

Step 1 Since centi- means one-hundredth, first convert the number of centimeters to meters by dividing by 100 (move the decimal point 2 places to the left).

Step 2 Since one meter = 39.37 inches, convert the meters to inches by multiplying the number of meters by 39.37. (If you're starting with meters, skip Step 1 and just go right on with Step 2.)

Let's do an example based on Antoine's height. We'll convert 180 centimeters to feet and inches, like this:

$$180 \text{ cm. (centimeter)} = 1.80 \text{ m. (meter)} \left\{ \begin{array}{l} \text{Divide by 100, or move} \\ \text{the decimal point 2 places} \\ \text{to the left.} \end{array} \right.$$

$$= (1.80 \times 39.37) \text{ in. (inches)}$$
$$= 70.866 \text{ in.}$$

Dividing by 12 inches (there are 12 inches in a foot), you find that 70.866 inches is about 5 feet 11 inches. (Recall that based on guesswork alone we estimated that 180 cm was equivalent to about 5 feet 10 inches.)

As a second example, convert 2 meters (m) to feet and inches.

$$2m. = (2 \times 39.37) \text{ in.}$$
$$= 78.74 \text{ in.}$$

That's about 79 inches, or 6 feet 7 inches—pretty close to our intuitive estimate for Pierre of 6 feet 6 inches.

> EXAMPLE: While watching the Olympic track and field events, you became curious about exactly how far 400 meters is in yards.
> SOLUTION: Convert the meters to inches by multiplying 400 by 39.37 because there are 39.37 inches per meter:
> $$(400 \times 39.37) \text{ in.} = 15,748 \text{ in.}$$
> Then divide by 36 because there are 36 inches in a yard:
> $$(15,748 \div 36) \text{ yards} = 437.4 \text{ yards}$$
> *By calculator:*
> PRESS 400 ⊠ 39.37 ⊟ 36⊟

The 400 meter run is thus quite close in length to the 440 yard run which is, in fact, one-quarter mile. (There are 5280 feet per mile divided by 3 feet per yard equals 1760 yards. Dividing 1760 yards by 4 equals 440 yards.)

For *approximation purposes,* think of the meter as an over-sized yard since 1 meter = 39.37 inches = 3 feet 3 inches (approximately), which is about 1 yard and 3 inches. So, if a sign announces an exit in 100 m., it's reasonable to think of that distance as a bit longer than 100 yards.

To Convert Kilometers to Miles:

Since 1 kilometer equals ⅝ (.625) mile, multiply the number of kilometers by .625 to get the equivalent number of miles:

5 km. (kilometer) = $(5 \times .625)$ miles = 3.125 miles
15 km. = $(15 \times .625)$ miles = 9.375 miles

If you want to do an easier approximate conversion from kilometers to miles, remember that one kilometer is close to two-thirds of a mile ($\frac{2}{3} = .667$). Therefore, *divide the number of kilometers by 3 and multiply the result by 2* to obtain the number of miles:

15 km. = $[(15 \div 3) \times 2]$ miles = 10 miles

(The exact equivalent we just saw was 9.375 miles.) Or, equivalently, *multiply the number of kilometers by 2 and divide the result by 3* to obtain the approximate number of miles:

15 km. = $[(15 \times 2) \div 3]$ miles = 10 miles

The conversions we have just done were from the metric system to the British (or U.S.) system. Converting in the other direction to metrics is no more (or less) complicated.

To Convert Inches, Feet or Yards to Centimeters or Meters Exactly:

Step 1 First, convert the number of feet to inches (by multiplying by 12) or convert the number of yards to inches (by multiplying by 36).

Step 2 Since 1 inch = 2.54 cm., multiply the number of inches by 2.54 to get the number of centimeters.

Step 3 If desired, the number of centimeters can be converted to meters by moving the decimal point 2 places to the left (which is the same as dividing by 100).

Let's do an example. Convert 5 feet to centimeters, then to meters.

5 ft. = (5×12) in. = 60 in.
= (60×2.54) = 152.4
= 1.52 m.

To do an *approximate* conversion from inches into centimeters, *divide the number of inches by 2 and multiply the result by 5* or *multiply the number of inches by 5 and then divide the result by 2*.

25 in. = $[(25 \div 2) \times 5]$cm. = 62.5 cm.
or
25 in. = $[(25 \times 5) \div 2]$cm. = 62.5 cm.

(The *exact* conversion of 25 in. = (25×2.54) cm. = 63.5 cm.) The approximation technique works because 2.54 is about equal to 2.5 and 2.5 equals 5 divided by 2. Multiplication by 2.54 is approximately the same as multiplication by $\frac{5}{2}$.

To Convert Miles to Kilometers:

Multiply the number of miles by 1.6:

60 miles = (60 × 1.6) km. = 96 km.

A rough estimate of the number of kilometers can be obtained by multiplying the number of miles by 3 and dividing the result by 2 (or by dividing the number of miles by 2 and multiplying the result by 3). This works because 1.6 is about 1.5 = $\frac{3}{2}$.

60 miles = [(60 × 3) ÷ 2] km. = 90 km.
        or
60 miles = [(60 ÷ 2) × 3] km. = 90 km.

We employ similar procedures when we want to convert weights to and from the metric system.

Here's how

$$\boxed{\text{MEASURING WEIGHTS}}$$

As with lengths, there is both a British (or American) system of weights and a metric system. While we and the British are familiar with pounds and ounces, in Europe one would commonly buy ½ kilo of tomatoes, 100 grams of cheese or 5 kilos of potatoes. The typical woman weighs between 50–60 kilograms, while the average man's weight is between 60 and 85 kilograms. Even in the United States, however, the standard dosage of an aspirin tablet is quoted as 325 milligrams. These quantities lose their mystery when you know some additional metric facts:

Kilo means one thousand.
Milli means one-thousandth.
One kilogram = 2.2 pounds.
One pound = 454 grams.

To Convert Kilograms to Pounds and Ounces Exactly

Step 1 Since one kilogram (kg.) = 2.2 pounds (lbs.), multiply the number of kilograms by 2.2 to obtain the number of pounds as a decimal.

Step 2 Multiply the decimal portion of the number of pounds by 16 to obtain the number of ounces. (Remember, there are 16 ounces in a pound.)

   5 kg. = (5 × 2.2) lbs. = 11 lbs.

   56 kg. = (56 × 2.2) lbs. = 123.2 lbs. In addition: .2 × 16 ounces = 3.2 ounces. So, 56 kilograms is about 123 pounds 3 ounces.

EXAMPLE: Convert ½ kilo (gram) to pounds.

   ½ kilo = .5 × 2.2 lbs. = 1.1 lb. (Notice that one pound is about the same as ½ kilo! That's why it's reasonable to buy ½ kilo tomatoes.)

EXAMPLE: Convert 100 g. (g = grams) to ounces.

   100 g. = ⅒ kg., since 1 kilogram = 1,000 grams

   100 g. = ⅒ kg. = ⅒ × 2.2 lbs. = .22 lbs.

   .22 lbs. = .22 × 16 oz. (ounces) = 3.52 oz.

Thus, 100 grams of cheese is close to one-quarter pound of cheese (4 ounces).

EXAMPLE: Convert 325 mg. (milligrams) to ounces.

   First, notice that since "milli" means one-thousandth (¹⁄₁₀₀₀):

   325 mg. = $^{325}/_{1000}$ g. = .325 g.

But one kilogram is 1,000 grams, so one gram is ¹⁄₁₀₀₀ kilogram.

   Then, .325 g. = .325/1000 kg. = .000325 kg.

This is a very small quantity, but, continuing our conversion, we have:

   .000325 kg. = .000325 × 2.2 lb. = .000715 lb.

   = .000715 × 16 oz. = .01144 oz.

Thus, a typical aspirin tablet weighs about one-hundredth (.01) of an ounce, a *very* small quantity indeed! But not necessarily a small amount of medication. Medication is generally given in very small doses, usually measured in milligrams rather than grams or ounces.

You can convert kilograms to pounds *approximately* by multiplying the number of kilograms by 2 (rather than by 2.2).

To Convert Pounds to Kilograms Exactly:

Divide the number of pounds by 2.2, since there are 2.2 pounds per kilogram:

   155 lbs. = (155 ÷ 2.2) lbs. = 70.5 lbs.

You can *approximately* convert pounds to kilograms by dividing the number of pounds by 2. The approximate conversion would be $155 \div 2 = 77.5$ pounds, and the result is a little higher because we are dividing by a lower number (2 rather than 2.2) than we should be.

To Convert Ounces to Grams Exactly:

Step 1 Convert ounces to pounds by dividing the number of ounces by 16.

Step 2 Multiply the result in Step 1 by 454 since there are 454 grams in a pound.

EXAMPLE: Convert 8 ounces to grams.
8 oz. $= \frac{8}{16}$ lb. $= .5$ lb.
$= .5 \times 454$g. $= 227$ g.
EXAMPLE: Convert 5 ounces to grams.
5 oz. $= \frac{5}{16}$ lb. $= .3125$ lb.
$= .3125 \times 454$g. $= 142$ g.

Of all the metric measures, none has had as great an impact on American society as the measurement of liquid volume. Pepsi, Coke and other soft drinks now come in one-liter or two-liter bottles, and cans are marked in both ounces and milliliters. Perhaps you're already accustomed to thinking of a liter as being a bit more than a quart and two-liter bottles as containing somewhat more than a half-gallon (two quarts).

Here's how

MEASURING LIQUID VOLUME

In the metric system, the liter is the basic unit of volume. By definition,

one liter $= 1000$ cubic centimeters (1000 cc.).

In the American system, the *exact* relation between liters, quarts and ounces is:

one liter $= 1.0567$ quarts
one liter $= 33.8$ ounces
one quart (qt.) $= .946$ liter
one ounce $= .03$ liters or 30 cc.'s

You can see that a liter is really quite close to a quart.

To convert liters to quarts, you have to keep in mind that the quart is divided into liquid ounces. There are 32 ounces in one quart.

To Convert Liters to Quarts and Ounces Exactly:

Step 1 Since one liter = 1.0567 quarts, multiply the number of liters by 1.0567 to get the number of quarts.

Step 2 To convert the decimal part of the number of quarts to ounces, multiply the decimal by 32, since there are 32 ounces in one quart.

EXAMPLE: Convert 2 liters to quarts.
2 liters × 1.0567 qts. per liter = 2.1134 qts.
.1134 qt. × 32 oz. per qt. = 3.63 oz.
2 liters = 2 qts. and 3.63 or about 4 oz.

To convert liters to quarts *approximately:*

Step 1 Multiply the number of liters by 1.1 (instead of 1.0567).
Step 2 Multiply the decimal part of the number of quarts by 32.

EXAMPLE: Convert 2 liters to an approximate number of quarts and ounces.
2 liters × 1.1 qt. per liter = 2.2 qts.
.2 qts. × 32 oz. per qt. = 6 oz. (approximately)
2 liters = 2 qts. and about 6 oz.

This is a little high in comparison with the exact answer of 2 quarts 3.6 ounces, but it is good enough for most practical purposes.

Dosages of liquid medicines are often given in cc.'s (cubic centimeters) or, equivalently, in ml.'s (milliliters). Notice that, since

one liter = 1000 cc.'s and one ml = $\frac{1}{1000}$ liter, one ml. = one cc.

To Convert Cubic Centimeters or Milliliters to Ounces Exactly:

Step 1 Note that one cc. = .0338 oz. (since one liter = 33.8 oz.).

Step 2 Multiply the number of cc.'s by .0338 to obtain the equivalent number of ounces.

EXAMPLE: The doctor prescribes 10 cubic centimeters of medicine every 3 hours. How much is this in ounces?
10 cc. × .0338 oz. per cc. = .338 oz., or about ⅓ oz.
10 cc.'s are about ⅓ oz.

You might also be interested in these facts:

> One tablespoon = ½ oz.
> One teaspoon = ⅓ tablespoon = ⅙ oz.

So, 10 cubic centimeters equal about 2 teaspoons!

To Convert from Quarts and Ounces to Liters Exactly:
Step 1 Since one quart = .946 liters, multiply the number of quarts by .946.

Step 2 Since 1 oz. = $\frac{1}{32}$ qt. = .03125 qt., first multiply the number of ounces by .03125 to get the number of quarts. Then, to convert these quarts to liters, multiply by .946.

EXAMPLE: Convert 2 quarts 3 ounces to liters.
3 oz. = 3 × .03125 qts. = .0938 qts.
Altogether, 2.0938 qt. × .946 liter per qt. = 1.98 liter

That's about all you need to know to convert between the American and metric measurements. With these simple conversion methods at your fingertips, you need never be mystified by the metric system again.

Section 4: Electrical Conversion, or Will My Hair Drier Blow Abroad?

You're about to start on your first European vacation. In preparation, you've bought some new clothes, refilled all your cosmetics and prescriptions, bought a travel iron and made a note to pack your electric razor and blow drier.

In truth, it's not necessary to pack much differently for a European vacation than for an American one. Soap, cosmetics and all kinds of nice clothes are available from Sweden to Spain, so if you forget something or run out of it, buying a replacement is really no problem. And shopping abroad for odds and ends like toothpaste, anti-acid tablets or band-aids can be quite an amusing adventure. Nevertheless, you'll probably want to pack everything you think you might need.

If you read the beginning chapters of your guidebook, you'll have learned that, in Europe, as well as in most other foreign countries, the standard voltage for electrical current is 220–240 volts. In the United States, it's 110–120 volts. This difference in voltage means that, all else being equal (and it's not—the plugs and sockets are different too), electrical equipment designed to run at 110–120 volts will not work at 220–240 volts. The motor will burn out. Similarly, 220–240 volt equipment can't be used on 110–120 volt lines.

So what do you do about the iron, razor and hair drier? You actually have a few options.

Here's how

CONVERTING VOLTAGE

Your object is to use the correct appliance on the appropriate electrical system. First, find out the voltage requirement of the appliance. All electrical appliances have this information printed on them, usually on the bottom or back of the device near the power cord. Electrical appliances can usually tolerate a 10% deviation from the quoted voltage requirements and still function effectively. Thus, if your TV requires 120 volts, it will work just fine with only 110–115 volts. It will not, however, work in Europe where the 220–240 volt system applies. The 220–240 volt system allows you to obtain the same wattage (electrical power) with half the current required in the 110–120 volt system. But, on the other hand, the 220–240 volt system is a bit more dangerous in that you'd receive a more severe electrical shock from that system should you accidentally put your finger in a live socket. If you would like to learn a little more about electricity, skip ahead to Chapter 12, Section 2.

One way of making sure that your appliance can be used in a foreign country is to buy a *converter*. This is a fist-sized gadget that converts 220–240 volt current to 110–120 volts. You can use the same converter interchangeably for all the electrical equipment you have.

Another alternative is to buy new appliances especially designed for foreign travel. This sort of equipment has special circuits built in which allow you to run on either electrical system at the flip of a switch. As more and more people do more and more travelling, these dual-system appliances are becoming increasingly common, although you may still have some difficulty finding one.

Alternatively, you can purchase electrical equipment made for the European market that works on 220–240 volts exclusively. That's what we did in Paris last year when our hair drier broke—but, remember, it can't be used on 110–120 volt systems back home. Other than in large U.S. cities, however, 220–240 volt appliances will be very difficult to find; so, if you really want a piece of equipment just to use abroad, we suggest you buy it on your trip.

If you do extensive travelling, it probably makes good sense to buy 220–240 volt appliances or dual-purpose ones. Consider these options carefully, especially when you're thinking of replacing your regular equipment with lighter-weight, travel-sized models.

So, packed and armed with your electric voltage converter you make the trip to Rome. After arriving, quite tired, and settling down in your hotel, you decide to take a shower and wash your hair. Locating your shampoo, you are a little surprised to find soap and towels laid out. A refreshing shower perks you up and you get out your hair drier . . . to find you can't plug it into the wall!

Here's how

ADAPTER PLUGS

Not only is the voltage system different in Europe, the outlets (sockets) are different too, a fact that many travel guidebooks fail to warn you about. Your made-in-America appliance, whether the 110–120 volt one with a converter or the dual-system one with a built-in converter, ends in a plug that looks like this:

and all the sockets at home look like this: or this:

except for the 3-pronged heavy duty ones:

To use your electrical appliance abroad, you need a *plug adapter* in addition to a converter. This is a gadget that looks like a plug without a cord. On the end where you'd expect to find the power cord, you'll actually find a socket into which you fit the plug of your appliance. The other end goes into the wall outlet.

There are a variety of plug ends that go into the various wall outlets of foreign countries—and there are different ones for different countries. They may look like these:

with different length prongs and spacing between the pins.

Wall outlets in most foreign countries look like this and require the type of plug that has thin, round pins:

Common in England and Central Europe.

These are some of the other common outlet configurations; they correspond to the plugs illustrated above:

England/Africa/Hong Kong   Caribbean/South America   Europe/Africa/Asia/Middle East

For a few dollars you can buy a 4- or 5-piece plug set useful worldwide. Remember, though, that adapter plugs do not affect the voltage. They only enable you to connect your appliance into the electrical system. You'll need an adapter plug *and* a voltage converter to make your blow drier blow— and not blow out its motor.

Section 5: Changing Time Zones

When traveling in the United States or abroad, you invariably have to deal with plane or train or bus schedules. Here are a few typical examples of the kind of situations you're likely to run into:

- You leave New York at 7:30 P.M., fly by commercial jet at a cruising speed of about 600 miles per hour and arrive in Paris (3,000 miles east) at 7:35 A.M.—it looks like 12 hours and 5 minutes later.
- A plane leaves New York at 11:00 A.M., travels west 3,000 miles to California and sets down in Los Angeles at 1:29 P.M.—is it really 2 hours and 29 minutes later?

On the New York to Paris run, you are really in the air for 6 hours, 5 minutes, while from New York to Los Angeles, the actual flying time is 5 hours, 29 minutes.

Are these differences due to typographical errors? Fancy arithmetic? Science fiction? No . . . changing time zones.

Here's how

STANDARD TIME

Prior to 1884, when delegates from 27 nations met in Washington, D.C. and agreed to adopt a worldwide uniform time system, each local community kept its own time. The need for a standard system arose with the development of rapid railway transportation in the 19th century (differences in local time along the rail routes caused confusion in schedules). In the United States and Canada, the need to standardize time was especially acute because of the long distances involved. Therefore, in the late 1870's, Sir Sandford Fleming, a Canadian railway planner and engineer, designed a plan—very similar to the one we now use—for worldwide standard time.

The present system divides the earth into *24 standard time zones,* the centers of which are designated by standard meridians of longitude, imaginary lines running from the North Pole to the South Pole which meet the equator at right angles. The equator, an imaginary line around the earth, measures 24,000 miles in circumference and is equidistant at all points from the North and South Poles.

These 24 meridians of longitude are set 15 (spherical) degrees (15°) apart at the North Pole, starting with the prime meridian (of 0°) at Greenwich, England. You can visualize this by thinking of how the sections of an orange meet at the stem. Any section designated as the starting place would be equivalent to 0°, like Greenwich, England. As you may remember from geometry, there are 360° in a circle. The 24 meridians of longitude multiplied by 15 degrees for each meridian equals 360 degrees, the number of degrees in an imaginary circle drawn at the top of the earth with the North Pole as center. (See drawing   on next page.)

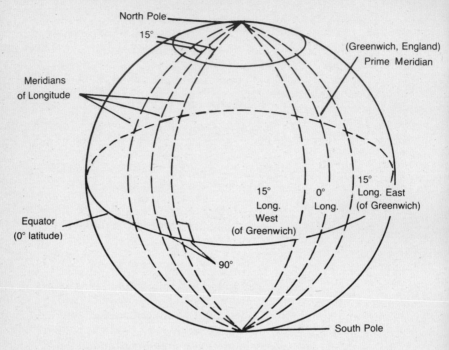

The 24 meridians of longitude do not form the boundary lines of the standard time zones, but rather, the zones' *theoretical centers*—like this:

In practice, however, the east-west boundaries of the time zones have been altered in shape, or subdivided in some cases, for the convenience of the inhabitants. For example, the time zone which would bisect Siberia has been redrawn with a bulge to take in all of Siberia.

If you look at the map of the United States in the front of the white pages of your telephone directory, you will see how the time zone boundaries zigzag down the country—not necessarily coincident with state boundaries. For example, Pacific time includes all of the states of Washington, Nevada and California, most of Oregon and small corners of Idaho and Utah. Mountain time's easterly boundary cuts through South Dakota, Nebraska and Kansas. Similar warps define the Central and the Eastern time zones. These are the four time zones of the continental U.S.

Clock time is the same everywhere within a zone (north and south, and to the zone's eastern and western boundaries) and usually differs from the starting base point at Greenwich by an *integral number* of hours (i.e., *whole hours*—minutes and seconds don't count). There are a few places in the world where local standard time differs from Greenwich mean time (GMT), the time at Greenwich, England, by half-hours (Afghanistan, Burma, Sri Lanka, for example) or quarter-hours (for example, Guyana).

Here's how

TRAVELING EAST

Local mean solar time (time measurement based on the earth's rotation around the sun) at the Greenwich meridian is the basis of clock time throughout the world. *As you go in an easterly direction from Greenwich, you add one hour of clock time for each time zone you travel through.* In other words, you add one hour *of clock time for every 15° to the east* to arrive at local time. Thus, when it's 1:00 P.M. in Los Angeles (Pacific time), it's 4:00 P.M. in New York to the east (Eastern time) because of the 3 time zone differences. When it's 10:30 A.M. in New York, it's 4:30 P.M. in Paris (6 hours difference), because New York and Paris are 6 time zones apart.

Plane, bus and train schedules use *local* times in listing the hours of departure and arrival. Thus, when a plane is listed as leaving New York at 7:30 P.M. New York time and arriving in Paris at 7:35 A.M. Paris time—an arithmetical difference of 12 hours and 5 minutes—you know that 6 hours have been added (you set your watch 6 hours *ahead*). To compute the amount of actual time you will be traveling involves two steps:

First, you must find the difference between the arrival and departure times (which means that you have to know how to subtract and add hours and minutes); then you must adjust for the time zone changes.

As an example, let's use the New York to Paris flight where you leave New York at 7:30 P.M. and arrive in Paris at 7:35 A.M. How long is this interval?

Subtract 7:30 P.M. from 7:35 A.M., like this:

From 7:30 P.M. until midnight   = 4 hrs. 30 min.
  +   +
From midnight to 7:35 A.M   = 7 hrs. 35 min.
                        Total time = 11 hrs. 65 min. = 12 hrs. 5 min.

The total difference is 12:05. Then, because you were going in an easterly direction through 6 time zones (for which you *added* 6 hours), you *deduct* these 6 hours for the *actual* time you'll be airborne:

    12:05 (local standard time difference)
  − 6:00 (time zone difference)
    6:05 of actual travelling time

When going in a westerly direction, you subtract hours.
  Here's how

TRAVELING WEST

When you go in a westerly direction from Greenwich, to compute local time, you subtract one hour for every 15° of longitude.

So, because New York and California are 3 time zones apart, there is a 3 hour time difference: if it's noon in New York, you subtract 3 hours to compute California time at 9:00 A.M. When it's 11:00 A.M. in New York, it's 6:00 A.M. in Hawaii, because Hawaii is 5 time zones away in a *westerly direction*. Therefore time is set *back* that many hours.

Now, let's figure out how many hours of actual flying time elapses during a plane trip going west from New York to Hawaii, via California.

From the earlier example, we know that the plane departs New York at 11:00 A.M. and arrives in Los Angeles at 1:29 P.M.

Therefore:

From 11:00 A.M. to 12:00 noon = 1 hour
  +   +
From 12:00 noon to 1:29 P.M.   = 1 hr. 29 min.
                      Total time = 2 hrs. 29 min.

However, you have to account for the 3-hour time difference. Since Los Angeles is 3 time zones to the *west* of New York, it is 3 hours "earlier" there. To compute the actual flying time, you have to *add* those hours back in, like this:

2:29 (standard time difference)
+ 3:00 (time zone difference)
= 5:29 (actual flying time)

Suppose the plane leaves California at 9:00 P.M. and arrives in Hawaii at 11:29 P.M.

11:29 P.M. (arrival, Hawaii time)
− 9:00 P.M. (departure, L.A. time)
2:29 (local standard time difference)

Then, add 2 hours for the 2 time zones' difference between California and Hawaii to get·

4:29 minutes of actual flying time.

In total, it took 5:29 minutes to fly from New York to California and another 4:29 minutes to go from California to Hawaii. Total flying time is:

5:29
+ 4:29
9:58

This does not count, of course, any layover wait between planes or other stops along the way.

If you circled the globe completely in either direction, east or west, you would travel through 24 time zones and, theoretically, gain or lose a whole calendar day. But this doesn't happen.

Here's how:

INTERNATIONAL DATE LINE

The international date line is an imaginary line in the middle of the Pacific Ocean which follows the meridian of 180°—exactly halfway around the world from Greenwich, England—but adjusted so as to include the Aleutian Islands with Alaska and some of the South Sea Islands with Australia. Selected by mariners because it was "convenient," it is arbitrarily defined as the place where each new date begins. When traveling across the international date line going *west*, the date becomes a day later; going *east* across the international date line, the date becomes a day earlier. To understand why a change of a full day must occur somewhere, consider the following example.

Suppose you could travel around the earth in 2 minutes. If there was no international date line, you could leave Greenwich, England at noon on December 24, go east though 24 time zones and arrive back in Greenwich at 12:02 P.M. This would be 12:02 P.M. on December 25, because when you arrived at the time zone in which it was midnight, you would start the next day.

But this doesn't happen because a correction is made at the international date line. Here, halfway around the world from Greenwich (and traveling east), the calendar date is set back by one day (to December 24). Since we left at noon and it takes 2 minutes to travel around the earth, halfway around would be 12:01 A.M. If there was no international date line, it would be 12:01 on the 25th. Instead, the international date line corrects this by setting the calendar back one day: it's still 12:01 A.M., but it's 12:01 A.M. on December 24. So one more minute and 12 time zones later, you arrive safely back in Greenwich at 12:02 P.M. on December 24.

In flying from California to Australia (going west through 6 time zones), you cross the international date line. The time between a scheduled takeoff of 9:00 P.M. on a Tuesday and a scheduled landing of 7:35 A.M. on Thursday is computed as before:

From 9:00 P.M. to midnight = 3 hrs.
+   +
From midnight to 7:35 A.M. = 7 hrs. 35 min.
                             = 10 hrs. 35 min.

Now add 6 hours (one for each time zone). The calendar date can be ignored since the clock times are independent of the date.

Moving clocks back and ahead are arbitrary decisions that have little to do with the earth's rotation on its axis (which defines a day and night and seasons) or with the earth's rotation around the sun. Daylight savings time is a good example.

Here's how

DAYLIGHT SAVINGS TIME

First proposed by Benjamin Franklin in 1784, used extensively during World Wars I and II and finally adopted by an act of Congress in 1966 (the Uniform Time Act), daylight savings time is a way of using more daylight, especially in the summer months when more daylight is available. By setting the clock ahead in the summer, we take advantage of the longer days.

In both the world wars, daylight savings time was in force as a means of saving fuel by reducing the need for artificial light. For a period of 3 years and 8 months during World War II, the United States stayed on daylight savings time continuously.

Most states (not all—some use a variation or stay on standard time year round) follow daylight savings time and set the clock one hour ahead (of local standard time), usually on the last Sunday in April. The clock is set back again one hour (to local standard time), usually on the last Sunday in October.

(Remember the mnemonic device that tells you the direction to set the clock? "Spring *ahead,* Fall *back.*")

Since plane, train and bus schedules are always stated in local times, they will reflect daylight savings time adjustments for those places in the United States or abroad that use it. But, since not all countries are on daylight savings time, a place 5 or 6 time zones away that is not on daylight savings time may actually differ from your time by only 4 or 5 clock hours in the summer months.

7

Sports and Car Math

Section 1: Miles Per Gallon

When you buy a new car today, information about expected gas consumption (mpg—miles per gallon) is included on the ticket. Yet surprisingly few people bother to compute the number of miles per gallon their car is getting on a regular basis, despite the fact that performing this easy computation can often enable you to detect early signs of engine trouble.

Some years ago, a friend of ours was driving his Volkswagen back from San Francisco to New York when, just outside of Sioux Falls, South Dakota, he recorded a sudden drop in gas mileage. Thinking it might be a fluke, he waited until the next time he filled up and again computed his miles per gallon. The figure was even lower than before. Nothing else seemed wrong, but he decided to stop at a VW dealer—just in case. It turned out that one of the valves was badly burned. The dealer was most accommodating. In fact, the mechanic came in at 4:30 the following morning to complete the repairs. If Jeff hadn't been alert to this early warning indicator, the VW would surely have suffered major engine damage.

Computing miles per gallon is relatively straightforward.
Here's how

$$\boxed{\text{MPG}}$$

Keeping track of your gas mileage involves noting the *odometer reading* each time you fill up your gas tank. If you don't already do this habitually, start now! And follow these easy steps:

Step 1 The next time you stop for gas, be sure to fill the tank up completely and make note of the odometer reading.

Step 2 Drive as you normally would and stop for gas whenever you want to. But be *sure* to fill up the tank again.

Note the current odometer reading and the number of gallons needed to fill the gas tank.

Step 3 Figure out the difference between the current and the previous odometer readings. This number is the number of miles you have driven between successive fill-ups.

Since you started out with a full tank, the number of gallons needed to fill the tank is the number of gallons you used in driving the number of miles since the last fill-up.

Step 4 Divide the number of miles between fill-ups by the number of gallons of gas used between fill-ups. The result is the *number of miles per gallon of gas (mpg)*.

These steps can be summarized with a formula:

$$\text{Mpg} = \frac{\text{New odometer reading}^* - \text{Previous odometer reading}^*}{\text{Number of gallons of gas needed to fill tank}}$$

Now for an example. Speedy filled up her tank in Boston when the odometer read 21,565. When she filled up the tank again in Philadelphia, she needed 13.4 gallons of gas. The odometer read 21,884. Find the number of miles per gallon of gas Speedy was getting on her trip South.

SOLUTION: Substituting in the formula, we have:

$$\text{Mpg} = \frac{21,884 - 21,565}{13.4}$$
$$= \frac{319}{13.4}$$
$$= 23.8$$

Speedy got 23.8 mpg's on the Boston to Philadelphia leg of her trip.

To keep track of your mpg's, it's a good idea to keep a small notebook in your car. You can use it to record the date, odometer reading, number of gallons of gas to fill the tank and the amount you paid for the gas—as well

---

(*NOTE: To compute mpg's, each odometer reading must be taken when the tank is filled up.)

as for computing your gas mileage. Remember, you can only compute miles per gallon from fill-up to fill-up, but it's worth your while for your car's sake to make this effort.

Section 2: RPM's and Gear Ratios

Here's some information about:

RPM's

In the olden days, about 35 years ago, phonograph records were quite brittle and played at 78 rpm's. That is, they completed 78 *revolutions per minute* on the turntable. Needless to say, lots of records broke and, since they revolved so fast, the needle spiraled from the record's outer edge to the center in just a very few minutes. As a result, not too much music could be recorded on one record.

Now, two types of records are produced: 45 rpm's and 33 ⅓ rpm's. The 45 rpm is smaller and has a big hole in the middle; it is most always used for "singles." Albums are recorded on the large 33 ⅓ rpm discs. Improved technology, including the use of superior materials, now permits recording of as much as 20 to 30 minutes of music on each side of these slowly revolving discs.

Rotational speed is generally measured in revolutions per minute (or per second), or in degrees per minute (or per second). For example, since a full rotation around a circle is 360 degrees, a rotational speed of 360 degrees per minutes would be equivalent to a rotational speed of one revolution per minute.

Many of today's cars are equipped with *tachometers,* which indicate how fast the drive shaft is being turned by the engine. For example, a reading of 6,000 rpm means the drive shaft is spinning at 6,000 revolutions per minute. Most tachometers have a red zone warning drivers of the maximum permissible rpm's before engine damage begins to occur.

Here's how gears work

GEARS

An automobile engine is connected to the car's rear wheels (or to the front wheels in a front-wheel-drive automobile) by means of a drive shaft and gears. These effect the transfer of power from the turning of the engine to the turning of the wheels.

Gears have teeth that mesh. The ratio of the number of teeth on one gear to the number of teeth on the gear with which it meshes is called the *gear ratio*. On a bicycle, pedaling turns a front gear, which, in turn, is attached by the chain to a gear attached to the rear wheel. The turning of the front gear that results from pedaling produces *torque* (rotary force) which is transmitted to the rear wheel.

When a small gear turns a larger gear, such as the gear on the back wheel of a bicycle, all of the rotary force created by pedaling one revolution of the small gear is transferred to the rear gear in such a way that the wheel moves only a little bit. All your effort in this case only creates a little movement—the bike goes slower. Carefully examine the gears of a 10-speed bicycle. You will discover that the "lowest" gear is when the gear in use at the pedal is smallest and the gear in use at the rear is largest: this is the most powerful, but slowest gear. Similarly, the highest gear is when the largest gear at the pedal turns the smallest gear at the rear.

Hi Gear   Lo Gear

Driving Gear   Driving Gear

The same principle also applies to automobiles. In first gear, which is the lowest gear, a small gear (the driving gear) drives a much larger gear (the driven gear). The car moves slowly at first, and it takes a very high torque (lots of rotary force—you hear it as the engine racing) to get it rolling.

In a typical car, the gear ratios are as follows:

GEAR	RATIO	
1st (lowest)	3.72	
2nd	2.04	
3rd	1.34	
4th	1.00	
5th (highest)	0.82	

The first gear ratio number, 3.72, means that the gear that turns the wheels (the driven gear) has 3.72 times as many teeth as the gear that is turned by the power of the engine (the driving gear). This means that it takes 3.72 revolutions of the driving gear to force one complete revolution of the driven gear.

Notice how the ratios drop as you move out of first. In fourth gear, acceleration would be very slow since the gear ratio is one-to-one. And in fifth gear, which is "overdrive," you go fastest but have almost no ability to accelerate (increase your speed) because the driving gear is actually larger than the driven gear.

In first gear it takes a great many revolutions of the engine to move the car. And it's revolutions of the engine that burn up gas. So, driving in "first" uses lots of gas. In contrast, in fifth gear it takes relatively few revolutions to move the car, making it the most economical gear.

On a 10-speed bicycle, the highest gear consists of a large gear driving a much smaller one. In this gear it is very hard to pedal, but each rotation of the pedal forces many rotations of the wheel so you will go much faster—if you have the strength!

Section 3: About Speed: Faster than a Speeding Bullet

Did you know that rockets travel faster than a speeding bullet? That light travels at 186,000 miles per second? That a rocket must achieve a velocity of 17,500 miles per hour to go into orbit around the earth?

These speeds make driving a car at 55 miles per hour seem like barely crawling along the ground.

Miles per hour (mph) is a typical measure of speed. Traveling at a speed of 55 miles per hour means that if this speed is maintained, a distance of 55 miles will be covered in one hour. When taking a long trip, figuring out your average speed of travel makes driving less boring and lets you better plan your stops.

Here's how

$$\boxed{\text{AVERAGE SPEED—MPH}}$$

There's a very easy formula for computing average speed:

$$\text{Average speed} = \frac{\text{Total distance covered}}{\text{Total time}}$$

EXAMPLE: Fast Fred drove from Denver to New York in 34 hours (not counting rest stops). He covered a distance of 2,100 miles. What was Fast Fred's average speed?

SOLUTION:

$$\text{Average speed} = \frac{2,100 \text{ miles}}{34 \text{ hours}}$$
$$= 61.8 \text{ miles per hour (mph)}$$

Fast Fred traveled at an average speed of 61.8 miles per hour—considerably over the national speed limit! To maintain this average, especially over as long a time period as 34 hours, means that Fast Fred probably drove for long stretches at very high speeds, perhaps even in excess of 80 mph—not the speed of sound certainly, but very, very fast . . .

Do you know why you see the flash of lightning before hearing the accompanying roll of thunder?

Here's how

MACH AND SONIC BOOM

Lightning "comes first" because light travels many times faster than sound. Light travels at about 186,000 miles per second—there is nothing in the universe faster—while sound travels through *air* (at 32°F or 0°C) at about 742 miles per hour. The speed of sound in *water* at 32°F is about 3,246 mph—much faster than in air. (The speed of the propagation of sound is not constant: it depends upon the medium in which it travels and upon temperature.)

Other things travel fast too. Commercial jet passenger planes travel at about 600 mph, while the Concorde travels at approximately 1,300 mph. The Concorde is called a *supersonic transport (SST)* because it travels faster than the speed of sound. When the SST travels through air at 32°F, it's going at the speed of Mach 1.8.

The Mach number (named after the Austrian philosopher and physicist, Ernst Mach, 1838–1916), *is the ratio of the speed of an object to the speed of sound in the medium through which the object is traveling*. Therefore, the Concorde's Mach speed was obtained by dividing its speed by the speed of sound through air:

$$= 1,300 \text{ mph} \div 742 \text{ mph}$$
$$= 1.8$$

This means that the SST travels 1.8 times the speed of sound! As the speed of an airplane or rocket reaches and exceeds the speed of sound, a shock wave is created which is heard on the ground as a *sonic boom*.

Imagine a rocket traveling at 25,000 miles per hour! That's at about Mach 34 (25,000 mph ÷ 742 mph), or 34 times the speed of sound. The more you think about speeds, the more like science fiction it seems.

Here's how

ROCKETS . . . AND SPEEDING BULLETS

Rockets must achieve a very high speed (much faster than a speeding bullet) in order to break free of the pull of the earth's gravity. If a rocket reaches a speed of 17,500 miles per hour, it will go into orbit around the earth. If it travels still faster (25,000 miles per hour, to be precise) it will break completely free of earth's gravity and head off into outer space. The speed which must be reached at the surface of a planet to escape the pull of the planet's gravity is called the *escape velocity*.

Venus is a smaller planet than earth and the force of gravity at its surface is less than on our planet. To escape from Venus's gravitational pull requires a velocity of a mere 22,883 mph. Jupiter, on the other hand, is far bigger than earth and exerts a much greater gravitational attraction on objects on its surface. The escape velocity on Jupiter is 134,548 mph. These large numbers may be a bit easier to imagine if we consider a comparison.

The muzzle velocity of a bullet fired from a .22 caliber rifle is 1,300 feet per second. That means that the bullet travels about one-quarter mile per second. Since there are 3,600 seconds in one hour, 1,300 feet per second is the same as $1,300 \times 3,600 = 4,680,000$ feet per hour. To translate this into miles per hour, we divide by 5,280 because there are 5,280 feet in a mile. Doing the division, we find that a bullet travels at the speed of 886.4 mph:

$$4,680,000 \div 5,280 = 886.4 \text{ mph}$$

The SST travels faster than a rifle bullet.

And a rocket headed toward the moon will reach a velocity of 25,000 miles per hour, or 28 times the speed of the bullet.

These speeds pale in comparison to the speed of light. Light travels at an incredible 186,000 miles per second (186,284 miles per second, to be precise). Yes, that's *per second*. At this speed it would take light about one-seventh of a second to travel completely around the earth.

Since there are 3,600 seconds in one hour, light travels $3,600 \times 186,000$ miles $= 669,600,000$ miles in one hour. In one year, light would travel about 5.87 trillion (5,870,000,000,000) miles. The term "light year" refers to the distance light travels in one year. So, a light year is the same as about 5.87 trillion miles.

It takes light about 8 minutes to travel from the sun to the earth, and about one second to come here from the moon. On the other hand, after the sun, the star nearest to the earth is Proxima Centauri, about 4 light years away. That is, it takes light 4 years to travel here from that star—a distance of about 24 trillion miles. And it would take our poor little rocket, which travels at a mere 25,000 mph, 960,000,000 hours (about 110,000 years) to get to Proxima Centauri.

In 1985, there were already plans to design a new plane that could make the New York–Los Angeles trip in 12 minutes. It would travel at Mach 21!

Superman, watch out!

8

Hobbies,
Games and Gambling

Section 1: Getting the Proper Exposure: Shutter Speed and Lens Opening

In 1898, when the first Kodak camera was marketed, it bore the slogan, "You press the button, we do the rest." All *you* had to do was line up the image, uncover the lens to admit light, press a button, and you had a picture.

As time went on, new discoveries in film and manual adjustments for focus, lens opening and shutter speed gave the photographer more control over the final picture image. Today, many cameras—from the Kodak disc to the fancy foreign imports—are fully automatic. They have now come full circle. The sophisticated developments in photography that occured in the last 100 years have all been built *into* the camera. All you have to do is press the button, and the camera does the rest.

Since many of today's high-quality cameras have both an automatic and manual mode, however, they give you the option of doing more than that. Typically, what they let you do (or in some models, require that you do) is:

- *Focus*. (There are several different, easy methods, some involving viewfinders or rangefinders, that are described in the directions that come with the camera.)
- *Control the light* (or exposure—more about this below).

The result is that you can take pictures under a wide variety of conditions and situations.

Your purpose in controlling the light entering the camera is to assure that the right amount comes through the lens onto the film. Too much light and the picture comes out too light (overexposed). Too little light and the picture is too dark (underexposed). When the needle on your light meter (don't forget to turn it on) balances at the center of the scale, you have the right amount of light.

There are, however, two manual adjustments for regulating the available light: you can vary the speed of the shutter and/or change the size (width) of the lens opening.

Here's how

SHUTTER SPEED

Simply stated, the shutter is a highly crafted lid inside the camera that covers the film, barring light. When you set the shutter speed, you determine how long the film will be uncovered and, as a result, how much light will pass through the lens and strike the light-sensitive particles on the film.

Shutter speed is measured in *fractions* of a second and is noted on your camera as 500, 250, 125, 60 (and maybe 30, 16 . . . and B—for bulb). By tradition, camera manufacturers have left off the top of the fractions, so that you have to interpret them. When you set the shutter to one of those numbers just noted, you are uncovering the film for exactly 1/500th, 1/250th, 1/125th, or 1/60th of a second.

Remember fractions? You might recall, for example, that 1/60th is a larger piece of a pie than 1/250th (just as 1/2 is more than 1/4th, and 1/4th is larger than 1/8th). Thus, at a shutter speed of 60, the shutter is open longer than at 125, 250, or 500. The longer the lens is open, the more light can reach the film.

The scale goes like this:

faster shutter speed	500 (1/500)		less light admitted
	250 (1/250)		
	125 (1/125)		
slower shutter speed	60 (1/60)		
	30 (1/30)		more light admitted

All other things being equal, under average light conditions, a shutter speed of 125 is the usual setting. When the light is exceptionally bright, however, (as at the beach on a sunny summer day) you must keep the shutter open a shorter time (use a faster speed—say 250 or 500) to admit the right amount of light. On a dark, cloudy day, or whenever there is not a lot of available light, the reverse is true: keep the shutter uncovered for a relatively long time—otherwise the picture will be too dark.

At shutter speeds of 60 or slower, it becomes difficult to hold the camera still enough for the entire fraction of a second so that the image doesn't blur from your own motion. (That's why the tripod was invented. If you don't have one, use your own body as one: lean against a solid object, press your elbows into your sides, take a deep breath and hold it while shooting.)

To capture a sharp, unfuzzy image of a moving object (whether it be a racer or leaves on a tree waving in a breeze), it is necessary to use a very fast shutter speed, such as 250 or faster. This can only be done if there is good light available. When the light isn't bright enough, the fast shutter speed probably won't admit enough light. And, if you slow down the shutter speed to let in the amount of light you need, you will lose the sharp image. Can you take a picture under these conditions? Probably yes, but you need to make a further adjustment for light.

Here's how

LENS OPENING

By varying the *width* of your lens opening (aperture—the hole the light goes through), you have added control over the amount of light hitting the film. A small opening lets through less light than a large one.

The size of the lens opening is typically noted on the camera as 2, 2.8, 4, 5.6, 8, 11, 16. These numbers are called f/stops. (Now, the photographic jargon.) An f/stop is the ratio of the distance from about the center of the lens to the film (this is the focal length of the lens) to the size of the lens opening. For example, with a 50mm lens, the distance from the center of the lens to the film is about 50mm. If the diameter of the lens opening measures 25mm, then the f/stop would be 2.0 or 50mm ÷ 25mm = 2.0. What this means is that smaller lens openings give large ratios, or higher-numbered f/stops (and vice versa).

Another way of saying this is that the higher the f/stop number, the smaller the lens opening. This is what it looks like on a simple chart:

smaller ratio	f/stop	size of lens opening		more light admitted
	2	●	☼	
	2.8	●	☼	
	4	●	☼	
	5.6	●	☼	
	8	●	☼	
	11	●	☼	
larger ratio	16	●	☼	less light admitted

(If you look through the lens of your camera when the back is open and there's no film in it, you can actually see the opening at the back of the lens enlarge and shrink in diameter as you go from low to high f/stops.)

Why use a particular f/stop? Why not just pick the best shutter speed for the kind of object you're photographing (stationary, moving) and for the available light conditions (bright, dim) and then fiddle around with the f/stop adjustment until your light meter balances?

With higher f/stops, the narrow lens opening has the effect of focusing the incoming light in a relatively narrow beam. This gives a clear image of objects *over a distance*. To test this, look at an object 10 to 20 feet away. Now squint your eyes (narrowing them) and see how much clearer the object becomes. (If you've left your reading glasses at home, squinting your eyes and holding the material farther away from you will make it more legible for short periods. On the same principle, looking at an object through a pinhole in a piece of paper has the effect of focusing the image more clearly.)

The improved focus resulting from a small lens opening (high f/stop) is referred to as "greater depth of field". With a larger lens opening, you can take a picture with less available light, but the trade-off is a shallow depth of field in which the only objects in focus in your final picture will be those you focused on—not the surrounding foreground or background.

What combination of shutter speed and lens opening will give the needed amount of light for highlight and shadow detail and also provide a clear, sharp image of details in the objects in the foreground and background?

Here's how

GETTING THE RIGHT BALANCE

There is rarely any one single combination that works because of the mathematical relationship between the two scales. If the two adjustments (shutter speed and width of aperture or f/stop) are made in equal numbers of steps in opposite directions, there is no change in the light coming into the camera. For example, all the shutter speed/lens opening pairings below admit the same amount of light:

Shutter Speed		f/Stop		
500	fast speed	4.0	●	wide opening
250		5.6	●	
125		8.0	●	
60	↓ slow	11.0	●	↓ narrow
30	speed	16.0	●	opening

Notice how many different combinations there are. Also, take note of the relationships:

• The lens opening decreases as the shutter speed decreases
• The slower the shutter speed, the higher the f/stop
• The smaller the f/stop, the faster the shutter speed

Using your camera, experiment with various combinations under different lighting conditions. Be particularly alert to the changes in depth of field in your final picture.

Here are some ideas for adjusting your camera for the proper exposure. Let's assume you have lots of light to work with. Unless the object you're photographing is in fast motion, start out by setting your shutter speed at 125. Look through the lens and adjust your f/stop until the light meter balances. OK? Take a deep breath, hold it, and . . .

Shoot!

If you're trying to get a sharp picture of, let's say, a racer under these same light conditions, you will want a faster shutter speed, say, 500. After you set this speed, see if there is an f/stop that will balance the needle; if not, you may be forced to use a slower speed, sacrificing some sharpness of image.

To find the fastest possible speed, open the lens as wide as possible (the smallest f/stop on your camera), look through the lens at the light meter and adjust the shutter speed until the needle moves past the halfway mark. Then make a final small adjustment in the lens opening to bring the needle into balance.

Let's take this further and suppose that depth of field is important. You want as much as possible, near and far, to be in focus. So, start by setting the f/stop at say, 11, and then manipulate the shutter speed until the light meter is in balance or comes close to balancing. (If it comes close, you can bring it into more exact balance by slightly adjusting the f/stop.)

Up to now, we've been assuming normal light. If the light is dim, you may have to forego great depth of field as you open your lens as wide as possible.

Light control is an important part of the technique that distinguishes Alfred Stieglitz from the Sunday shutterbug. Manually setting the lens opening/shutter speed combination allows you to supersede external conditions of light and motion and gives you more say in the kind of image you want. You will be less limited in your picture-taking, and your new skills will help satisfy your secret suspicion that you are indeed an exceptional photographer.

Section 2: Playing the Odds: An Introduction to Probability

If knowing the odds was all it took to win at backgammon, poker, blackjack or craps, then anyone could become a mathematics major specializing in probability and statistics, go to Las Vegas, Reno, Atlantic City or Monte Carlo and become rich—provided that the casinos did not ask you politely, but firmly, to leave because of your dazzling skill and phenomenal winnings.

But it takes more than an understanding of probability to win at games of chance. Winning also requires strategy, the ability to bluff, luck and many other factors which are not quantifiable. Indeed, knowing the odds may lead you to conclude that you don't stand a chance.

While understanding probabilities won't assure your success as a gambler, most professional gamblers and dedicated amateurs are certainly keenly aware of probabilities, at least in an intuitive way. Experienced backgammon or craps players, for example, know the possibilities of various possible outcomes of rolls of the dice.

Here, we provide a brief introduction to the concept of probability and odds. In the next section, we discuss some of the important probabilities for backgammon, poker and craps. We also present tables of some of these probabilities, for, while we don't encourage memorization as the way to master mathematics, we certainly don't expect you to interrupt an intense card game in order to carefully compute the probabilities before deciding on your next move. If you did this, your opponent would have a fit—justifiably—if he or she didn't overturn the table and walk away instead.

What are probabilities and how are they determined?

Here's how

PROBABILITY

Ask yourself what is the *probability* (in other words, the likelihood) of getting a head when flipping a fair (meaning a two-sided and well-balanced) coin one time? If you answered 50%, even, 50–50, ½, or .5, you would be right to some degree, although, strictly speaking, only the last two answers (½, .5) are correct. Let's see why.

Flipping a coin is an example of a *random experiment*—an act in which the outcome is determined entirely by chance. With a fair coin, the outcomes of "getting a head" or "getting a tail" are equally likely. *To determine the probability of getting a head, we compute the ratio of number of favorable outcomes to the number of possible outcomes:*

$$\text{Probability of a head} = \frac{\text{Number of favorable outcomes}}{\text{Number of possible outcomes}}$$

In flipping a coin, the number of possible outcomes is 2 (heads or tails). The number of favorable outcomes (by which we mean the number of outcomes that is of interest to us) is 1 (heads). Therefore:

$$\text{Probability of a head} = \frac{1}{2}$$

(Notice that the probability of getting a tail is also ½). We could write ½ as .5 and also say the probability of getting a head is .5, as is the probability of getting a tail.

In a random experiment in which all outcomes are equally likely, the *probability of an event (an outcome or set of outcomes) is the ratio of favorable to possible outcomes*. In this kind of situation, the following facts about probability are important:

1. P (Probability) = 0 means the desired (favorable) outcome is impossible. There are no favorable outcomes.
2. P = 1 means the desired (favorable) outcome is certain. For example, the probability of getting a head *or* a tail when flipping a coin once is one, because the number of favorable outcomes is 2 (heads or tails) and the number of possible outcomes is also 2:

$$\frac{2}{2} = 1$$

Thus, the ratio of favorable outcomes to possible outcomes is 1.

3. If P is the probability of a particular event, then $0 \leq P \leq 1$ (P is greater than or equal to zero and less than or equal to 1.) In other words, the value of P falls between 0 and 1.

Now let's look at some examples of probabilities involving dice.

A die (the singular of dice) is a cube with 6 faces, each of which is imprinted with between 1 and 6 dots corresponding to the numbers 1 to 6. When you roll one die, there are exactly six possible outcomes: 1, 2, 3, 4, 5 or 6. Let's figure out the probability of rolling a 4. Here there is one favorable outcome and 6 possible outcomes. So the probability of getting a 4 is ⅙.

Now, what is the probability of rolling either 2 or a 3? In this case, there are 2 favorable outcomes (2 *or* 3) and 6 possible outcomes. Thus, the probability of rolling a 2 *or* 3 is ⅖ or ⅓.

Probabilities become more difficult to compute as the number of favorable and possible outcomes become more difficult to count. We'll do a few more examples with dice to give you an idea of what this means.

In most games involving dice, you roll a *pair* of dice. Before we begin computing the probabilities of various outcomes, we need to count the number of possible outcomes. To do this, it is important to understand that even though the two dice may look alike, there are really two distinct dice being rolled. This is most easily imagined by thinking of the pair as consisting of one Red die (R) and one Green die (G). Now, we'll count all possible outcomes by listing all R–G combinations:

Table 1
Possible Outcomes of Rolling Two Dice (R and G)

R	G	R	G	R	G	R	G	R	G	R	G
1	1	2	1	3	1	4	1	5	1	6	1
1	2	2	2	3	2	4	2	5	2	6	2
1	3	2	3	3	3	4	3	5	3	6	3
1	4	2	4	3	4	4	4	5	4	6	4
1	5	2	5	3	5	4	5	5	5	6	5
1	6	2	6	3	6	4	6	5	6	6	6

The first column shows that when we roll 1 with the R die, we can roll from 1 to 6 with the G die. The second column shows rolling a 2 with the R die and 1 to 6 with the G die. The rest of the columns are read the same way.

Getting a 2, 3 means getting a 2 on the R die and a 3 on the G die. This is not the same as getting 3, 2 or a 3 on the R and a 2 on the G die, although the sum, 5, is the same in both cases.

Altogether, we have listed a total of *36 possible outcomes*.

Now for some examples.

First, what is the probability of getting a sum of 5 when rolling a pair of dice?

To answer this, we are required to count the number of favorable outcomes (keeping in mind that there are 36 possible outcomes). That's the number of different outcomes which result in a sum of 5.

We could get a five in each of the following four ways:

1,4   4,1   2,3   3,2

Therefore:

$$\text{Probability (sum} = 5) = \frac{\text{Number of favorable outcomes}}{\text{Number of possible outcomes}} = \frac{4}{36} = \frac{1}{9}$$

In the next example, we want to know the probability of rolling a 7 (that is, getting a sum of 7) using a pair of dice. To solve this problem, we first list the number of favorable outcomes:

1,6   6,1   2,5   5,2   4,3   3,4

Since there are 6 favorable outcomes and 36 possible outcomes, the probability of rolling a 7 is $\frac{6}{36}$ or $\frac{1}{6}$.

The probability of getting every other sum from 2 through 12 can be computed in the manner we just described. The following is a list of the probability of each sum when rolling a pair of dice:

SUM	PROBABILITY
2	$\frac{1}{36}$
3	$\frac{2}{36} = \frac{1}{18}$
4	$\frac{3}{36} = \frac{1}{12}$
5	$\frac{4}{36} = \frac{1}{9}$
6	$\frac{5}{36}$
7	$\frac{6}{36} = \frac{1}{6}$

8	$5/36$
9	$4/36 = 1/9$
10	$3/36 = 1/12$
11	$2/36 = 1/18$
12	$1/36$

Note that the most difficult outcomes to roll are a sum of 12 or a sum of 2. That's because there is only one way to get a 12 (6,6) or to get a 2 (1,1). In contrast, a sum of 7 has the highest probability, $6/36$ or $1/6$, because there are more ways to get a sum of 7 than there are ways to get any other sum. You might want to see if you can list all the ways to get a few of the other sums.

Odds are related to but a bit different from probability. The concept of "odds" is an integral part of betting.

Here's how

AGAINST ALL ODDS

If you were asked to bet on the outcome of the flip of a coin, you would be likely to offer "even money." That is, you might bet $1 on heads against your opponent's $1 on tails. Intuitively (and quite correctly), you are likely to think of odds as the *ratio of the number of outcomes favorable to your bet to the number of outcomes which are not favorable to your bet.* When flipping a coin, for example, the odds in favor of a bet on heads against tails are 1 to 1. This is commonly phrased as "50–50." Notice that the ratio 50 to 50 is equivalent to the ratio 1 to 1.

Now think about rolling a pair of dice again. We already figured out that the probability of getting a sum of 7 was $6/36$ or $1/6$. The odds in favor of getting a sum of 7 is the ratio of the number of outcomes which are favorable to this result (namely, 6) to the number of outcomes which are not favorable. The unfavorable outcomes are all the outcomes which do not result in 7. Since there are 36 possible outcomes, that's 36 minus 6 or 30 outcomes which are not favorable. So the odds in favor of getting a sum of 7 are 6 to 30 or 1 to 5. Clearly, the odds are not in your favor (although they are better than for any other sum). If you wanted to bet on getting a sum of 7, you should bet $1 against $5.

A horse named Turtle is a "20 to 1 shot." In horse racing, this means that the odds in favor of him *losing* are 20 to 1. In this case, a fair bet would be your $1 in favor of Turtle's winning to someone else's $20 bet against him. In probabalistic terms, out of every 21 races, you should expect poor Turtle to win only once and lose 20 times. Thus, the probability of his winning is $\frac{1}{21}$.

If you know the probability, you can always compute the odds.

If the probability of an event is $\frac{a}{b}$, the odds in favor of the event are a to $(b-a)$. For example, when rolling a pair of dice, the probability of the event "snake eyes" (that's 1,1) is $\frac{1}{36}$. The odds in favor of snake eyes are a to $(b-a)$ or 1 to $36-1=1$ to 35. (The odds *against* snake eyes are 35 to 1.)

As another example, suppose that the feeling is that the chances of the New York Yankees winning the pennant are about 7 out of 10 because of their new manager. That's the same as $\frac{7}{10}$. Then, according to this estimate, the *odds in favor* of the Yankees would be 7 to 3 (or 7 to $[10-7]$). The odds against the Yankees would be 3 to 7. A fair bet in *favor* of the Yanks would be $7 against $3, or $14 to $6 and so on in a 7 to 3 ratio.

Now, you may feel ready to place a bet. We hope not. There's no such thing as a sure thing. Remember, if there's an 80% chance that you'll win, there's also a 20% chance that you'll lose. That's 1 out of every 5 chances against you. We hope that knowing the odds will make you aware of those against you as well as those in your favor.

Section 3: Games of Chance: Some Facts about Backgammon, Poker and Craps

Now that you've read Section 2 and know the principles of computing probabilities, you're ready to consider some probabilities that are basic to the games of backgammon, poker and craps. If you don't know these games, parts of this section will not make much sense, although you may still find the discussion of probabilities interesting.

We'll start with backgammon.

Here's how

BACKGAMMON: "THE BLOT"

In the game of backgammon, the number of moves of your men is controlled by the outcome of rolling a pair of dice. Here, however, it is not the total sum that counts, but the numbers appearing on each of the "up" faces of the two dice. For example, a roll whose outcome is 5,3 enables you to move one man 5 and the same or another man 3 spaces. The choice of which man to move how many spaces is not always up to you. If, for example, your opponent has made a point (has 2 or more men on a position), you are not permitted to terminate a move at that position. Thus, you may not be able to move, say, one of your men 3 spaces because the point you would land on has been made by the other player.

On the other hand, you can be "hit" (bumped off the board) if your opponent lands a man on a position on which you have only one man. Such a position is called a "blot." Let's consider the probability of a blot being hit. To simplify the computation, we will assume that your opponent is free to land anywhere before your blot.

If your blot is 5 points (positions) away from one of your opponent's men, what's the probability that you'll be hit? A hit requires that one of the numbers appearing on the face of the dice is a 5 or that the sum of numbers which appear is 5. Here's a list of all the ways that a 5 can appear or that the sum of the two dice will total 5:

5 APPEARS:		SUM = 5:	
5,1	1,5	1,4	4,1
5,2	2,5	2,3	3,2
5,3	3,5		
5,4	4,5		
5,5			
5,6	6,5		

Counting, there are 11 ways for a 5 to appear and 4 ways for the sum to be 5. Therefore, your blot can be hit in 15 (11 + 4) ways. The probability of being hit is $15/36$ (36 is the number of possible outcomes of throwing the dice). The fraction $15/36$ is equivalent to about 42%. This means that if your blot is 5 points away from the other player's man, you can expect it to be hit about 42% of the time.

Now, suppose that your blot is 7 units away from your opponent. The chance of being hit becomes much slimmer, because you cannot be hit by a 7 appearing directly, but only by the sum of the outcomes of the roll of the two dice. We saw in the last section that there are 6 ways the two dice can total 7:

1,6	6,1	2,5	5,2	3,4	4,3

The probability is $6/36 = 1/6 = 17\%$. The dramatic drop in the likelihood of being hit is due entirely to the fact that there is no way for a 7 to appear on one die only, since a die has only 6 faces.

Below is a table of all the relevant information on the probability of a blot being hit:

Table 1
Probability of "Blot" Being Hit in Backgammon

DISTANCE AWAY	WAYS TO BE HIT	PROBABILITY OF A HIT	PROBABILITY AS A %
1	11	11/36	31%
2	12	12/36	33%
3	14*	14/36	39%
4	15*	15/36	42%
5	15	15/36	42%
6	17*	17/36	47%
7	6	6/36	17%
8	6*	6/36	17%
9	5*	5/36	14%
10	3	3/36	8%
11	2	2/36	6%
12	3*	3/36	8%

*These outcomes can be reached in extra ways by getting doubles.

In backgammon, when you roll doubles, you can move the amount you get twice. For example, double 4's means you can move 4 and 4, and then 4 and 4 again. This can be done with either the same man or with different men. If your opponent got double 4's, he or she could possibly hit your blot 12 points away by moving one man 4, 4, 4. In fact, a blot 16 points away would also be vulnerable to a hit when double fours are rolled (4, 4, 4, 4). However, the probability of rolling double 4's is only 1/36, or 3%.

It's worth examining the figures in Table 1 a little more closely. Instinctively, you may feel most at risk when your blot is closest to your opponent, but the figures show this is only partly true. If your blot is more than 12 points away, it is either very unlikely or impossible to be hit. And, if you look at the table, you'll see it's safer to be 10 points away than 5 points away. But notice that 12 is less safe than 11 and no more safe than 10. And it is much safer to be 1 point away than it is to be 6 points away. One conclusion to be drawn from these probabilities is that, if you must expose a blot less than 7 points away from your opponent, than the closer the better!

There's another important situation in backgammon that involves probabilities. This occurs when you've been hit and knocked off the board onto the bar.

Here's how

BACKGAMMON: ENTERING FROM THE BAR

Rolling a number between 1 and 6 enables you to land on points 1–6 on your opponent's inner table and thus return your man to the game. This becomes more difficult if your opponent has made some of the points on her/his inner table. Then the number of points you can enter on is reduced accordingly.

If all 6 points are open, you are sure to reenter the game on the next roll of the dice. Suppose, however, that your opponent has made one of the points on the inner table—say, point 5. In that case, you will be able to reenter the board with any throw *except* double 5's. So the probability of reentering would be $35/36 = 97\%$. If your opponent has made 2 points, 4 and 5 for example, you would be able to reenter with any throw of the dice except:

4,4   5,5   4,5   5,4

There are only 4 ways you can't enter, so there are 32 ways (36 − 4) in which you *can* enter. Thus, the probability of returning from the bar when the other player has made two points is $32/36 = 89\%$. The following is a table of probabilities of entering from the bar, varying by the number of points your opponent has made:

Table 2
Probability of "Entering from the Bar" in Backgammon

NUMBER OF POINTS MADE BY OPPONENT	NUMBER OF WAYS TO COME IN FROM THE BAR	PROBABILITY OF ENTERING	PROBABILITY AS A %
1	35	35/36	97%
2	32	32/36	89%
3	27	27/36	75%
4	20	20/36	56%
5	11	11/36	31%

Looking at the probabilities, you can be pretty sure of being able to return your man to play after being hit if your opponent has made 1 or 2 points in his/her inner table. If she/he has made 3 points, there is a 25% (100% − 75%) chance that you will be unable to reenter on a given throw of the dice and will, therefore, lose your turn. Things look increasingly bad after this, so you might become more careful about exposing blots as your opponent gets to the position of having made 3 or more points in his/her inner table.

In the last section we pointed out that in real play you can't stop to compute probabilities. Instead, you might memorize some of the probabilities we illustrated so that you will have them at your disposal while you play. You might also improve your game by reading through any of several good books that offer extensive discussions of backgammon probabilities and strategy.

Good luck! Here's hoping you win . . .

Craps is *not* a dirty word! It's the name of a popular gambling game which developed from an old English game called Hazard. It was introduced into the United States in the early nineteenth century.

Here's how

SHOOTING CRAPS

Craps is usually played as follows. The shooter (of a pair of dice) keeps on rolling the dice until she/he either wins or loses. There are several different ways to win or lose.

1. Rolling a sum of 7 or 11 on the first roll wins.
2. Rolling a sum of 2, 3 or 12 on the first roll loses.
3. Rolling any other sum (4, 5, 6, 8, 9, 10) on the first roll means you continue to roll the dice until you either match your first sum or roll a 7.
4. Matching your first sum before rolling a 7 wins.
5. Rolling a 7 before matching your first sum loses.

The probability of winning at craps is not easy to compute. But the basic game just described is very fair. In fact, under these rules, the probability of winning is almost ½. It's actually about .493 as we show you on the next page. That is, you would have about a 49.3% chance of winning. In casinos, the rules may change slightly, resulting in changes in the probabilities. (You can be sure the change is in the casino's favor, not yours.)

Let's figure out the probability of winning and the probability of losing on the first roll of the dice. To win, you must roll a sum of 7 or 11. Earlier in this chapter (Section 2), we found that were 6 ways to roll a sum of 7 and two ways to roll a sum of 11. Thus, the probability of rolling a 7 or 11 is $(6+2)$ $8/36 = .22$. You have about a 22% chance of winning on your first roll.

You'll lose if your first roll is a 2, 3 or 12. There is one way to roll a sum of 2, two ways to roll a sum of 3, and one way to roll a sum of 12. Therefore, the probability of rolling a 2 or 3 or 12 is $4/36 = .11$. So there's about an 11% chance that you will lose on your first roll.

The difficult computation is in figuring out the probability of winning *after* rolling a 4, 5, 6, 8, 9 or 10. You can roll any number of times *as long as you don't roll a 7!* We have figured out these probabilities for you and listed them below:

Table 3
Winning Probabilities in Craps

IF YOUR FIRST ROLL IS:	THE PROBABILITY THAT YOU'LL MATCH NUMBER BEFORE GETTING A 7 IS:
4	$1/3 = 33\%$
5	$2/5 = 40\%$
6	$5/11 = 45\%$
8	$5/11 = 45\%$
9	$2/5 = 40\%$
10	$1/3 = 33\%$

Because there are more ways to make 6's and 8's, you stand a better chance of matching those numbers before rolling a 7 than you do if your "point" is 4 or 10. The adventurous reader might check that the probability of winning at craps, .493, is obtained by computing the following:

$$P(4) \times \tfrac{1}{3} + P(5) \times \tfrac{2}{5} + P(6) \times \tfrac{5}{11} + P(8) \times \tfrac{5}{11} + P(9) \times \tfrac{2}{5} + P(10) \times \tfrac{1}{3} + P(7 \text{ or } 11) \times 1$$

Here, for example, P(4) stands for the probability of rolling a 4 and $1/3$ is the probability of matching that 4 before rolling a 7 as given in the table above. The values for P(4), P(5), etc. are given in the table on page 162 of Chapter 8, Section 2.

This is just a sample of the most basic probabilities involved in the basic game. The game gets more complicated with side bets and different combinations of points.

Craps can be fun *and* you have a reasonable chance of winning, yet we still don't recommend gambling. After all, you also have a more than reasonable chance of losing.

Poker is one of the classic card games. It is also a gambling game conjuring up images of a windowless back room filled with the heavy aroma of cigar smoke, a round table piled high with chips and a group of serious, professional gamblers.

Here, we take a more mathematical view of the game.

Here's how

PLAYING FIVE-CARD POKER

In five-card poker (one of the many variations of the game), each player is dealt 5 cards from a deck of 52. The object is to get groupings of cards which form pairs (two of the same numbered cards), 3 of a kind (three of the same numbered cards), 4 of a kind (four of the same numbered kind), a straight (five cards in numerical order), a flush (all five cards of the same suit), a full house (three of a kind and a pair) and, best of all, a straight flush (all five cards of the same suit in numerical order). The ideal is the famous royal flush—from 10 to the ace in the same suit.

Computation of probabilities in poker requires an understanding of permutations and combinations. This is a complicated topic that is best learned in a college course in finite mathematics or statistics and probabilities. Here, we will just show you some of the results and offer you some tips.

The difficulty in calculating probabilities in poker comes from the large number of possibilities that exist. We just can't list them all as we did with the 36 possible outcomes with dice. The number of possible poker hands (5 cards out of 52) is enormous—2,598,960!

The probability of being dealt a pair is .42. That's a pretty good chance. On the other hand, the probability of being dealt four of a kind from a full deck is .00024. Hands with the lowest probability are the most valuable—because they are the most rare—and always beat hands with higher probabilities.

Below, we have listed the probability of being dealt various hands:

Table 4
Probability of Types of Poker Hands

TYPE OF HAND	NUMBER OF WAYS	PROBABILITY
one pair	1,098,240	.42
2 pair	123,552	.05
3 of a kind	54,912	.02
Straight*	10,200	.004
Flush*	5,108	.002
Full house	3,744	.001
4 of a kind	624	.0002
Straight flush	40	.00002

---

*Straight flushes are not included in these figures.

You can see from the table that while the pair is fairly likely, straight flushes are truly rare occurrences, happening in only 2 out of 100,000 chances. And of the 40 ways to be dealt a straight flush, only 4 of them are royal flushes.

These probabilities are just the rudiments of what you have to know before you can play the game of poker effectively. As we've said before, in poker as in all games of chance, just knowing the basic rules and probabilities is not enough—although it is very important. Experienced gamblers also have well thought-out strategies, know when to bluff and understand the value of luck. Most importantly, *successful* gamblers know to quit when they're ahead.

PART THREE

INDOOR MATH

9

Media
Math

Section 1: Dealing with Price Fluctuations:
The Consumer Price Index

Suppose for a moment that apples sold at an average price of 20¢ last year but cost an average of 25¢ apiece today. To answer the question, "By what percentage has the price of apples increased?", we calculate the percent increase (see Chapter 1, Section 1) by subtracting last year's price from today's price, dividing the answer by last year's price, and multiplying by 100:

$$25 - 20 = 5$$
$$5 \div 20 = .25$$
$$.25 \times 100 = 25\%$$

Another way of looking at the change in price is to consider the old price as 100% of itself. Then the new price is 125% (100% + 25%) of the old price. These computations answer the question, "What is the cost today of some amount of goods and services compared to the same amount in some base period year?"

Assuming the apple represents all the goods and services we are interested in, last year can be considered the base year in which the price is 100%. This year's price (125%) is called an *index number*. The 125 simply says that this year's price is 125% of the base year's price. Since the base year price is 100(%), this year's price is 25% higher.

The *Consumer Price Index* (CPI) is a monthly economic index number of the Bureau of Labor Statistics that measures *changes in the average price of goods and services*. In its present form, the CPI dates back to World War

I, when very rapid rises in prices, especially in geographic centers heavily involved in the war effort, made such an index essential for calculating cost-of-living adjustments in wages. To this day, the CPI is used to determine wage policy in all kinds of labor negotiations, as well as in calculating adjustments to social security payments and in other situations (food stamps, the school lunch program) where cost-of-living changes need to be considered to maintain the real purchasing power of the dollar.

In addition to its usefulness as an indicator of change in the cost of living, the CPI is a measure of inflation/deflation in the economy and is also valuable as a means of studying trends in prices of various goods and services. In these ways, the CPI can be taken as a measure of the effectiveness of national economic policy.

How did the CPI originate?

Here's how

INDEX NUMBERS

Historically, interest in economic indexes peaked at times of great price fluctuations. The earliest economic index was little more than the average of prices paid for grain, wine and oil at two different time periods. The Napoleonic wars and other major events like the California and Australian gold discoveries stimulated new investigations of price fluctuations. In 1864, the economist, Étienne Laspeynes, developed index formulas that are the basis of those used today by the Bureau of Labor Statistics.

Defined by the Bureau of Labor Statistics as *the relative change in income necessary to maintain an unchanged standard of living,* the Consumer Price Index is the ratio of the cost of a particular series of consumer items now to the cost of the same series of items at some set time in the past (the base or reference period).*

The current Bureau of Labor Statistics' formula is rather impressive. It is essentially unchanged since first developed by Laspeynes and looks like this:**

---

*This Section is based extensively on the Bureau of Labor Statistics' *Handbook of Methods, Volume II, The Consumer Price Index,* April 1984, U.S. Department of Labor, Bureau of Labor Statistics. The Bureau of Labor Statistics has been publishing economic indexes since 1919.

** Although the Bureau of Labor Statistics distinguishes between the base period for prices and for quantities, we have simplified the discussion by avoiding this distinction.

$$I_{to} = \frac{P_{1t}Q_{1o} + P_{2t}Q_{2o} + \cdots P_{it}Q_{io}}{P_{1o}Q_{1o} + P_{2o}Q_{2o} + \cdots P_{io}Q_{io}} \times 100$$

Before skipping ahead, let us define the symbols.

I_{to} is the index number for t, the comparison period, and 0 is the base period. The letter i stands for the total number of items in the market basket. P_{1t}, P_{2t}, etc. are the prices for items 1, 2, etc. in the comparison (present) period t; P_{1o}, P_{2o}, etc. are the prices for the items in the base period o; and Q_{1o}, Q_{2o}, etc. are the quantities of items 1, 2, etc. consumed in the expenditure base period.

$P_{1t}Q_{1o}$ is the total cost of the first item in the market basket at time t because you multiple the price of the item by the quantity. The numerator of the I_{to} formula is thus the total cost of the market basket at time t. $P_{1o}Q_{1o}$ is the total cost of the first item in the base period, so the denominator is the total cost of the same market basket at the base period. I_{to} is the ratio of the cost of the market basket now its cost in the base period. (We multiply by 100 to convert the ratio to a percent.)

What, you may ask, are the series of items that are included in the fixed market basket of goods and services, and how are they priced?

Here's how

CPI

The CPI is based on a sample of actual prices of goods grouped under 7 major categories of consumer expenditures: food and beverages, shelter and fuels, apparel and upkeep, transportation, medical services, entertainment and "other goods and services" that people buy for day-to-day living.

Each major group is subdivided. Take "food and beverages" as an example. The first division is "food at home—outside the home." Under "food at home" there are cereals and bakery products; meats, poultry, fish and eggs; dairy products, fruits and vegetables; and "other foods at home." Within "meats, poultry, fish, and eggs," for example, there is beef and veal, pork, other meats, poultry, fish and seafood and eggs. A further subdivision of "pork," as an illustration, includes: bacon; pork chops; ham other than canned; pork other than bacon, chops, ham, sausage; sausage; and canned ham. In total, there are 382 of these items that are priced for the CPI.

Price change, according to the Bureau of Labor Statistics, is measured by "repricing essentially the same market basket of [382] goods and services at regular time intervals [monthly] and comparing the aggregate costs with the costs of the same market basket [both the same items and the same *quantity* items] in a selected base period.''

The base period for the Consumer Price Index is 1967. Thus, the cost of today's market basket can be compared with the cost of the same goods and services for each year for almost the past 20 years.

The CPI is continuously undergoing revision. The most recent major revision was introduced in January 1987. While it naturally did not change the items comprising the market basket of goods and services, it reapportioned them to reflect a decade's worth of changes in the nation's spending patterns—such as more money for cable TV, legal fees and dinners away from home and less for car repairs, red meat, dry cleaning and pastry.

There are two national indexes, the CPI-U for all "urban families" (supposed to reflect the "buying habits of approximately 80% of the noninstitutionalized population of the United States") and the original CPI-W, which represented the buying habits of only urban wage earners and clerical workers. The CPI-W, however, is still the basis of cost-of-living adjustments in most wage negotiations.

The Consumer Price Indexes are also presented in "seasonally adjusted" and "seasonally unadjusted" ways. (Unless otherwise noted, the CPI is quoted for unadjusted data.) Seasonally adjusted data are often preferred for analyzing general price trends in the economy because they eliminate the effect of changes in buying patterns that occur at the same time every year—such as price movements resulting from holidays, sales and model changeovers.

Consumer Price Indexes are also available for various geographic locations and specific segments of the total market basket: food and beverages at home, for example, or energy prices. It is not unusual to read or to hear on the news that "the New York-Northeastern New Jersey [one of the local areas] CPI went up 0.3% in April—3.6% from a year ago" or, "Grocery prices in the Buffalo metropolitan area up 1.3% in March—2.1% from a year ago."

How are the calculations done?

Here's how

CPI PERCENT CHANGE

The index measures price changes from the 1967 reference data, which equals 100(%). An increase of 125%, for example, is shown as 225. According to the Bureau of Labor Statistics, the price of a base period market basket of goods and services can also be expressed in dollars: from $10 in 1967 to $22.50 today (225% of $10 = 2.25 × $10 = $22.50).

"Movements of the indexes from one month to another are usually expressed in percent changes rather than changes in index points because index point changes are affected by the level of the index in relation to its base period while percent changes are not." The index number is always a percent of the *base period price* (1967). In contrast, a percent change can compare any two periods.

The following example reproduced from the *Handbook of Methods* illustrates how index points and percent changes are calculated

Index point change

CPI (in Period B) .... 299.3 (% of 1967)
Less previous index (CPI in Period A) .... 298.1 (% of 1967)
Equals index point change .... 1.2 (% of 1967)

Percent change

Index point difference (between Period A and B).... 1.2 (% of 1967)
Divided by the previous index (Period A)........ 298.1 (% of 1967)
Equals 0.004
Results multiplied by 100 .... 0.004 × 100
Equals percent change....... 0.4 (% increase above Period A index)

Percent changes for 3-month and 6-month periods are expressed as annual rates (computed according to standard compound growth rate formulas), which means they indicate what the percent change would be if the current rate were maintained for a 12-month period.

The national CPI–W for April 1985 was 316.7. (Remember, 1967 is equal to 100.) Therefore, since 1967, there has been a 216.7 percent change—increase—in prices.

However, from April 1984 when the national CPI-W was 304.1, the percent change in inflation was only 4.14% (316.7 − 304.1 = 12.6 ÷ 304.1 × 100%). This means that the typical wage earner or clerical worker would have had to spend 4.14% more in April 1985 to maintain the April 1984 standard of living.

For any particular individual, however, the Consumer Price Index is not necessarily an exact indicator of the effects of price changes. First, the CPI does not count income taxes or social security taxes that affect you as a consumer. (The CPI does incorporate all other sales and excise taxes that accompany the market basket items.) Second, the CPI does count items which may *not* affect you (for example, the cost of public transportation in New York City). Finally, integral to the CPI is the *fixed* market basket (always the same goods in the same quantities), while in reality, individual consumers adjust their purchases to cut down on higher-priced items and take advantage of more moderately priced ones.

Section 2: Word Pictures: Reading Tables and Graphs*

Numbers are inescapable. They're all around us on the pages of daily newspapers and magazines, on radio and television—statistics about crime, inflation, unemployment, industrial productivity, number of TV viewers. Here's a recent sampling:

"NBC's ratings increased 9%"

"Texaco will reduce its worldwide work force by about 14,500 or 21%, by the end of the year"

"The utility's preferred stock climbed 31.7%, closing at $13.50, up $3.25 for the day"

Examples like these abound. Understanding them requires knowing how percentage increases (or decreases) are computed. For this we refer you to Chapter 1, Section 1.

Frequently, however, statistical information is not presented in words, but in *word pictures* in the form of tables and graphs. Reading them intelligently does not take sophisticated mathematical knowledge, but it does require a few moments of carefully focused attention. In fact, as we'll show you here, the old saying, "One picture is worth 1,000 words" is really very meaningful when it comes to the presentation and interpretation of data.

Here's how

---

*The graphs in this section were adapted from *The Math Solution: A Skill Building Course with Business Applications,* by Stanley Kogelman and Victor D'Lugin (1982), AMACON Special Products Division, New York.

READING TABLES

Tables and graphs are a way of quickly and efficiently presenting large amounts of numerical data in a form that can be readily digested. They are also helpful in demonstrating relationships between 2 or more sets of facts, and they have dramatic appeal which catches the reader's attention and makes points forcefully.

Suppose, for example, that we wanted to communicate information about the financial status of The Company, including information about total annual sales, cost of goods sold, other costs, income before taxes, net income and amount of dividends declared. Such a wealth of information is hard to absorb when it is presented orally or in writing. Instead, summarizing it, as in the table below, enables it to be read quickly and easily.

Table 1
Summary of Financial Information (1985)
The Company
(In millions of dollars)

Annual Sales	$1,304
Cost of Goods Sold	1,069
Other Expenses	111
Income Before Taxes	124
Net Income	96
Amount of Declared Dividends	39

(A question that usually comes to mind at this point is, "What am I supposed to do with all this information?" The answer is to just read it and absorb what's there.)

To begin to interpret the figures given, first notice that the table says the numbers are "In millions of dollars." This means that the annual sales figure, for example, which looks like $1,304, is actually $1,304,000,000. That's more than one billion dollars.

Now let's see if the figures check in some way. As you look down the column, you see a breakdown of annual sales. Note that the cost of goods sold (1,069) + other expenses (111) + income before taxes (124) adds up to the total annual sales (1,304). Also, notice that the difference between total annual sales (1,304) and total expenses (1,069 + 111) is equivalent to income before taxes (124).

The difference between the income before taxes (124) and the net income (96) is the amount of the taxes (28), which is *not* shown in the table but has to be deduced from the data that is available.

This type of analysis gives you a feel for the figures, but it's not an automatic process. It is the result of careful study of the detailed information.

Often, information for only a single year doesn't tell very much about a company. In some cases, tables of multi-year summaries provide a better picture of trends—how a company is doing from one year to the next.

Consider the illustrative table below:

Table 2
Five-Year Summary of Financial Information (1981–85)
The Company
(In millions of dollars)

	1981	1982	1983	1984	1985
Annual Sales	772	842	860	1,042	1,304
Cost of Goods Sold	556	577	638	806	1,069
Other Costs	90	106	75	118	111
Income Before Taxes	126	159	147	118	124
Net Income	56	62	76	57	96
Amount of Declared Dividend	14	48	79	14	39

It's now possible to follow year-to-year trends in any category listed by reading horizontally across a row from 1981 through 1985. For example, the first row shows what's happened to annual sales over the years. (You could also read down any column to find the complete financial information for any given year.)

If you find such a vast array of numbers confusing, use a piece of paper to cover up everything except the row or column you are interested in.

Starting to interpret the data, we find a few items worthy of note:

1. Look across the first row and see that annual sales increased year to year.
2. Read across the fourth row. Notice that while sales increased from year to year, the income before taxes did not. This is because costs increased faster than sales in some years.
3. A glance at the last row shows that, in terms of dividends, the best year by far was 1983. This is true despite the fact that annual sales and net income were highest in 1985.

Observations like these are at the heart of reading tables. There's no magic, just patience with detail.

While tables can present a great amount of information in very compact form, they still require study of the detailed figures in order to ascertain trends. Graphs, on the other hand, enable you to see trends more quickly and with much less effort.

Here's how

READING GRAPHS

The figure below pictures the 5-year annual sales data of The Company in the form of a *line graph*. On this graph, the horizontal axis represents years, and the vertical axis represents millions of dollars in annual sales.

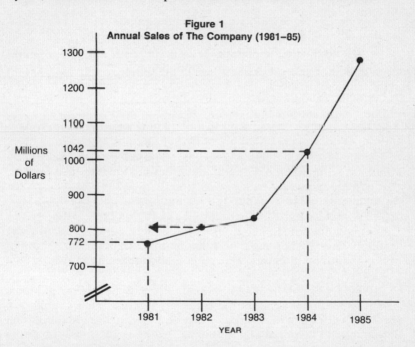

Figure 1
Annual Sales of The Company (1981–85)

The first point on the line graph stands for 1981 annual sales of $772 (million). The point is located by finding the intersection of a vertical line through 1981 and a horizontal line through the value 772. Similarly, you can plot 1984 annual sales of $1,042 on the graph by finding the point of intersection of a vertical line through 1984 and a horizontal line through 1,042.

It's possible to read information from the graph. The annual sales in 1982, for example, can be found by following an imaginary vertical line from the 1982 mark on the horizontal axis until it hits the line. Then move horizontally until you meet the vertical axis where you'll read sales of about

$840. The actual value as we saw from the table was $842, but $840 is certainly a good enough approximation.

While it's more exact to read actual values from a table than from a graph, it's easier to see patterns in the data from a graph. Notice, for example, that the line we have drawn connecting the points in Figure 1 is rising from 1981 to 1985. This means that sales steadily increased during that period. The fastest rise (steepest segment of the line) took place between 1984 and 1985. This means that sales increased at the fastest rate during this period. In other words, this is the period of the greatest percent increase in sales. And we found this out without doing any computations!

Take note of the following features of the graph:

- The small double hash marks at the beginning of each axis indicate that the axis doesn't start from zero.
- The vertical axis is just a little shorter than the horizontal one. This is the conventional way to draw the axes.

The reason why graphs are drawn this way is that changing the relationship of the axes can give you a distorted impression of the data. In the two graphs that follow, Figures 2 and 3, we present the same data as in Figure 1. But, in Figure 2, the vertical scale is greatly contracted; in Figure 3, it is greatly expanded.

With the contracted vertical scale, Figure 2 shows sales still rising, but apparently not as fast as before. Also, the distinction between the period 1981–83 and the period 1983–85 is not portrayed nearly as dramatically as it was in Figure 1. In contrast, with the expanded vertical scale, the later period rise in sales pictured in Figure 3 appears far more impressive than it is in actuality.

When reading graphs, take note of the size of the axes. If the vertical axis is about ¾ the length of the horizontal axis, the graph is likely to present a fair picture of the data. If the vertical axis is much longer or shorter than the horizontal axis, be sure to read the numbers on the scales. This will help you to correct the possibly misleading picture presented by the graph.

So far, we've considered data on annual sales for The Company in two different forms: a table and a line graph. There is another type of graph that is often used with this type of data. It's called a *bar graph*. Figure 4 on page 186 is a bar graph representation of the annual sales of The Company. The axes are drawn exactly as in Figure 1 and the points that are plotted on the graph are also located the same way we described before. (For example, the dot above 1981 represents 1981 sales of $772 [millions].) Now, however, instead of connected dots, we have a collection of vertical bars each

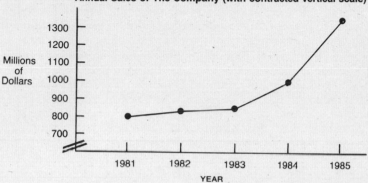

Figure 2
Annual Sales of The Company (with contracted vertical scale)

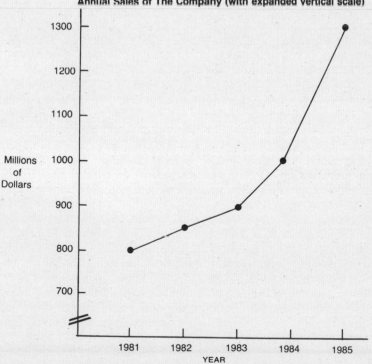

Figure 3
Annual Sales of The Company (with expanded vertical scale)

Figure 4
Annual Sales of The Company

of which rises to the level of one of the dots. Be careful though! While the height of the bars does represent sales, they are not proportional. A bar that appears twice as high as another bar does not represent twice the amount of sales because the vertical axis does not begin at zero (as indicated by the hash marks on the lower part of the vertical axis). If the vertical lines had started at zero, then the height of one bar being double the height of another would be indicative of twice as much.

So, when looking at graphs, *be sure to check where they begin.*

Now that you're familiar with line and bar graphs, let's look at an example of a type of graph commonly found in the newspaper. Reading Figure 5 requires careful study because the axes are not presented in the traditional way. However, since we know what to look for, we can systematically seek out the information.

First, we need to determine what the axes represent. Since months are listed along the bottom of the graph, the horizontal axis must be time in months.

The vertical axis is located on the right of the graph. The title of the graph, "Trading Activity of Pacific Stocks," indicates that the graph must somehow represent trading. Looking further, we see the sentence, "New purchase or sales of Pacific stocks listed on all exchanges in millions of dollars." This tells us that the right scale measures millions of dollars. The words "Net Purchases" written near one of the peaks shows us that the upper part of the graph (the portion above the zero line) represents purchases. Therefore, the lower part must represent sales.

Figure 5

Trading Activity of Pacific Stocks

Net purchase or sales of Pacific stocks listed on all exchanges in millions of dollars.

Now we can see that sales were highest in September 1984 (at more than $300 billion). We can also see that there was a shift from net purchases to net sales between September and October. But between October and November, Pacific Stocks again moved to a net purchase situation. This didn't last, however, and the stock dropped to a net sales position for the remainder of the graph (until February 1985).

The last type of graph we'll consider is a *circle graph*. Circle graphs are used to show the breakdown of some fixed quantity into subdivisions. The graph pictured on page 188 represents the average age of students enrolled in advanced mathematics courses in the United States. One hundred percent is being broken down in this instance. One hundred percent refers to 100 percent of the students in these courses.

The circle graph is sliced so that percentages correspond to appropriate portions of the circle. Since 20-year-olds comprise 32.7% of the total, for example, roughly 33% of the circle (that's nearly one-third) is marked off for this age group. Since about 11% of the total is 22-year-olds, this is represented by a slice which is one-third as large as the slice apportioned to 20-year-olds. In well-done circle graphs, the relative size of the slices are proportional.

You can read circle graphs at a glance, slice by slice, or you can combine the slices. For example, age groups can be combined by adding to-

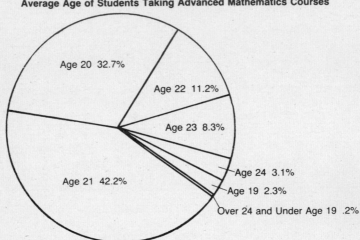

Figure 6

Average Age of Students Taking Advanced Mathematics Courses

Age 20 32.7%

Age 22 11.2%

Age 23 8.3%

Age 21 42.2%

Age 24 3.1%

Age 19 2.3%

Over 24 and Under Age 19 .2%

gether the corresponding percentages. Of the students taking advanced mathematics, the percent aged 19–21 inclusive can be found by adding the percentages of 19, 20 and 21-year-olds (2.3 + 32.7 + 42.2) to obtain 77.2%.

There is no end to the various combinations of line, bar and circle graphs that can be produced. And they are very handy for providing a quick view of complicated information. Reading graphs requires a little practice. Reading the really complex ones requires lots of patience as well.

Section 3: Lies, Damned Lies and Statistics (Average vs. Median)

Linda's father used to tell her a bedtime story about a ship's captain who took his little daughter on a sailing trip. To save her from drowning one day when a storm threatened to capsize the boat, the captain strapped her to the mast.

It was not until many years later in a high school English class that Linda learned this story was the plot of "The Wreck of the Hesperus," a famous poem by Henry Wadsworth Longfellow.

We had much the same experience with "averages." We started computing arithmetic averages way back in third or fourth grade. It was one of the first things we did when we got our report card . . .

It wasn't until much later in college that we learned that average or *mean* was a *statistical concept.*

REPORT CARD	
SUBJECT:	GRADE:
Arithmetic	89
English	93
History	84
Social Studies	95
Art	90
French	88
Physical Education	92

90.14 = AVERAGE

But it was still computed in the same way we did it in fourth grade. *Here's how*

AVERAGE or MEAN

We added up all the grades and divided by the number of them we added together.

The mean is defined as the sum of all the scores (or grades or measures) divided by their number. In *statistical notation*, the formula for the the mean (which is symbolized by X) is:

$$\bar{X} = \frac{X_1 + X_2 + \cdots X_n}{n}$$

In this formula:

X_1 stands for the first score (or measure or grade), X_2 stands for the second score $\cdots$ and X_n stands for the "n th" or last score.
n stands for the total number of scores.

When applying this formula to the fourth grade scores, you have $X_1 = 89$, $X_2 = 93$ and so on; and $n = 7$. Then:

$$\bar{X} = \frac{89 + 93 + 84 + 95 + 90 + 88 + 92}{7} = \frac{631}{7}$$
$$= 90.14$$

Notice that the result, 90.14, does not coincide with any of the scores in the distribution of grades. Actually, it's not even a whole number like the other scores. Nonetheless, the mean grade *summarizes* how we performed in the several different subjects. In statistical terms, the mean depicts the central "value" or "tendency" of a distribution or collection of scores in the sense that the scores are *evenly balanced* about the mean. This should not be interpreted to mean that the mean falls in the center of a distribution of scores.

To illustrate first how the scores in a distribution balance about the mean, let's compute all the scores' "deviations" from the mean. We do this by subtracting the mean from each score, like this:

Score	(Minus)	Mean	(Equals)	Deviation
89	−	90.14	=	−1.14
93	−	90.14	=	2.86
84	−	90.14	=	−6.14
95	−	90.14	=	4.86
90	−	90.14	=	− .14
88	−	90.14	=	−2.14
92	−	90.14	=	1.86

In this example, note that the negative values (−) indicate that the score fell below the mean, while the positive deviations (by tradition, the " + " sign is left out) indicate that the score was above the mean.

Now, if we add up the values of the deviations that are below the mean (1.14 + 6.14 + .14 + 2.14 = 9.56) and add up the values of the deviations above the mean (2.86 + 4.86 + 1.86 = 9.58), we find that they just about balance. In fact, the scores would be *exactly* balanced about the mean if the mean score had not been rounded off to 90.14 (but left as 90.14285714).

The mean is the "balance point" of any distribution of scores. However, it can be very misleading when there are extreme scores. For example, suppose we had gotten 65 in French instead of 88. When we recompute the mean, we find it falls to 86.86 as a result of this one low grade. While the new mean is the balance point of the new distribution in that the sums of the positive and negative deviations balance (or come to zero), you would be mistaken to interpret the mean as the point around which most of the actual scores fall. They do not; actually, all scores fall above this mean except for the just-passing grade we got in French.

Let's consider another example of a distribution with an extreme score. These are the times of 6 people running a 100-yard race: 9.6, 9.7, 9.8, 9.9, 10.0 and 14.0 seconds. Applying the formula for the mean, we find that:

$$\overline{X} = \frac{9.6 + 9.7 + 9.8 + 9.9 + 10.0 + 14.0}{6}$$
$$= \frac{63.0}{6}$$
$$= 10.5$$

Here you can clearly see that the mean of 10.5 seconds does not satisfactorily describe the typical runner's time because of the distorting effect of the extremely slow racer.

In almost any instance where there are *extreme scores in one direction,* the mean is probably not the statistic that is most "typical" of the distribution. There's another statistic that gives a more typical description in the case of extreme scores.

Here's how

THE MEDIAN

The median is defined as the middle value (score, measure, grade) in a distribution so that half of the scores fall above it and half fall below it. (It is also a measure of "central tendency.") If there is an *odd* number in the distribution, the median is the value of the middle score. When there is an *even* number in the distribution, the median lies between the two middle scores and is computed to be the average of these two scores.

To calculate the median, you must *first arrange all the scores in order.* Let's stick with the report card, for which we'll arrange the grades from low to high. (We could also arrange them from high to low.)

84   88   89   90   92   93   95

Since there is an odd number in the distribution of 7 grades, the middle score is the fourth one. The median is 90. Three scores fall above the median and 3 scores fall below it.

Let's assume we didn't take French that semester and had only 6 subjects (an even number), like this:

84   89   90   92   93   95

The median still falls halfway into the distribution, in this case, halfway between 90 and 92. To find the median, add the 2 middle scores:

$$90 + 92 = 182$$

And divide by 2:

$$182 \div 2 = 91$$

The median is 91. The median is thus not one of the actual scores in a distribution with an even number of data points.

Now, we're going to compare means and medians to illustrate when you would want to use one rather than the other.

Here's how

MEAN VS. MEDIAN

Using all 7 report card grades, we had calculated the mean as 90.14 and the median as 90. They are very close together, and either of the two satisfactorily describes how we did in school. When we dropped French from the distribution and used only 6 scores, the mean (90.5) and median (91) were still pretty close together and either one could be used to describe the typical score.

But, in a distribution that has extremely high or extremely low scores, the values of the mean and median are not similar. Consider the times in the 100-yard race:

9.6   9.7   9.8   9.9   10.0   14.0

Here, the mean is 10.5. The median (which falls halfway between 9.8 and 9.9; $[9.8 + 9.9] \div 2$) is 9.85. In this instance, the median gives a better picture of how most of the racers performed.

Now let's take a look at the salaries of 9 people, including the president of the Freehold Company. They earn:

$12,500
78,000
15,225
22,750
13,800
21,375
15,175
20,650
23,425

Calculating the mean:

$$\bar{X} = \frac{222,900}{9}$$
$$= 24,767$$

We find the average salary to be $24,767, which is a higher salary than all but the company's president. The mean falls at the very upper end of the distribution, a result we obtained because of the effect of the extreme salary: the president's.

The median, on the other hand, is not so affected. Arranging the scores in order to compute the median (we'll arrange them from high to low as in case A below), we find the median to be the *fifth value:* $20,650. (This is an odd-number distribution, so the middle score is the median.)

Table 1
Freehold Workers' Earnings

CASE A	CASE B	CASE C
78,000	178,000	30,000
mean (24,767)	mean (35,878)	23,425
23,425	23,425	22,750
22,750	22,750	21,375
21,375	21,375	median 20,650
median 20,650	median 20,650	mean (19,434)
15,225	15,225	15,225
15,175	15,175	15,175
13,800	13,800	13,800
12,500	12,500	12,500

Compare the median of $20,650 with the mean of $24,767. Which statistic shows better what most Freehold Company workers earn?

Because the median is not affected by the size of the extremes, we could raise the president's salary to $178,000 without changing the median (Case B above). Similarly, if we reduced the President's salary to $30,000 we would not affect the median (Case C above). *But we would affect the mean in each of these Cases.* When we raised the president's earnings, we increased the mean salary to $35,878. When we reduced the president's salary so that it wasn't too much higher than the other salaries, the median was not changed, but the mean dropped to $19,434. In the case of the lowered president's salary, the effect of eliminating the extreme score was to bring the mean and median into alignment.

But it's not only the mean that can give a distorted view. The median can too. For example, suppose you were dealing with the following salaries:

$ 15,000
    20,000
    25,000
    60,000
    70,000
    80,000
    90,000
   100,000

In this distribution, the median is 65,000 ([60,000 + 70,000] ÷ 2), while the mean is 57,500. Neither statistic gives a good picture of the salary structure—that is, of the wide range of salaries—but consideration of *both* the mean and the median makes it more apparent that there are many very high salaries, but also some low ones. Here's why. To better understand this, think about how you could have a median of $65,000 and a mean of $57,500. A median of $65,000 implies that half of the scores were $65,000 or more (and half were less). But the mean was much lower than this amount. Therefore, there must have been some very low salaries to pull the mean down that low.

With salaries in particular, where there tend to be extreme scores in one direction, the median is probably a better indicator of typical earnings. In fact, when you see the mean (or average) salary reported, you might well question whether there is some distortion resulting from the use of this statistic. After all, if we wanted to make the Freehold Company look like it pays *all* its employees high salaries, we would report the *mean* salary. These are the kind of "lies" Benjamin Disraeli meant when he talked about ". . . lies, damned lies and statistics."

10

Kitchen Math

Section 1: Timely Thoughts, or "We're Having Company for Dinner"

Let's roast a turkey!

"What," you ask, "does cooking a holiday dinner for 18 people have to do with math?"

Plenty!

First, we need to figure out how large a turkey to buy. Then, we need to calculate how long to cook the bird. And, finally, we have to know whether to double or triple our stuffing recipe to make sure we have enough.

Here's how

BUYING A BIRD: POUNDS/PERSON

A good rule of thumb is to allow from three-quarters to one pound of turkey per person, because of the bones. When you're buying steak (or fish where the bones are negligible), the per person allowance is one-half pound. So, for 18 guests, at ¾ pound per person, we should order a 13 to 14-pound turkey. To arrive at the total weight, multiply the per pound allowance by the number of people:

$$¾ \times 18 = .75 \times 18 = 13.5 \text{ lbs.}$$
Change the fraction (¾) to a decimal by dividing the numerator (3) by the denominator (4).

If we allow one pound per person, we'd buy an 18-pound turkey.

To be on the safe side, and to make sure we have leftovers and enough for doggy bags, we'll order a 20-pound bird. This should feed 20 very hungry people (at one pound per person) or 26–27 moderately hungry guests at ¾ pound person, like this:

20 lbs. ÷ ¾ lb./person = 20 ÷ .75 = 26.7 people

It will certainly be more than adequate for 18 holiday dinners, plus next day turkey soup, sandwiches and hash.

With fresh turkey selling at $1.29 per pound, what is the cost of a 20-pound turkey?

$1.29 × 20 = $25.80

To carry this one step further, we can compute the per person cost by dividing the total cost by the number of *diners*:

$25.80 ÷ 18 = $1.43 per person

Or we can compute the per serving cost by dividing by the expected number of *dinners:*

$25.80 ÷ (18 + leftovers for 6) = 25.80 ÷ 24 = $1.08 per serving

Turkey is really quite an inexpensive dish. How does it compare with steak, for example, which is selling for $3.59/pound? At one-half pound per person, to feed 18 people, we'd need 9 pounds of steak. Nine pounds of steak cost $32.31 (9 × $3.59), which represents a per person cost of $1.80 (32.31 ÷ 18).

Steak compares so favorably to turkey when calculated on a per person basis because of the difference in the amounts recommended per person and because so much "extra" is generally not built in for leftovers.

Now that we have it home, for how long must we roast the turkey? Our cookbook indicates 20 minutes per pound in a moderate (325°–350°) oven.

Here's how

COOKING TIME

To compute the total cooking time, multiply the minutes per pound by the total number of pounds:

20 lbs. × 20 min./lb. = 400 minutes

Now, divide by 60 (there are 60 minutes per hour) to get the total cooking time in hours and minutes:

400 ÷ 60 = 6.66

This is *not* 6 hours and 66 minutes but, rather, 6 hours and .66 of an hour. To compute a fraction of an hour, multiply the fraction (or decimal) by 60 minutes:

.66 × 60 = 39.6 or, rounding off, 40 minutes

So, 400 minutes equals 6 hours and 40 minutes. We can check this by multiplying 6 hours by 60 minutes (6 × 60 = 360) and then adding the 40 minutes (360 + 40 = 400).

Let's do some other examples. How long will it take to roast an 18-pound turkey?

18 × 20 = 360 minutes
360 ÷ 60 = 6 hours of cooking time
    (check: 6 × 60 = 360)

A 12-pound turkey will require 4 hours of cooking time at 20 minutes per pound:

12 × 20 = 240
240 ÷ 60 = 4 hours

And a 13½-pound turkey should cook for 270 minutes. This is 4 ½ hours:

13.5 × 20 = 270
270 ÷ 60 = 4.5, which is 4 hours and .5 of one hour or one-half an hour
(.5 × 60 = 30 minutes)

Going back to our original example (the big bird), we need 6 hours and 40 minutes of cooking time. Assuming we want to serve dinner at about 4:00 in the afternoon, at what time do we put the turkey in the (pre-heated) oven?

There are basically 2 methods for subtracting hours and minutes (and for adding time) when both times are in the A.M. or both are in the P.M.

Here's how

SUBTRACTING TIME

Let's start with *Method 1*.

Step 1 Set up the problem as a subtraction problem with hours and minutes listed side by side. For example, the time difference between 8:40 A.M. and 11:20 A.M. is set up as follows:

$$
\begin{array}{l}
11 \text{ hours} \quad 20 \text{ minutes} \\
-\ 8 \text{ hours} \quad 40 \text{ minutes} \\
\hline
\end{array}
$$

Step 2 In this example, since 40 is "bigger" than 20, it is necessary to borrow 1 hour (60 minutes) from the 11 hours and add it to the 20 minutes:

$$
\begin{array}{l}
11 \text{ hours} \quad 20 \text{ minutes} \ = \ 10 \text{ hours} \quad 80 \text{ minutes} \\
-\ 8 \text{ hours} \quad 40 \text{ minutes} \ = \ 8 \text{ hours} \quad 40 \text{ minutes} \\
\hline
\end{array}
$$

Step 3 Do an ordinary subtraction:

$$
\begin{array}{l}
10 \text{ hours} \quad 80 \text{ minutes} \\
-\ 8 \text{ hours} \quad 40 \text{ minutes} \\
\hline
2 \text{ hours} \quad 40 \text{ minutes}
\end{array}
$$

The result is the time difference.

Method 2 is called *Use Your Fingers!* Yes, counting on your fingers is highly recommended. For many calculations, it is the preferred and most accurate procedure you can use.

Step 1 Start by counting the number of minutes from the earlier time to the *next full hour*. (For example, from 8:40 to 9:00 is 20 minutes.)

Step 2 Count the number of hours from this next full hour to the *last full hour*. (For example, from 9:00 to 11:00 is 2 hours.)

Step 3 Count the number of minutes from the last full hour to the *final time*. (For example, from 11:00 to 11:20 is 20 minutes.)

Step 4 Add together the results from Steps 1, 2 and 3 to find the total time difference. (For example, 20 minutes + 2 hours + 20 minutes = 2 hours 40 minutes.)

Our real-life cooking problem is a little different. Here, we know the time interval (equivalent to the total time difference, 6 hours and 40 minutes), and we know the time we want it to be finished (by 4:00 P.M.). What we are looking for is the starting time. We need to count back 6 hours and 40 minutes from 4:00 P.M.

Let's first use *Method 2* and count backwards on our fingers.

From 4:00 P.M. backwards to noon equals 4 hours. Counting back 2 more hours, from noon to 10:00 AM., gives us a total of 6 hours. We need another 40 minutes:

$$\underline{-\begin{array}{r} 10 \text{ hours and } 0 \text{ minutes} \\ 40 \text{ minutes} \end{array}} = \underline{-\begin{array}{r} 9 \text{ hours and } 60 \text{ minutes} \\ 40 \text{ minutes} \end{array}}$$
$$9 \text{ hours and } 20 \text{ minutes}$$

We have to put the turkey in the oven at 9:20 A.M.

Here's how we'd do it with a 24-hour clock.

24-HOUR CLOCK

A 24-hour clock is not so much a physical apparatus as a way of counting the hours from midnight to midnight. Both the 24-hour clock (the clock used by the military) and the 12-hour clock (the clock we normally use) start at midnight. Therefore, the morning times are the same on both clocks: 10:15 A.M. or 1015 means 10 hours and 15 minutes past midnight; 11:30 A.M. (1130) means 11 hours and 30 minutes past midnight; and 12:00 noon (1200 hours) means 12 hours past midnight.

The two types of clocks differ in how they present the times *after* noon. For example, 1:30 P.M. (which on a regular clock is one and one-half hours after noon) is 13 hours and 30 minutes past *midnight* on a 24-hour clock. This would be presented as 1330. As another illustration, 3:00 P.M. is equal to 15 hours after midnight, or 1500 on a 24-hour clock. Thus, *to convert a P.M. time to a 24-hour clock time, just add 12!* Here are some additional examples:

7:35 P.M. = 1935 hours
10:42 P.M. = 2242 hours
11:59 P.M. = 2359 hours

To convert times greater than 1200 on a 24-hour clock, just subtract 1200 to arrive at a P.M. reading. Going back to our cooking problem, if we wanted the turkey ready at 1600 hours (4:00 P.M.), and it had to cook for 6 hours and 40 minutes, by *Method 1,* subtraction, we'd have to put it in the oven at 0920 (9:20 A.M.):

$$
\begin{array}{rcl}
\underline{-\ \ 16 \text{ hours and }\ \ 0 \text{ minutes}} & & \underline{-\ \ 15 \text{ hours and } 60 \text{ minutes}} \\
6 \text{ hours and } 40 \text{ minutes} & = & 6 \text{ hours and } 40 \text{ minutes} \\
& & 9 \text{ hours and } 20 \text{ minutes}
\end{array}
$$

We use more math when we prepare the stuffing.
Here's how

INCREASING RECIPES

The New York Times Cookbook (Craig Claiborne, ed., New York: Harper & Row, 1961) says that about ¾ to 1 cup of stuffing is needed for each pound of ready-to-cook bird and then proceeds to present a "Basic Bread Crumb Stuffing" recipe for a 5-lb bird, as follows:

one small onion
one stalk of celery with leaves,
  chopped
⅓ to ½ cup butter
1 to 2 teaspoons poultry seasoning
  or sage
Freshly ground black pepper

2 tablespoons chopped parsley (op-
  tional)
5 cups of stale bread cubes or
  crumbs
½ teaspoon salt
Water, milk or giblet gravey (op-
  tional)

We need to quadruple (multiply by 4) these ingredients to fill our 20-pound turkey. (Here, it might be helpful to refer to Section 3 of this chapter.)

one small onion $\times 4 = 4$ small onions or 2 medium-sized ones
one stalk celery $\times 4 = 4$ stalks of celery
⅓ cup butter $\times 4$ to ½ cup $\times 4 = 1$ ⅓ to 2 cups butter
1 to 2 teaspoons poultry seasoning $\times 4 = 4$ to 8 teaspoons
freshly ground black pepper $\times 4 =$ only taste will tell!
2 tablespoons of chopped parsley $\times 4 = 8$ tablespoons or ½ cup
5 cups of bread cubes $\times 4 = 20$ cups
½ teaspoon salt (no proportional increase of salt)
liquid $\times 4 =$ enough to barely moisten bread

To finish the recipe:

1. Sauté the onion and celery in the butter until tender but not brown.
2. Combine the seasonings and bread crumbs, toss together with the onion mixture and, if a moist dressing is desired, add enough liquid to barely moisten crumbs.

Then, lightly fill the cleaned and salted body cavity and the neck or wishbone cavity: do not pack the dressing since it greatly expands in cooking. Close the cavities (with skewers and/or by sewing); place the bird on its back in a pan; cover the breast with generous amounts of butter or with a cloth soaked in melted fat; pop it into a moderate oven; and cook for 6 hours and 40 minutes, basting often with the fat from the pan.

Dinner will be ready at 1600 hours.

Section 2: Not So Small Differences: Comparison Shopping

We just returned from a grocery shopping expedition which confirmed our suspicions that it would be difficult to decide upon the best buy. For example, we found three bags of the same brand, same type of potato chips priced as follows:

WEIGHT	PRICE
7½ oz.	$1.39
11 oz.	$1.99
16 oz.	$2.49

Odd quantities such as 7½ ounces or 11 ounces make it hard to compare prices in your head. If, for example, the quantities had been 8, 12 and 16 ounces, the comparisons would be quite straightforward. You would expect the price of the 16-ounce bag to be twice the price of the 8-ounce bag since it is twice the weight. If the price was less than double, the larger package would be a good buy.

While it's not as easy to compare a 12-ounce bag with an 8-ounce bag as it is to compare 16 ounces and 8 ounces, it's still not too bad. You could reason this way: a 12-ounce bag is one and one-half times the size of an 8-ounce bag, so the price of a 12-ounce bag should be one and one-half times the price of an 8-ounce bag. If the price is lower than this, the 12-ounce package is the better buy; if it's higher, buy the smaller bag of chips.

In the market we visited, odd quantities and uneven prices, such as those on the potato chip packages, were the rule rather than the exception. The only reasonable way to comparison shop given such incompatible weights and such "hard" pricing structures is with a calculator. That's the way we recommend you determine *unit prices,* although, at first thought, bringing a calculator to the supermarket seems terribly embarrassing. In fact, current pricing is designed to discourage you from comparison shopping in a rigorous way. So, do consider using a calculator. It takes only a moment to compare prices with it. . . . And it can really save you money.

Here's how

UNIT PRICING

Prices of different amounts of similar items can be compared by computing the price per pound, per ounce, per quart or any other measurement unit. To figure out the cost per unit of weight (or volume), divide the price of the item by the quantity that you can buy for that price. Expressed as a formula:

$$\text{Unit price} = \frac{\text{Price}}{\text{Quantity}}$$

The required division is best done on a calculator.

The goal of comparison shopping is to determine the best buy. *This is the item with the lowest unit price.* However, you may sometimes decide to buy a smaller or a larger size box (or bag or bottle) than the one with the lowest unit price because of other factors, such as spoilage or convenience. As an illustration, a gallon of milk may be a better buy than a quart of milk (it also may not be), but if you use only a little milk, the gallon size might spoil before you can come close to finishing it. Similarly, the limitations of home storage space may also mitigate against purchasing giant-sized packages.

Now let's look at some examples. These are not "textbook" cases but are the actual prices we found in a large local supermarket on a Saturday morning, not too long ago.

Let's start by figuring out which bag of potato chips is the best buy:

7½ oz. for $1.39
11 oz. for $1.99
16 oz. for $2.49

Solving this problem requires us to find the unit price for each of the three bags. To repeat the *unit price formula:*

$$\text{Unit price} = \frac{\text{Price}}{\text{Quantity}}$$

Substituting in the formula, the unit price for the smallest bag is:

$$\text{Unit price} = \frac{\$1.39}{7.5 \text{ oz.}}$$
$$= \$0.185 \text{ per oz.}$$

Translating this into cents by multiplying by 100 (100 cents in a dollar), the first bag costs 18.5¢ per oz.

By calculator:
PRESS 1.39 ÷ 7.5 × 100 =

For the middle-size bag, the unit price is:

$$\text{Unit price} = \frac{\$1.99}{11 \text{ oz.}}$$
$$= \$0.181 \text{ per oz.}$$
$$= 18.1¢ \text{ per oz.}$$
By calculator:
PRESS 1.99 ÷ 7.5 × 100 =

And the largest bag's unit price is:

$$\text{Unit price} = \frac{\$2.49}{16 \text{ oz.}}$$
$$= \$0.156 \text{ per oz.}$$
$$= 15.6¢ \text{ per oz.}$$
By calculator:
PRESS 2.49 ÷ 16 × 100 =

The largest bag has the lowest unit price by about 1½ cents per ounce. (Incidentally, unit price labels appear on market shelves by law, but anyone who shops regularly knows that they are hard to read, hard to find or missing altogether.)

Is the best buy the largest package of potato chips? Yes, in the sense that it's cheapest, ounce for ounce. (There really is very little difference between the unit cost of the 7½-ounce bag and the 11-ounce bag (.4 cents per ounce). But unless you expect to use a large quantity of chips, you should probably consider one of the smaller sizes. Potato chips get soggy quickly and, besides, having a very large bag around might just be too much temptation.

Intuitively, or because you've often been told so, you may have felt that the biggest size would be the best buy. While it turned out to be so with potato chips, it's not always the case, as we'll now see.

The same Saturday in the supermarket, paper towels were on sale in 2 different packages. You could get one jumbo roll for 93¢ or a package of two smaller-looking rolls for $1.25. A careful reading of the labels revealed that the jumbo roll contained 90 sheets of two-ply towels, which measure 11 inches by 10.6 inches for a total area of 73 square feet. The two-roll package contained a total of 100 square feet, including 62 two-ply towels per roll. Each sheet in this package also measured 11 inches by 10.6 inches. Which package was the better buy?

Given so much information it's difficult to sort out the relevant from the irrelevant to find a common basis for comparison. Best to use the total square footage because that is a true measure of what's in the package. (But you could also use the number of sheets since both packages give this information and, in this example, both contain two-ply sheets of the same dimensions.)

Since the two-roll package contains 100 square feet and costs $1.25, the unit price can be computed as follows:

$$\text{Unit price} = \frac{\$1.25}{100 \text{ sq. ft.}}$$
$$= \$0.0125 \text{ per sq. ft.}$$
$$= 1.25\text{¢ per sq. ft.}$$

For the jumbo roll, we have:

$$\text{Unit price} = \frac{93\text{¢}}{73 \text{ sq. ft.}}$$
$$= 1.27\text{¢ per sq. ft.}$$

The .02 cents per square foot difference in the unit prices is really insignificant, so it makes no difference (price wise) which pack you purchase.

Let's do a third example.

We looked at mayonnaise, which was available in three sizes:

32 oz. for $1.99
48 oz. for $2.99
One gallon for $7.99

Which size is the best buy?

Notice that these sizes lend themselves to very easy comparison. Remember that thirty-two ounces equals one quart, so one quart is about $2. (We've rounded off.) The next larger size, 48 ounces, is 1½ quarts $(48 \div 32 = 1½)$, so it should cost about one and one-half times as much as the smallest size. The middle size is just about $3, which is one and one-half times $2. So the small and medium-sized jars really cost the same. You might think that the gallon size would be a great bargain (assuming, of course, that you could use so much mayo), but it's not.

One gallon is the same as 4 quarts. The very large size costs exactly 4 times the one quart size $(4 \times $2)$. Here again, the largest size was no bargain. The only reason to buy this size is convenience, or because you use vast quantities (maybe you have a very large family or a restaurant) and don't want to keep several smaller jars in stock, or maybe you don't want to shop for mayonnaise often.

The examples we just considered were chosen more or less randomly from the supermarket shelves. The same principles apply whether you're buying corn flakes or cookies, butter or bug spray. And while convenience, brand loyalty or color preference are all legitimate approaches to decision-making, it really pays to first compute unit prices!

Section 3: Equalities: Measure for Measure

When in the middle of cooking some complicated dish, it's annoying to find that the recipe either calls for a measurement you don't have readily accessible (for example, *our* measuring cup is marked only in quarters and thirds, not in eighths) or for an amount that you're not generally familiar with. Then, in the midst of all the preparations, you have to stop and figure out a way to decode what a jigger is or to measure out seventh-eighths of a cup.

What we're presenting first in this Section is a listing of common measurements in more than one form. Some of this information may be found at the back of your all-purpose cookbook; in developing the guides below, we used several different cookbooks to compile the information. Whenever you see a measurement, keep in mind that, unless it specifically calls for a "heaping" teaspoon, all measurements given are for level amounts.

Let's start with what equals what, beginning with small quantities and moving up to larger amounts.

Here's how

TABLE OF WEIGHTS AND MEASURES

When a recipe calls for a "few grains," it means less than ⅛ of a teaspoon; this is equivalent to a "pinch." Similarly:

Table 1
Common Household Measurements and Their Equivalents

HOUSEHOLD MEASURE	EQUIV. HOUSEHOLD MEASURE	APPROX. EQUIV. WEIGHT OF WATER IN GRAMS	APPROX. EQUIV. WEIGHT OF WATER IN OUNCES (SOLID MEASURE)
80 drops	one teaspoon (tsp)	5 grams	.2
one teaspoon	⅓ tablespoon	5 grams	.2
one tablespoon (tbl)	3 teaspoons	15 grams	.5
2 tablespoons	one (fluid) ounce	30 grams	1.1
one jigger (3 tablespoons)	1½ fluid ounces	45 grams	1.6
¼ cup	4 tablespoons	60 grams	2.1
⅓ cup	5 tablespoons + 1 teaspoon	80 grams	2.8
⅜ cup	6 tablespoons	90 grams	3.1
½ cup (1 gill)	8 tablespoons	120 grams	4.2
⅝ cup	½ cup + 2 tablespoons	150 grams	5.3
⅞ cup	¾ cup + 2 tablespoons	210 grams	7.3
1 cup (½ pint)	16 tablespoons	240 grams	8.4 (½ lb.)
2 cups	one pint (16 fluid ounces)	480 grams	16.7 (1 lb.)
one quart	2 pints (4 cups)	946 grams	33.4 (2 lb.)
one gallon	4 quarts (16 cups)	3784 grams	133.5 (8 lb.)
one peck (Dry measure)	8 quarts (Dry measure)		
one bushel (Dry measure)	4 pecks (Dry measure)		

Aside from tables of weights and measures, other interesting things that you'll find tucked away in the back of cookbooks may include "household hints," ways to clean common stains, "serving suggestions," table service and menu planning and "definitions" of cooking terms. The tables of equivalents below show the weights of selected foods.

Here's how

TABLE OF EQUIVALENTS

Did you ever wonder how much a stick of butter weighed? One stick weighs 4 ounces or one-quarter of a pound. It is also the equivalent of ½ cup, or 8 tablespoons. Different foods have different weights, as you can see by glancing at the following table.

Table 2
Household Measures and Equivalent Weights

HOUSEHOLD MEASURE	EQUIVALENT WEIGHT
one cup of dried beans	½ pound
one cup of chopped nuts	⅘ pound, shelled
2 cups of butter	one pound
2 cups of cottage cheese	one pound
2 cups of granulated sugar	one pound
2 cups of water	one pound
2½ cups of shortening	one pound
2½ cups of uncooked rice	one pound
3 cups of dried apricots	one pound
3 cups of uncooked macaroni	one pound
4 cups of cocoa	one pound
4½ cups of sifted cake flour	one pound
5 cups of grated cheese	one pound

Whether food is cooked or raw also affects the quantities involved, as illustrated below:

one cup of raw macaroni	= 2 cups of cooked macaroni (the rule is that macaroni doubles, although some cookbooks say pasta grows by ⅓)
one cup of raw rice	= 3 to 4 cups of cooked rice
one cup of whipping (heavy) cream	= 2½ cups of whipped cream

Other equivalencies that you might find useful are:

3 small eggs	= 2 large eggs
5 whole eggs	= one cup
8 egg whites	= approximately one cup
16 egg yolks	= approximately one cup

one square of cooking chocolate	= one ounce
juice of one lemon	= approximately 2 to 3 table-spoons
juice of one orange	= approximately 6 to 8 table-spoons
one grated orange rind	= one tablespoon

Many tables of equivalents and lists of "substitutions" (such as using honey instead of molasses, or baking soda and cream of tartar for baking powder) date back to the time, not too long ago, when it was not uncommon for women to bake cakes and breads as a matter of routine. Then, especially, it was crucial to be able to determine which items could be substituted for others and what were the weights and measure of the ingredients.

Today, however, there is considerably less home baking and newer, "gourmet" and speciality cookbooks often omit both lists of "equivalents" and "substitutions." Instead, you may find such things as conversion tables for foreign equivalents (see Chapter 6, Section 3–Metrics) and approximate can sizes.

Here's how

CAN SIZES

Obviously, different sized cans weigh varying amounts and contain different quantities. Did you know that there was a time when cans were also numbered? Presented below is a list of what used to be considered standard sized cans and their contents.

Numbered cans with nice, neat even amounts of food (like 12 or 16 ounces) are rapidly disappearing. In their place are slightly smaller cans

Table 3
Standard Can Sizes and Equivalents

CAN SIZE	WEIGHT	CONTENTS
6 ounces (frozen juice)	6 ounces (171 grams)	about ⅔'s cup
6½ ounces (tunafish)	6½ ounces (184 grams)	about ¾'s cup
No. 1	11 ounces (312 grams)	1⅓ cups
12 ounce can	12 ounces (340 grams)	1½ cups
No. 303	16 ounces (454 grams)	2 cups
No. 2	20 ounces (567 grams)	2½ cups
No. 2½	28 ounces (794 grams)	3½ cups
No. 3	33 ounces (936 grams)	4 cups
No. 10	106 ounces (3,005 grams)	13 cups

containing odd-sized amounts and their metric equivalents; 19 ounces (1 pound 3 ounces or 539 grams) instead of a No. 2 can; 27 ounces (one pound 11 ounces or 765 grams) replacing the No. 2½ can; and 13.5 ounces (383 grams) that appears to approximate the size of a one pound No. 303 can.

We could find no *good* explanation for the slightly diminishing size of canned goods; the real reason seems to be that this is a way to increase prices without an obvious price increase: selling a 13.5 ounce can for the same price as a 16 ounce can is an example of this kind of marketing strategy. Take a look at some of the cans on your shelf and notice that not only are they smaller than the once standard cans, but they also contain *odd* amounts. Also packaging goods in 19 ounce amounts, or 13.5 ounces, certainly makes finding the unit cost of the item that much more difficult, as we saw in Section 2.

11

Home Improvement

Section 1: Let's Cut a Rug: Computing Areas

Did you ever read the label on a can of paint? Typically, it will say something like, "spreading rate is 400–450 square feet per gallon." Area is always measured in square units, such as square inches, square feet, square yards and so on—except for acres which are already squared units of measure. Buying carpeting, paint or wallpaper requires an understanding of how *area* is measured.

Before we get to actually measuring rooms, let's review the concept of area. Then we'll show you how to do the computations you need to buy the materials to decorate.

The area of a flat region such as a wall or floor *is the number of square units that it would take to fill that region.* For example, the drawing below represents the floor of a rectangular room that is only 6 feet wide and 8 feet long. The square drawn next to the room measures one foot on a side and is called a *square foot*. The area of the room is the number of square feet you'd need to cover the floor.

Here's how

FINDING AREA OF RECTANGLES

To find the area of a rectangle like the one pictured above, *multiply the length by the width.*

   EXAMPLE: Find the area of a rectangle that is 6 feet wide and 8 feet
      long.
   SOLUTION: Area $=$ Length $\times$ Width
                  $= 8$ ft. $\times 6$ ft.
                  $= 48$ sq. ft.

The diagram below illustrates how 48 square feet fit inside the rectangle.

The area of a square is computed in a similar manner.
Here's how

FINDING AREA OF SQUARES

To find the area of a square, multiply the length of a side by itself.
Notice that finding the area of a square is really the same as finding the
area of a rectangle because a square is just a rectangle with all sides equal.
There also are ways to find the area of other-shaped figures.
Here's how

FINDING AREA OF TRIANGLES

To find the area of a triangle, take one-half the product of the base times the height.

This can be written as the formula:

$$A = \frac{1}{2} \times B \times H$$

A stands for area, B stands for the base, and H is the height.

The height of a triangle is the distance from a vertex (corner) to the side opposite that vertex. *That* side is called the base. It does not matter what pair of sides and vertex you use—the area is always the same.

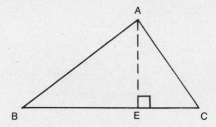

In this diagram, A is one vertex (B and C are the others). The height of the triangle is represented by the dotted line AE. To measure the area of this triangle using the A vertex, use the base side BC.

EXAMPLE: Find the area of the triangle illustrated below.

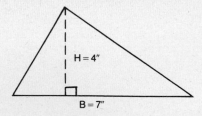

SOLUTION: In this triangle, the height is 4 inches and the base is 7 inches. Therefore:

$$A = \frac{1}{2} \times B \times H$$
$$= \frac{1}{2} \times 7 \text{ in.} \times 4 \text{ in.}$$

$$=\frac{1}{2}\times 28 \text{ sq. in.}$$
$$= 14 \text{ sq. in.}$$

Now we'll show you how to find the area of a circle.
Here's how

FINDING AREA OF A CIRCLE

Finding the area of a circle requires using the following formula:

$$\text{Area} = \pi \times R^2$$

In this formula, R is the radius of the circle, and the Greek letter π (pi) stands for the number 3 14 (approximately). Taken to nine decimal places, π is:

$$= 3.141592654$$

(Also, R^2 is read "R squared" and means $R \times R$.)

Let's do an example. What is the area of a circle that has a radius of 5 inches?

To solve this problem, substitute in the formula:

$$\text{Area} = \pi \times R^2$$
$$= 3.14 \times 5 \text{ in.} \times 5 \text{ in.}$$
$$= 78.5 \text{ sq. in.}$$

The area of a circle with a 5 inch radius is 78.5 square inches.

Sometimes it's necessary to convert from one measurement of area to another. For example, carpeting is generally priced by the square yard. If you've computed the area in square feet, it'll be necessary to convert them to square yards.

Here's how

CONVERTING AREA MEASURES

These are the rules for the most common conversions:

A. *To convert square feet to square yards, divide the number of square feet by 9.* There are 9 square feet in a square yard because a square yard measures 3 feet by 3 feet. This yields an area of 9 square feet.

B. *To convert square yards to square feet, multiply the number of square yards by 9.* (This computation is the inverse of the one described in (A) above.)

C. *To convert square inches to square feet, divide the number of square inches by 144.* There are 144 square inches in a square foot because a square foot measures 12 inches by 12 inches; 12 inches multiplied by 12 inches equals an area of 144 square inches.

D. *To convert square feet to square inches, multiply the number of square feet by 144.* (This computation is the inverse of the computation described in (C) above.)

By the way, we just thought you might like to know:

one acre = 4,480 square yards
one square mile = 3,097,600 square yards
one square mile = 691.4 acres

Now that we've reviewed the concept of area, let's turn to some practical applications, like carpeting and paint.

Here's how

MEASURING FLOOR AREA

Even if you're not going to lay carpet or linoleum yourself, it's a good idea to have some notion of how much carpet (or linoleum) will be needed for the job. Let's start by assuming that the room you're going to carpet is rectangular.

First, measure two adjacent sides of the room, *including* in your measurement all open spaces such as doorways and closets. Suppose one side measures 11 feet 9 inches and the adjacent side measures 9 feet 8 inches.

Next, find out from the store or manufacturer the width of the carpeting you are interested in. Most carpeting, for example, comes in 12-foot widths although wider widths are available in very expensive carpeting and by special order.

If the direction that the pattern will go when laid on the floor does not matter, consider as the *width* of the room the side that is closest to but less than the width in which the carpet is sold. The other dimension (that is, the other side of the room) is the *length* of carpeting you will need to order.

The measurements given in the example above, 11 feet 9 inches by 9 feet 8 inches, indicate that the longer dimension of the room is close to the 12-foot width in which the carpet is sold. Therefore, only a 9 feet 8 inches length of carpet is needed to cover the room. Don't cut it too close! Allow some extra. You probably wouldn't be able to order "and 8 inches" anyway, so order 10 feet.

Note: If the width in which the carpet is sold is smaller than either dimension of the room, or if the pattern is asymetrical and direction is important, then it will be necessary to buy two runs of carpet, have them sewn together and then trimmed to the proper width.

To compute the amount of carpeting to be ordered, find the area by multiplying the length and width of the *carpeting*. In the example we are using, the length is 10 feet and the width is 12 feet, so the area of the carpeting we would need is 120 square feet. (Compare this to the area of the *floor*, which measures 11 feet 9 inches or 141 inches by 9 feet 8 inches or 116 inches; 141 inches by 116 inches equals 16,356 square inches, divided by 144 equals 113.6 square feet.)

Since carpet is sold in square *yards,* it is now necessary to convert the number of square feet to square yards by dividing by 9. In our example, it is $120 \div 9$ equals 13.3 square yards. This is the amount of carpeting for which you will have to pay.

Measuring for wallpaper is similar in theory to measuring for carpeting, but in actuality it's quite a bit more complicated. You need to know the width and height of your walls and the width and lengths of the rolls in which paper is sold. You also need to figure in the size of the "repeat"— the amount of space one whole pattern takes up. Since patterns have to be carefully matched, you may have to buy much more paper than you might think. Unless you're very handy, we suggest you leave wallpaper measurement (and hanging!) to the paper-hanger or to the wallpaper specialty store manager. Part of their service is that they will come to your house to measure.

Paint will cover the area of your walls or ceiling at a predetermined rate which is generally indicated on the paint can. A typical spread rate is 400–450 square feet per gallon. This means that one gallon of paint will cover an area of from 400 to 450 square feet. How much paint will you need to buy for the bedroom?
Here's how

| MEASURING FOR PAINT |

To determine how much paint you'll need:

(1) *Measure the length, width and height of the room.* Round each measurement up to the next largest footage. Be generous. Don't subtract out windows, doors or closet space.
(2) The next step involves *computing the area of each wall* by multiplying its width (in feet) by the height of the room (also in feet).
(3) *Add together the areas of the walls* to get the total wall area.
(4) To figure out how much paint to buy, *divide the total wall area to be painted by the spread rate of the particular type and brand of paint you are planning to use.*

The answer is the number of gallons of paint you'll need to do the walls. Remember, don't cut it too close. Always err on the high side. It's better to have some paint left over (for touch-ups) than to run out in the middle of the job.

If you're painting the ceiling the same color as the walls, using the same paint, then you have to figure the ceiling area in your computations. If you're going to use different paint on the ceiling, keep this measurement separate. In either case, you need to know the area of the ceiling.

To find the ceiling area, multiply the length of the room by the width. Notice that *the ceiling area is the same as the floor area!*

Assuming the ceiling is to be a different color, divide the ceiling area by the spread rate for the ceiling paint to find the number of gallons of paint needed for the ceiling.

After some discussion, we've decided to paint the bedroom walls coffee and the ceiling bone white. The room measures 13 feet 3 inches by 16 feet 7 inches. The height of the ceiling is 8 feet. The coffee-colored wall paint has a spread rate of 450 square feet and the bone paint will cover 500 square feet per gallon. Now let's figure out how much wall and ceiling paint we need.

First, round up the room measurements to 14 feet by 17 feet.

Then compute the areas of two adjacent walls by multiplying the length by the height of the room:

14 ft. × 8 ft. = 112 sq. ft.
17 ft. × 8 ft. = 136 sq. ft.
        Total = 248 sq. ft.

Since the other two walls have the same area, 248 square feet:

Total area of the walls = 2 × 248 sq. ft. = 496 sq. ft.

Next, calculate the number of gallons of paint needed by dividing the total area of the walls by the spread rate of the paint. (If a spread rate range is given, use the lower end in this calculation to be on the safe side.)

Gallons needed = 496 ÷ 450 = 1.1

This comes to one gallon and one-tenth of a gallon, but it would be best to buy one gallon and an additional *quart* of paint. If the quart is not a custom mix, you can probably return it if you don't open it.

Painter's hint: Save one of the small walls to paint last. That way, when you get to this wall, if it looks like there's enough paint in the gallon can to complete it, go ahead and finish the job. If, however, it looks like you might run out of paint, use the extra quart instead of finishing the gallon can. Paint color varies slightly from can to can. You won't notice the difference on adjacent walls, but will see the color variation if you start a new can in the middle of a wall.

Finally, determine the area of the ceiling:

14 ft. × 17 ft. = 238 sq. ft.

And divide by the spread rate of the ceiling paint (500 square feet per gallon):

238 ÷ 500 = .48

This is slightly less than one-half gallon, so two quarts will do. You can avoid color variation by mixing the two quarts together before starting on the ceiling. (That's another experienced painter's hint.)

Final hint: Transfer left-over paint into small jars. Try the kind used for canning because they have air-tight seals. Be sure to label the jar with the brand of paint, name/number of the color, base (oil, latex) and which room was painted that color. Using small glass jars for leftover paint takes up less room than old paint cans. They are also more tidy to store and easier to use for touch-ups.

Section 2: How to Make a Round Tablecloth

To make a round tablecloth, you first need to make a square whose side is equal to the diameter of the required circle. Then you draw the circle and cut it out, hem it and, *voilá,* you have a round tablecloth.

Let's go through these steps a little more slowly and in greater detail, taking into account some of the geometric concepts involved in circles and squares as well as the sewing suggestions that will make this a truly professional job.

What we have in mind is a floor-length table covering that can be used as a cloth but that is more likely to be used decoratively, perhaps with another cloth draped over it. The following pictures illustrate (A) the table we want to cover, (B) the table covered by the cloth, (C) an "x-ray" view of the covered table and (D) the table covering spread out flat. As you can see in the last drawing, the cloth is a perfect circle.

Note that the same principles work for any type of round table top—of any height, with any kind of base or size top.

The first step involves making a square of fabric whose side is the diameter of the circle you need. What exactly is the diameter, and how do you find the diameter of the table covering you want to make?
Here's how

FINDING THE DIAMETER

The diameter of the floor-length round cloth is equal to 2 times the height of the table *plus* the diameter of the round table top *plus* another 2 inches (for the hem).

Step 1 Measure the height of the table from the floor to the top of the table (most dining-type tables are about 29 inches tall) and multiply by 2:

29″

2×29 in. $= 58$ in.

Step 2 Find the diameter of the table top. Drawings A, B, and C are aerial views of the top of a round table. (The dot, "O", represents the center of the circle.)

(A)   0

(B)   0

(C)   0

The diameter is the distance of the imaginary line that goes from one point of the circle to another through the center point. It is the length of the longest line you can draw from point to point.

The broken line in Drawing A is the diameter and, as an example, in the table we are covering, it is 36 inches across. Drawing B shows that no matter which way you measure the diameter of this same circle, it is always the same length.

Hint: Since your real-life table doesn't have the exact center marked for you, it might help in finding the diameter to remember it is the *longest* length from one point on a circle to another. In Drawing C you can visually compare the length of the diameter with the length of any other line that cuts across the circle but doesn't go through the center. Take a ruler and make the measurements for yourself so that you don't have to rely on visual data alone.

So, *to find the diameter of the table top, take your tape measure and find the longest length across the top.* (If the table top is too big for your arm span, fasten the tape measure at one edge of the table and swing the tape along the top until you find the longest length.)

In our example, the diameter measured 36 inches.

Step 3 The diameter of the floor-length table covering is equal to 2 times the height plus the diameter of the top plus 2 inches.

58 in. + 36 in. + 2 in. = 96 in.

Now we have to make a 96-inch square piece of fabric.
Here's how

MAKING A SQUARE

A square is a rectangle with all four sides equal in length and, like all rectangles, it has four right-angle corners. Large and small squares are illustrated below:

A 96-inch square is a square whose sides measure 96 inches. It is a large square and looks like this:

The problem is that, while squares are very simple things, a 96-inch square piece of fabric is a little difficult to make in real life because fabric doesn't usually come in 96-inch widths. If it did, all you'd have to do is to measure out a 96-inch length and you'd have the square you need. Similarly, if fabric came in widths wider than 96 inches, all you'd have to do to get a square this size would be to trim the width down to 96 inches, then measure out the required length.

Fabric traditionally comes in 36-inch, 48-inch, and 52-inch widths. Let's assume that the pattern we want for the table covering comes in a 52-inch width.

To make a 96-inch square from a 52-inch wide fabric, you'll have to add 44 inches to the width:

$$96 - 52 = 44$$

So your square would look like this:

The 44 inch piece of fabric, which is 96" long, has to be trimmed down from a piece 52" × 96". Note that you have to buy two runs of 96" lengths, or 2 × 96" = 192 inches of fabric (which is 16 feet or 5 yards and 1 foot of material.)

In the illustration, the dotted line represents where the two pieces of fabric could be joined together. (If your fabric comes in a 48-inch width, you couldn't make a 96-inch square from two runs because you have to allow about one-fourth to one-half inch on each run for sewing the pieces together.)

Hint: If you sew the pieces together like this—

52"   44"

your tablecloth will have a seam running across the top. To get the seams on the sides near the bottom where they'll be less noticeable, divide the 44-inch piece in half *lengthwise* to get 2 pieces, each of which measures 22 inches by 96 inches. Then sew one of these pieces to each side of the 52-inch by 96-inch piece like this:

22"   52"   22"

This will guarantee that no seams will fall on the flat surface of the table top.

Now from the 96-inch square we are going to cut out a circle that has a 96-inch diameter.

Here's how

CUTTING THE CIRCLE

The picture above illustrates what we want to accomplish. The circle we want will touch the square on all four sides. Can you see how this circle has a 96-inch diameter?

In school, to draw a circle you used a compass. The pointy leg left a teeny hole that marked the center of the circle you were drawing, and the distance to the pencil point was called the *radius* of the circle.

If you recall, the *radius of a circle is equal to one-half the diameter* (or, the diameter was 2 times the radius). So, we need a compass that can draw a circle with a 48-inch radius (96 in. ÷ 2). That's a mighty big compass: 4 feet. It's certainly not an instrument we'd find lying around the house so . . . Let's make a compass.

Hint: To make a compass, we'll need a pin, a long length of string (more than 48 inches) and a piece of chalk or charcoal. Some tape would also be helpful.

Tie the string securely around the chalk and tape it down so it won't slip. Measure out 48 inches of string starting from the knot and mark the length on the string with a pen. Use a pin to mark this spot which will become the "pointy" leg of the compass.

Now find the center of the square, which will also be the center of the circle, either by locating the point of intersection of the diagonals (drawing A), or by folding the square in quarters (Drawing B). Mark the center point with the chalk.

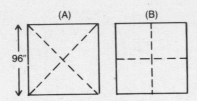

Now spread the cloth out flat on a surface such as the floor and pin the string at the place you marked (48 inches from the end knotted around the chalk) at the exact center of the square. Holding down the center with one hand, carefully extend the string and start drawing the outer edge of the circle. Remember, the string is equal to the radius of the circle, which in our example is 48 inches.

Hint: Try not to either stretch the string or let it sag. Hold it taut, but not tight. Also, it helps if the fabric can be held firmly in place. You might want to borrow another set of hands for this part of the operation.

Once you've outlined the circle, all that remains is cutting it out and hemming it. Use a sharp scissors and cut along the chalk line you've made. Incidentally, the chalk line is the *circumference* of the circle, which is:

$$C(\text{circumference}) = 2\pi r$$

That is, circumference is 2 times pi (the Greek letter) times the radius. Since π equals 3.14159 and, in our example, r = 48 inches:

$$C = 2 \times 3.14159 \times 48 \text{ in.}$$
$$= 301.6 \text{ (or } 301.593) \text{ in.}$$
$$= 25.13 \text{ ft. or } 8.38 \text{ yds.}$$

It's important to be able to figure the circumference of the circle if you want to buy trim to edge the cloth with. In our case, you'd buy 9 yards of trim. (Trim is sewn on after the hem is made.)

The last step involves sewing the hem.

Hint: We've left 2 inches, an inch all around, for the hem. Since a round tablecloth is always cut on the bias (that is, on an angle to the weave of the fabric), a "rolled" hem works best. A rolled hem is the type you'll find on most handkerchiefs and requires a "hemming" stitch. If you're going to roll the hem, you will have to trim off a little fabric all around first.

You now have a round tablecloth which should cover your table and just reach the floor on all sides. If you want a round tablecloth that doesn't come to the floor, go back to the first step in this section, where we first measured the height of the table. Instead of measuring from floor to table top, measure from the point you want the tablecloth to reach, like this:

Measure this distance

Double it, add the diameter of the table top plus a couple of inches for the hem and proceed as we've outlined.

While we were writing this section, we described it to a friend who asked, "Why on earth would you want to make a round tablecloth?" I guess we forgot to start by telling her that we had a round table.

Section 3: . . . With the Fringe on Top: Computing Perimeters

Molding is generally put along the base of walls or along the top edge where the wall and ceiling meet to give a room a more finished look. Edging is usually sewn around the border of area rugs. Round tablecloths, like the one we made in Section 2, often have fringe around the bottom. And many people enclose their property by placing a fence around it.

These constructions all involve the concept of *perimeter*.

The perimeter of a flat area is the distance around it. So to calculate, say, how much edging or fencing you need to buy for your home improvement project, you need to know how to compute the perimeter of variously shaped areas.

Here's how

FINDING PERIMETERS OF RECTANGLES

To find the perimeter of a rectangle add the length and width and multiply by two.

This can be summarized by the formula:

Perimeter $= 2 \times (L + W)$

EXAMPLE: Find the perimeter of a rectangle like the one pictured below that is 6 feet wide and 8 feet long.

SOLUTION: Perimeter $= 2 \times (L + W)$
$= 2 \times (8 \text{ ft.} + 6 \text{ ft.})$
$= 2 \times 14 \text{ ft.}$
$= 28 \text{ ft.}$

This amount, 28 feet, is the length of molding needed to go completely around the baseboard of a room which is 6 feet wide and 8 feet long. Actually, the required amount of molding would be a bit less, depending on how many feet are taken up by doors and closets. But, when buying molding, edging, fringe, border or even fencing, always get a bit extra—just in case!

Calculating the perimeter of a *square* is done similarly.

Here's how

FINDING PERIMETER OF A SQUARE

To find the perimeter of a square multiply the length of a side by 4.

Note that computing the perimeter of a square is really the same as finding the perimeter of a rectangle, because a square is just a rectangle with all sides equal.

EXAMPLE: Find the perimeter of a 7-foot square
SOLUTION: 4×7 ft. $= 28$ ft.

Perimeters of other-shaped flat figures, even odd-shaped ones like the one pictured below, are found in much the same way.
Here's how

FINDING PERIMETERS OF ANY REGION

To find the perimeter of any region or area bounded by straight line segments add up the lengths of the bounding segments.

EXAMPLE: What is the perimeter of the figure illustrated below?

SOLUTION: In this figure we add up the lengths of the edges as we move around the figure, counterclockwise, starting with the left side.
Perimeter $= 12 + 15 + 7 + 8 + 3 + 2 + 2 + 5$ ft.
$= 54$ ft.

The distance around a circle is called the *circumference* rather than the perimeter. There is a special formula for finding the circumference (perimeter of a circle).

Here's how

FINDING CIRCUMFERENCE

Use this formula:

Circumference $= 2 \times \pi \times R$

In this formula, R is the *radius* of the circle and the Greek letter π (pi) stands for the number 3.14 (approximately).

> EXAMPLE: If a circle has a radius of 7 inches, what is the circumference?
> SOLUTION: Circumference $= 2 \times 3.14 \times 7$ in.
> $\qquad\qquad\qquad\qquad = 43.96$ in. or 44 in. (Rounded off that's about 3 feet and 8 inches.)
> EXAMPLE: Find the circumference of a circle that has a radius of 5 inches.

> SOLUTION: Circumference $= 2 \times \pi \times R$
> $\qquad\qquad\qquad\qquad = 2 \times 3.14 \times 5$ in.
> $\qquad\qquad\qquad\qquad = 31.4$ in.

Since the *diameter* of a circle is twice the radius, another formula for the circumference is:

Circumference $= \pi \times D$

In this formula D is the diameter of the circle.

EXAMPLE: Find the circumference of a circular running track that has a diameter of 140 yards.

SOLUTION: Circumference $= \pi \times D$

$= 3.14 \times 140$ yds.

$= 439.6$ yds.

That's about ¼ mile since one mile $= 1,760$ yards and ¼ mile $= ¼ \times 1,760$ yards $= 440$ yards.

EXAMPLE: Find the amount of fringe needed to finish a round rug that has an 8-foot diameter.

SOLUTION: The amount of fringe needed is equal to the circumference of the rug.

Circumference $= \pi \times D$

$= 3.14 \times 8$ ft.

$= 25.12$ ft.

So, you would buy 26 feet of fringe just to be on the safe side.

12

Figuring
Your Bill

Section 1: It's a Gas! Gas Meters and Gas Rates

When you use gas for cooking (assuming, of course, that you have a gas stove) or for heating, the flow of gas through the gas lines is measured by a meter. Gas meters are usually installed inside your home or apartment, in the basement. Once a month, the gas company sends someone to read your meter in order to determine how much gas you have used. If you are not at home and they are unable to read the meter, the utility will estimate your monthly usage based on your past usage patterns. When they next read your meter, they will make corrections in your bill, up or down, if the estimate did not agree with the actual usage.

Gas consumption has traditionally been measured in *cubic feet* and you are billed for the number of *hundreds of cubic feet* you use. As of June 1983, Consolidated Edison in New York City changed from a base of one-hundred cubic feet to "therms."

A therm is a measure of the heat content of the gas supplied to you. It is generally a little more than one-hundred cubic feet (100.3 cubic feet) but, for all practical purposes, one therm and one Ccf (as one-hundred cubic feet is abbreviated) can be considered equivalent. Actually, the *heat content* of the gas you get varies slightly from month to month.

Low gas usage would be about 200 cubic feet (2 therms) per month. That's the amount you would use for running the pilot light on your stove and for light cooking. Obviously, gas usage would be far higher if you did a lot of cooking and baking and if you also used gas for heating or for hot water.

You can, if you wish, read the gas meter yourself—we'll show you

230

how. But the gas company will not allow you to call in a reading. They always want to read it themselves.

Gas meters are of two types: the older meters are made up of dials; the newer ones are digital and extremely easy to read.

First, we'll discuss how digital gas meters work.

Here's how

DIGITAL GAS METERS

A digital meter looks something like this:

The numbers on the display represent the number of hundreds of cubic feet used since the meter was first installed. The dials let you see how fast you are consuming gas. The small dial on the left makes one complete revolution for every $\frac{1}{4}$ cubic foot of gas used. The small dial on the right makes one revolution per one cubic foot of gas. Thus, 4 revolutions of the dial on the left correspond to one complete revolution of the dial on the right.

To see how it works, put up a kettle of water to boil and then go and look at the gas meter. You will see the hand on the dial on the left moving rather quickly, while the hand on the dial on the right moves more slowly: 4 revolutions to one. (The digital display dials will probably not move because the smallest unit of measurement there is 100 cubic feet.) If you were to do the same experiment when roasting a turkey in the oven and cooking a pot of soup on the stove, you would see the dials moving more rapidly because of the increased rate of gas consumption.

In the illustration above, the meter reads 106 hundreds of cubic feet. That's actually 10600 or 10,600 cubic feet. One month later the meter looks like:

It reads 108 hundreds of cubic feet. The difference in the digital readings from one month to the next represents the gas usage for that month. The gas usage in our example is: $108 - 106 = 2$ hundreds of cubic feet. Your gas bill is computed by multiplying the monthly usage by the gas rate—plus minimum charges, taxes and any gas adjustment factor.

Now, let's examine dial gas meters.

Here's how

DIAL GAS METERS

A dial gas meter looks something like this:

To read these meters, begin with Dial #3. The "one thousand" written above the dial means that one complete revolution of the hand represents 1,000 cubic feet of gas consumption. (Note that the arrow ⌒➤ on the face of this dial indicates that the hand moves *clockwise*.) Since 10 hundreds makes one thousand, the numbers 1–10 represent 100,200,300, etc. cubic feet of gas consumption. The hand is pointing between 7 and 8, so this dial indicates 700+ cubic feet.

Now go to Dial #1, the first dial on the left. One revolution of the pointer represents 100,000 cubic feet and each number on the dial stands for 10,000 cubic feet (since $10 \times 10,000 = 100,000$). The arrow ⌒➤ indicates that the rotation direction is clockwise. Since the hand is between 1 and 2, this dial reads 10,000 + cubic feet.

Dial #2 moves *counterclockwise* as indicated by the arrow ![arrow] Each number represents 1,000 cubic feet and a complete revolution is 10 × 1,000 or 10,000 cubic feet. The pointer is between 5 and 6, representing 5,000 + cubic feet.

The three dials taken together read 15,700 cubic feet (10,000 + 5,000 + 700). (The small unnumbered dial on the right is not part of the gas company's meter reading; it helps you see how quickly you are consuming gas, with one revolution representing one cubic foot of gas consumption.) Notice that although the three dials read 15,700 cubic feet, the reading would be recorded as 157, meaning 157 hundreds cubic feet.

Suppose that at the end of one month the meter looks like this:

Dial #1	Dial #2	Dial #3
100 Thousand	10 Thousand	One + Thousand
Per Revolution	Per Revolution	Per Revolution

The reading would be 16,000 cubic feet or 160 hundreds cubic feet. The difference between this reading and the prior month's reading of 157 hundreds cubic feet is 3 hundred cubic feet. This is the amount of gas you consumed and for which you would be charged.

Here's how

COMPUTING YOUR GAS BILL

Consolidated Edison in New York City charges its residential customers a minimum of $7.13 a month, which includes charges for billing, meter reading and other customer services, and also covers the first 3 therms of gas consumption. If you don't use gas for heating, you are then charged 68.5¢ per therm for all therms over 3. If, however, you do have gas heat, your additional therms are less costly (since the utility figures that you'll be using so many more of them): 66.81¢ per therm for from 3 to 3,000 therms and 60¢ per therm for therms over 3,000 per month.

If, as in our example, you used only 3 therms (or 3 hundred cubic feet), you'd pay only the minimum usage charge (plus the other charges described below). If you used 5 therms you'd pay:

$7.13 (which includes the cost of 3 therms)
+ $1.37 (2 × 68.5¢)
$8.50

In addition to the minimum charge and excess usage charges, this power company also has a 5¢ per therm adjustment factor. Some gas companies now use adjustment factors to compensate for changes in the price they pay for gas. The adjustment factor is the way they pass along to you increases or decreases in price.

If we used 5 therms at a total of $8.50, and if there had been a pass-along adjustment reflecting increased gas costs, the charge for your gas consumption that month would be:

$8.50 + (3 × 5¢) = $8.65

That's not all. Calculated into your bill, but not shown, is a 6.86% gross receipts tax. There's also a 4% sales tax if you are a residential customer. That's an additional 94¢ (10.86% × $8.65):

8.65 + .94 = $9.59

So, using only a minimal amount of gas, your bill quickly adds up to almost $10. It's a gas, alright!

Section 2: Electrical Charges or How Your Electrical Bill Is Computed

When you turn on a light switch, electrons immediately begin to move through the wire, generating electricity. The *rate of flow* of electrons through a wire is measured in units called *amps,* which is short for amperes, after the French physicist, André Marie Ampère (1775–1836), a principal architect of electromagnetic theory. The symbol i is generally used for amps or *current*.

All electrical devices exhibit *resistance* to the flow of current. This resistance is similar to the friction which is present in all mechanical devices. The energy that is dissipated in overcoming resistance (friction) appears as heat. Electrical resistance is measured in units called *ohms,* named after the German physicist George S. Ohm (1787–1854). The usual symbol for resistance or ohms is r.

It takes work to overcome resistance, and *the volt* (named for the Italian physicist Alessandro Volta (1745–1827), *is the unit of electromotive force required to move a current of one amp through a resistance of one ohm.*

Voltage, current and resistance are related through Ohm's law:

$v = ir$

In this law i is the current in amps, r is the resistance in ohms and v is the voltage in volts.

The "electricity" we pay for, however, is electrical *power.* *Here's how*

WATTS AND KILOWATTS

Although we tend to think of power in informal terms, it has a precise meaning in physics and to the "power" companies. *Power is defined as the rate at which electrical energy is transferred.* Power is measured in *watts* to acknowledge the Scottish inventor, James Watt (1736–1819).

Watts (power) is the product of voltage and current measured in volts and amps, respectively. That is:

$p = vi$

In this formula p stands for power in watts.

We'll see in a moment that it doesn't take much to use one watt of electrical power. Since watts are used rather quickly, electrical power is generally quoted in *kilowatts:*

1 kilowatt = 1,000 watts

Actually, we don't pay for electrical power per se, but for how long that power is used. After all, it is clear that we should be charged more for using one kilowatt of power for an hour rather than for a second. So electric rates are based on the cost per kilowatt-hour (kwh). *One kilowatt-hour means that 1 kilowatt (1,000 watts) is transferred continuously for a period of one hour.*

Now let's examine what this means in practical terms.

Consider light bulbs. A typical light bulb might be rated as 100 watts. It takes 100 watts of electrical power to light the bulb! Since 1,000 watts equals 1 kilowatt, this means that it takes .1 (¹⁄₁₀) kilowatt of power to light the bulb. If the lamp is on all evening, say from 6:00 P.M. to 11:00 P.M., the light burns for 5 hours. Therefore, you will be charged for .1 kilowatt × 5 hours = .5 kilowatt-hours of electricity.

Electricity rates range from about 5 to about 15¢/kwh, depending upon the region of the country in which you live and the amount of power you use. In New York City, for example, the residential rates are 13.281¢/kwh for the first 250 kwh's, then 12.756¢/kwh for kilowatt-hours in excess of 250. These are the winter rates, when you pay less per kilowatt hour for using more electricity. There is an inverted rate for the summer months (from June 1 through September 30): 13.281¢/kwh for the first 250 kwh's, then 14.256¢/kwh for anything over 250 kwh's. In the summer when more power is in demand (mostly to run air conditioners), you pay a penalty of a higher per kilowatt-hour rate for using more power.

Let's suppose you are paying a high rate of 15¢/kwh. Keeping the 100-watt bulb burning for 5 hours will cost you:

$$.5 \text{ kwh} \times 15¢ = 7.5¢$$

That doesn't sound like much for having the lamp on all evening. But wait!

During a typical evening, you may have 5 lights on, 2 of which are rated 60 W (watts), another 2 at 100 W and the final one at 150 W. You also have the television set on and it is rated at 120 W. (The wattage of an electrical device is generally printed on the bottom or at the back near the power cord.) Suppose all these devices are on for 5 hours. Let's figure what the cost will be at the New York City rate of 13.281¢/kwh.

First, you compute the total number of watts that are used by adding together the wattage of all the equipment:

$$\text{Total watts} = (2 \times 60) + (2 \times 100) + 150 + 120 = 590$$

Now compute the total number of kilowatts by dividing by 1,000:

$$\text{Total kilowatts} = 590 \div 1,000$$
$$= .59$$

Then compute the number of kilowatt-hours by multiplying the number of kilowatts by 5 (hours):

$$\text{Total kilowatt-hours} = 5 \times .59$$
$$= 2.95$$

Finally, compute the cost by multiplying the number of kilowatt hours by 13.281¢:

13.281¢/kwh × 2.95kwh = 39.18¢

That still doesn't sound too bad. But suppose you do the same thing every day, 30 days a month. Now the cost for the 5 lamps and the TV set for 5 hours per night is 30 × 39.18¢ or $11.75—and this doesn't even begin to account for all the electrical equipment you probably use!

Electrical appliances that are *very* heavy consumers of electrical power are toaster ovens, hair dryers, air conditioners, electrical stoves, irons and refrigerators. For example, a toaster oven is rated at 1350 W and an iron at 1100 W. That's 2 to 3 times more wattage than those 5 light bulbs and TV set combined!

How does the power company keep track of the number of kilowatt-hours of electrical power you use?

Here's how

ELECTRIC METERS

The electric meter, installed by the power company and usually mounted outside the house or in the basement, constantly records your use of kilo-watt-hours.

The newer electric meters are digital, in which case there are no complexities in reading the display: what you see is what you get. The older meters are similar to the gas meters discussed in the previous section. If you have one of the older-type meter boxes, it will probably have a four-dial display like this:

Dial #1	Dial #2	Dial #3	Dial #4
10,000 Kwh's	1,000 Kwh's	100 Kwh's	10 Kwh's

One complete revolution of the hand in Dial #1 represents 10,000 kwh's. Since the hand in the example is between 5 and 6, it represents between 5,000 and 6,000 kwh's. We read this as 5,000.

One complete revolution of the hand in the second dial (#2) represents 1,000 kwh's, so each digit represents hundreds of kwh's. In our example, the hand is between 3 and 4—between 300 and 400 kwh's. (If the hand had gone full circle, it would be 1,000 kwh's). We read the second dial as 300. Thus far we have used 5,300 kwh's.

One complete revolution of Dial #3 represents 100, so each digit represents 10. Since the hand is between 2 and 3, this means between 20 and 30. We read it as 20, and we now have 5,320 kwh's.

The last dial (#4) represents ones, since one complete revolution is 10 kwh's. Since the hand is between 7 and 8, we read it as 7 kwh's. Taken together, the 4 dials read 5,327 kwh's. (Notice that in reading the meter we always read the *lower* of the numbers between which the hand falls.)

The number you read on the meter is not the number of kilowatt-hours you used this month, fortunately, but rather, the total number of kilowatt-hours that have been used since the meter was first installed. The meter is read each month, and the difference in readings from one month to the next is the amount of electricity you have used.

Your total bill for the month includes:

1. A monthly customer charge (of $4.58 in New York City) that covers the utility's cost of reading your meter, billing you and other customer services.
2. Taxes, including local sales tax.
3. The amount of electricity you have used multiplied by the rate which gives you—pun intended—your monthly charge.

Section 3: Buddy, Can You Spare a Nickel? Dime? Quarter?: Figuring Your Phone Costs

Once upon a time, before deregulation of the telephone industry, it was all comparatively simple. A telephone call cost a dime, double the price of only a short while before that. For a set fee you had a wired phone and were permitted a certain number of local calls. Additional charges got you additional local and long-distance calls. And, while you never quite understood "message units," you got *one* bill each month, from *one* telephone company, most typically a subsidiary of the Bell system. In those days, repairs were generally free or easy to come by and, if you wanted a new instrument, your choice was limited to about 5 basic models in a narrow range of colors.

Today it's all changed. A federal court decision broke the AT&T monopoly, encouraging competition. One early consequence of "deregulation," which went into effect in 1984, has been an increase in the cost of local calls, the result of an attempt to bring the price of basic telephone service closer to its actual cost. Now there's also a late payment charge on unpaid balances. Long-distance rates, however, have tended to stay the same or, in some cases, to decrease. We now have a choice of long-distance carriers (and must learn to be better informed consumers) and a staggering array of new phone instruments to choose from.

Let's start by looking at the price of a local call made from your home telephone.

Here's how

TYPES OF HOME SERVICE

The cost of a local telephone call depends on a number of factors—whether you're using a pay phone, a home phone or an office phone, whether you've requested operator assistance, the type of service you've purchased and so on.

There's a basic monthly service fee for every phone which consists of: (a) the cost of an exchange access line from the phone company's central office to your home, and (b) an inside wire charge to connect your phone to that line. Your local telephone company owns the wire. Their *wire charge* for each phone consists of two parts: (b–1) a wire maintenance charge and (b–2) a wire investment charge. Our phone company, New York Telephone, charges us 87¢/month per phone (including extensions) for wire maintenance and $1.21/month per line for wire investment.

The *exchange access line* cost depends on the type of service you have. New York Telephone offers its customers three choices:

1. *Basic budget service,* which is the lowest-priced individual phone line service. This costs $3.28/month for the exchange access line (all prices are quoted without taxes and other local surcharges). Users of this service get no monthly allowance for outgoing calls—it's designed principally for people who want to receive calls but make very few outgoing ones.
2. *Unlimited service,* for which the basic monthly exchange access line charge is $7.08, of which $4 is a monthly allowance for local usage that covers both primary and extended area calls.
3. *Timed service,* where the basic monthly exchange access line cost of $6.11 includes a $4 allowance for local usage (both primary and extended area). In this option, even primary area calls are timed, with additional charges for each minute of overtime after the first 5 minutes.

As of June 1985, there was an additional $1 "subscriber line charge" for every line going into the 90 million households and 5.7 million small businesses that have phones!

These are basic charges, exclusive of the lease or purchase cost of equipment. AT&T Consumer Sales and Service owns the instrument—unless you've purchased yours. You can buy a single-line phone from AT&T, the standard black table top model, for $39.95 plus tax. Or, you can continue to rent the equipment—for $1.50 per month plus tax for the standard black model.

The cost of a phone call is based on distance, when (the time of day and day of week) you make the call and the length of your conversation. *Here's how*

LOCAL CALLS

Each telephone company has a defined "local calling area." A call to an exchange within this area is considered a local call. Our telephone company, New York Telephone Company, defines the local calling area as New York City's 5 boroughs and all or parts of several surrounding counties. In the front of your telephone *Directory*'s "white pages," you'll find the definition of your *local calling area*.

There are two types of "local" calls: *primary area* calls (Area A in our *Directory*) to your own or to nearby exchanges, and *extended area* calls (Areas B–F in our *Directory*), which include exchanges beyond the primary area but within your local calling area. Primary area calls may be *timed* or *untimed*, depending on your type of service, but all extended area calls are *timed*, meaning you get billed for an initial period (of one minute) and for each additional minute that you're on the line. (Calls beyond your local calling area are considered to be long-distance calls. We'll talk more about these later.)

Your telephone *Directory* has tables that help you determine your primary and extended area exchanges. To find this for any particular exchange you're calling involves three easy steps. *First*, you find the zone your exchange is in. *Next*, you look up the zone of the exchange you are calling. (The first 3 digits of the phone number are the exchange.) *Then* you read a table to find if the zone you are calling is in your primary or in (one of) your extended areas.

The final table in the *Directory* lists the charges for each primary and extended area call.

Our telephone company's *day period rates* for primary area calls are 8.7¢ for untimed and basic budget service calls and 7.7¢/5 minutes for timed service plus 1¢ for each additional minute of overtime. Extended area calls are all timed, and all are at higher rates. The table in the New York Telephone Company *Directory* shows a charge of 10.6¢ for a one-minute initial period in Extended Area B plus 2.9¢/minute for overtime; this is the area contiguous to our primary area. In Area F, the farthest away geographically, there is a 27.9¢/minute charge for the initial call plus 12.5¢/minute for overtime.

These charges can mount up quickly. One way to keep costs down is to try to take advantage of discounted rates.

Here's how

DISCOUNTED RATES

Telephone companies have different rates depending upon whether you make your calls during peak business periods (expensive) or during slack, off-hours (cheaper). The discounted rates are also shown clearly by your telephone company.

Our phone company has *day period rates* which apply weekdays from 8:00 A.M. to 9:00 P.M., except for 5 holidays (Christmas, New Year's, Thanksgiving, Independence Day and Labor Day) when evening rates apply from 8:00 A.M. to 11 P.M. and night rates apply from 11:00 P.M. to 8:00 A.M. Day period rates are most costly.

Evening period rates, which are in effect from 9:00 P.M. to 11:00 P.M., Mondays–Fridays, are discounted by 35%. (See Chapter 5, Section 2 for a complete discussion of discounts and an explanation of how to compute them.)

The least expensive time to call, if you can, is when *night period rates* are in effect; there's a 60% discount on the cost of calls made Monday to Friday from 11:00 P.M. to 8:00 A.M., all day and night Saturday, and Sunday from 8:00 A.M. to 5:00 P.M. and from 11:00 P.M. to 8:00 A.M..

The phone company suggests that the "most accurate way to figure the cost of an evening or night call is to use the full week day rate for the total time, then subtract the 35% or the 60% discount and round to the lower penny."

Let's compare the cost of the same call made when the three different rates are in effect.

Suppose we had timed service and made a primary area call for which we are charged the rate of 7.7¢/5 minutes plus 1¢/minute overtime. These are day period rates. If we talked for 18 minutes, the charge for this call (exclusive of taxes and local surcharges) would be:

$$7.7¢ + (13 \times 1¢) = 20.7¢$$

If, however, we made this call between 9:00 P.M. and 11:00 P.M. when evening rates were in effect, we would get a 35% discount. The best way to compute the discount is to: (a) compute the total day period cost of the call, (b) calculate 35% and (c) subtract the 35% from the total day cost, rounding to the lower penny:

(a) 20.7
(b) $.35 \times 20.7 = 7.245$
(c) $20.7 - 7.245 = 13.455$ or 13¢ rounded to the lower penny

If we made the same call at a 60% discount during the night hours, it would cost:

(b) $.60 \times 20.7 = 12.42$
(c) $20.7 - 12.42 = 8.42$ or 8¢ rounded to the lower penny

What happens if you start your call in one rate period and end it in the next one? Charges are billed at the rate that applies for each period. So if you started your call Monday at 10:50 P.M. and talked for 18 minutes, you'd be billed overtime at the evening period rate for 5 minutes and at the night period rate for the next 8 minutes:

(a) $7.7¢ + (5 \times 1¢) = 12.7¢$
(b) $.35 \times 12.7 = 4.445$
(c) $12.7 - 4.445 = 8.255$
               +
(a) $(8 \times 1¢) = 8¢$
(b) $.60 \times .08 = .048$
(c) $.08 - .048 = .032$
_____
$8.255¢ + .032¢ = 8.287$ or 8¢

In making any kind of call, even a local one, you pay extra for such services as an operator-assisted person-to-person call ($3.75 by our telephone company!), an operator-assisted station-to-station call ($1.10), a calling card call and for billing the call to a third number. Discount rates never apply to these extra charges but continue to apply to the timed charges.

In the olden days, before deregulation, you had local calls and long-distance calls. Whatever happened to long-distance?

Here's how

LATA'S—LONG DISTANCE

LATA stands for Local Access and Transport Area. According to the phone company, "A LATA is a geographic area within which the local telephone company provides local and long-distance services, plus access to the telephone network." What this means is that for some defined distance beyond your local calling area your local telephone company provides you with long-distance service from one LATA to any other, even if the LATA's are served individually by the same company.

The New York Telephone Company has 6 LATA's. We live in the "metropolitan" one which covers our local calling area plus some other counties as well as parts of other states. According to our *Directory,* a call to part of Connecticut is a long-distance call handled by our local phone company. But a long-distance call to another part of that state would be handled by the company we have selected as our long distance carrier—AT&T, SPRINT, or MCI, to name the 3 largest competitors. This long-distance call is billed separately by the long-distance company (although the AT&T billing for residential long-distance calls is still included on the New York Telephone bill) and, in the case of companies other than AT&T, may involve separate dialing instructions.

As we said before, it's least expensive to make a direct dial long-distance call, whether within or outside your LATA and irrespective of which long-distance service you have bought. They all charge extra for extra services (like operator assistance), although the basic calling charge reflects distance, the time of day and day of the week you call and the length of your conversation.

The *Directory* lists some sample rates for long-distance calls within our LATA. Shown are full day rates (between 8:00 A.M. and 5:00 P.M.), 35% evening discounted rates (from 5:00 P.M. to 11:00 P.M.) and 60% night and weekend discounts from 11:00 P.M. to 8:00 A.M. and Saturdays and Sundays. Charges are based on the rates in effect at the place the call originates, and our telephone company has an initial one-minute period with each additional minute charged as overtime for long-distance calls within the LATA.

Our local phone company also offers a package that would be very attractive if we were planning to make several long-distance calls per month within our LATA—such as to a child attending a state college or to a special friend who has a job upstate. Check with your phone company to see whether they have similar deals.

Long-distance calls to other LATA's, even if those are within your local company's area, are not provided by your local company but by long-distance carriers. Rates for these types of long-distance calls are determined by the companies that provide these services. When examining rates, remember that you are comparison shopping; you'll want the least expensive service with the fewest "extra" charges, smallest monthly fees and best package deals to places you call frequently. But you also want reliable service and ease of dialing. Look for a company that has applied for "equal access!"

Until deregulation, all customers using traditional long-distance dialing procedures (a "1," where required, followed by the area code and phone number) had their calls handled by AT&T. Currently, local companies are modernizing their equipment and facilities to allow all long-distance companies that request it equal access to these traditional dialing procedures so their customers will no longer have to use more cumbersome dialing instructions. Shortly, your long distance company may have equal access privileges; if they signed up, they'll probably notify you of any changes in dialing procedures.

How does deregulation affect your bill?

Here's how

PHONE BILLS

Although for many residential customers who have chosen AT&T as their long-distance carrier there is still only one bill, the long-distance carrier charges are clearly separated. However, anyone using SPRINT or MCI, for example, receives a monthly bill from them as well as one from the local company.

Our phone bill is several pages long. Page 1 consists of a summary statement that includes the total amount of the last bill and the payments applied to it. It then shows the prior unpaid balance, if any, and the 1.5% per month (that's 18% annually) late payment charge.

Also on the summary are total current charges for local service, AT&T communications' charges (long-distance) and the due date of the bill after which any unpaid balance is subject to the interest penalty. The *total amount due,* incorporating all of the charges mentioned above, is clearly indicated.

What you should remember when examining your bill is that the charges for local service and equipment are *billed one month in advance,* while local usage, long-distance calls and any installation and/or repair charges are shown after the fact.

Let's turn to the back-up pages.

If you subscribe to AT&T for long-distance, the long-distance calls are itemized on page 2 of the "AT&T Communications" section of the bill. You get a printout of the date and time of each call, the location and number called, an indication of whether day, evening or night rates applied to that call, the length of the call (in minutes) and the amount of each call. Also shown is the total charge for all itemized calls.

There's also a "NY Tel Page 2" that details the current charges by your local telephone company. First, there's the "monthly service" charge which includes the monthly fee for the type of service you own plus the wire charges plus a charge for the dial tone. Also included by our telephone company is a new $1.00 subscriber line charge. Your local phone bill may contain this or a variety of other charges and/or credits.

Local usage totals appear next and should be fairly easy to interpret. Our bill shows the details of local usage for the local calling areas, together with the rates. Last month, for example, we made 63 calls to Area A during the day (no discount!) and spoke for 51 additional minutes. The number of calls we made to each of Areas B–F is also shown, as is the number of calls made during each time interval when different discounted rates were in effect. Total amounts are given for all the calls to each calling area and, these totals together with any local surcharges, amount to your "total local usage charge."

Knowing what you know now, if you take the time to examine your bill, you'll find it's pretty straightforward but, once upon a time, long ago . . .

Section 4: Keep Your Cool: Btu's and Air Conditioners

Buying an air conditioner, like buying any other major appliance, requires careful consideration. Not only is there style and price to worry about, but there's also Btu's and EER's.

You don't have to understand what a Btu is to buy an air conditioner or to use one, and understanding them won't keep you any cooler in the summer. But we think the concept behind Btu's is interesting and will give you a better feel for what air conditioners do.

Here's how

BTU's

Although on an intuitive level we all know what heat is, it was only about 150 years ago that scientists came to recognize that heat is a form of energy. One Btu *(British thermal unit)* is the quantity of heat (energy) that enters (or leaves) one pound of water when the temperature of the water is raised from 63°F to 64°F (or lowered from 64°F to 63°F).

In the metric system, the calorie is a measure of heat. One calorie is the quantity of heat (energy) that enters (or leaves) one gram of water when the temperature of this water is raised from 14.5°C to 15.5°F.*

A little computation would show that:

1 Btu = 252 calories

The output of air conditioners is rated in Btu's per hour because they must cool—lower the temperature—of your room(s). But how do you know how many Btu's are necessary for the size room(s) you wish to cool?
Here's how

THE PROPER AIR CONDITIONER SIZE

Actually, in this book we're not able to provide all the information needed to determine the right size air conditioner for you. But we'll tell you generally what you need to know and where to find additional information. We'll also give you a rule of thumb used by our local appliance dealer to get an approximation of your Btu needs.

Determining the proper air conditioner capacity warrants study. The size you need, measured in Btu's, is based on the size of your room, the height of the ceiling, the number of doorways and arches, the number of windows and the directions in which they face, the type of construction of your walls, whether you're cooling the top floor of the building or a lower floor, the electrical equipment you use and other minor factors.

You can come up with a rough estimate by *multiplying the square footage (area) by 30 for rooms on lower floors* and *multiplying the square footage (area) by 35 for rooms on the top floor* of the building. Thus, if your first-floor room measures 12 feet × 16 feet:

(1) Compute the area (see Chapter 11, Section 1):
    12 ft. × 16 ft. = 192 sq. ft.
(2) Multiply the area by 30: 192 × 30 = 5,760

---

*Reference temperatures such as 63°F or 14.5°C are used in definitions because the amount of heat needed for a one-degree rise in temperature varies a bit with temperature.

According to this guide, your air conditioner should be about 5,800–6,000 Btu's.

But this is only an approximation. It's worth the trouble to more precisely determine the right size. The Association of Home Appliance Manufacturers (AHAM) has developed a form that helps you to compute the Btu-per-hour capacity needed to properly cool your room. Ask your local appliance dealer for this form or to help you obtain a copy. Or write directly to the AHAM. Here's the address:

Association of Home Appliance Manufacturers
20 N. Wacker Drive
Chicago, IL 60606
(312) 984-5800

An adaptation of the AHAM form appeared in the *1983 Consumer Reports Buying Guide*. We used the *Consumer Reports* form and found it to be easy to follow and remarkably helpful. It saved us considerable money because it turned out we didn't need as large an air conditioning unit as we thought we did. An air conditioner that is too large serves no purpose and will cost you more money to purchase and to run. On the other hand, an air conditioner that is too small will never cool your room adequately—except maybe in the late fall or winter when it's already cool enough!

Another factor to consider in buying an air conditioner is its Energy Efficiency Ratio (EER).

Here's how

```
EER
```

The Energy Efficiency Ratio (EER) is *the ratio of net cooling capacity, measured in Btu's per hour, to the total rate of electrical input, measured in watts, under designated operating conditions*. This ratio is indicative of how efficiently the air conditioner will use electricity. The higher the EER, the more efficient the air conditioner and the less it costs to operate. EER's range from 4.0 to 12.0. Low efficiency units are rated 6.5 or less; the efficient ones have an EER of 8.5 or more. A unit with an EER of 4.0, for example, will cost about 3 times as much to operate as a model with a EER rating of 12.

In our local appliance store, the tag on one typical air conditioner said that it costs 13.5¢/hour in electricity to operate a 6,000 Btu air conditioner unit with an EER rating of 7.6. In contrast, it costs 11¢/hour to operate a more efficient (EER = 9.5) model of the same size by the same manufacturer. If you run your air conditioner for about 700 hours per year, the average number of operating hours for the New York area, you'll save $17.50 a year by using the more efficient unit. There'll be bigger savings if you have a larger-size air conditioner.

Generally, high efficiency air conditioners cost more than lower efficiency units of the same size. We priced two models recently, each of 6,000 Btu's. The one with the EER rating of 9.5 had a list price of $424, while the model with the lower EER rating (7.6) listed for $335. Based on purchase price alone, the higher cost of the energy-efficient air conditioner would take 5 years of average use to make up. If you expect your air conditioner to last longer, you will save money in the long run, and you'll be making a contribution to the conservation of our energy resources.

Whatever your choice, happy shopping and have a cool and efficient summer!

13

Room to Grow: Personal Computers

In this "computer age," it's hard to resist the push and pull of the deluge of advertisements and articles about personal computers. There are dozens of magazines devoted exclusively to them; business magazines are full of ads for computers and software programs; even your daily newspaper may have a regular computer column in addition to scores of articles about computers. They're constantly mentioned on television and radio and in nontechnical publications of all kinds. Schools clamor for more computers, and computer literacy is the talk of the day.

Essentially, personal computers (PC's) or home computers process sequences of coded instructions extremely rapidly. Their power and versatility stem from this ability to quickly and accurately follow commands. Their disadvantage is that they are quite inflexible and unforgiving. A misspelled command is completely incomprehensible to a computer; if it expects a colon and you accidently type in a semi-colon, for example, the computer will be totally baffled and unable to proceed.

In our opinion, not everyone needs a computer. But we do think that everyone should know a little about what they can do. To that end, this chapter covers some computer basics, to help you assess whether or not you really need a computer and to provide some guidelines on what to look for if and when you decide to buy one.

Here's how

WHAT COMPUTERS DO

The following are the most common uses of home computers (micro-computers), although not necessarily in the order of popularity:

- Video games
- Word processing
- Data manipulation
- Spreadsheet analysis
- Programming
- Telecommunications

We'll discuss these applications one by one.

Video Games

It wouldn't be unusual if your first introduction to PC's was through PACMAN. There's no question about it, video games are fast, exciting, absorbing and fun. It's easy to become "hooked." If you've never tried one, visit your local video arcade and try some out. At first, you may feel clumsy as you try to manipulate the figures on the screen with the *joystick* (the handle with the control buttons). It does require some good hand-eye and motor coordination. But after some time, and lots of quarters, you may find yourself eagerly trying to beat your own score.

Of course, not everyone enjoys games, and a game that appeals to one person may not appeal to another. However, if you generally enjoy this sort of thing, we have a feeling that you could get the video game bug. There are games written for just about every PC, certainly for all the major ones.

Should you spend between $500 and $3,000 on a computer *just* to play games? That's your choice, but your decision may also depend on what other uses you expect to make of your computer. If you want one just for games, buy the least expensive computer that has the largest number of games written for it. Ask your dealer to show you the catalog or list of available games.

Word Processing

Word processing is typing—but much, much better. It's an understatement to say that word processors are as much of an improvement over the old manual typewriter as the compact laser disc player is over the old Victrola.

When we speak of word processing capability, we really mean that a disk (the size of a 45 RPM record, or smaller) with thousands of instructions, collectively called a *word processing program,* is inserted into a slot in the computer (disk drive) and is "read" by the computer. By reading a disk containing instructions, computers learn how to do word processing or any other task.

Doing word processing means a person types at a computer keyboard and has the words appear on a computer screen or *monitor.* Ultimately, the text will be stored on a disk. When the person wishes, she can instruct the computer to read that disk and transmit the information on it to a *printer* (which looks like a typewriter without keys), where her material will be typed automatically.

The advantage to typing on a computer screen is that you can make corrections quickly and easily *before your work is actually typed (printed)!* Have you ever had to retype an entire page because you left out a word or a line or paragraph? With a word processor, that will never happen again. Every imaginable change can be made on the screen. Here are just a few of the things you can do, and it doesn't take terribly long to learn how:

* Type over and correct errors.
* Insert or delete words, lines or paragraphs.
* Interchange the order of words, sentences or paragraphs.
* Number pages automatically.
* Change from single-space to double-space and vice versa.
* Rearrange margins, making them narrower or wider.
* Center text automatically.
* Create special effects, such as boldface and shadow print.
* Type subscripts and superscripts.
* Automatically find and correct spelling errors.

There are many excellent word processing programs available for all kinds of personal computers. They are regularly reviewed in computer magazines. Your local computer store can also give you some idea of the options you have.

Does it pay to buy a computer *just* to do word processing? If you type 5 to 10 letters a week or an occasional term paper, probably not. But if you do a great deal of writing or typing, it's a remarkably worthwhile investment. It can result in a 25% to 50% increase in speed of production, mainly because of the ease with which errors can be corrected. And, for some reason, it seems to help many people compose: for them, looking at a blank screen is not as intimidating as staring at a blank piece of paper.

Data Manipulation

Data manipulation is *data base management,* which is another way of saying that PC's have the capability to organize all types of data. At home and on the job, people collect information (data) and keep it in files, note-books and on index cards. A data base management program consists of thousands of instructions to the computer which enable it to act as filing cabinet, index card file or telephone directory.

Data entered into the computer and handled by a data base management program is stored, in turn, on a disk (or disks) in a form that makes it very easy to retrieve. But a data base program enables you to do much more than just store and retrieve information. Here are some of the other possibilities:

- Randomly entered information can be quickly sorted alphabetically.
- In just a few moments, a computer file of addresses and telephone numbers can be sorted by city, state or zip code.
- A file of employee records can be almost instantly sorted by date of employment or by any other characteristic, if it is one of the items in the employee records.
- A checkbook file can print out and total all checks issued by cate-gory, if the category was part of the file.
- An inventory file can be used to print out a report of the total pur-chases made, by category.
- An index file of authors, books and articles on a variety of topics can be rapidly searched. For example, all works by a single author or all articles on a specific topic could be found and listed almost instanta-neously.

Do you need a data base management program? Probably not, unless you work with very large quantities of data like those involved in a small business or a major research project. Otherwise, it's simply not worth the effort of setting up a system which requires that you enter (by hand) every single letter and number into the computer file. If you have a file of, let's say, 100 addresses and phone numbers, you would do just as well keeping them in an address book, or in a card file or rolodex. But if you have 10,000 addresses and phone numbers and do mass mailings, you'd be foolish not to set up a data base system.

There are many excellent ones available either as stand-alone products or as part of integrated packages which include spreadsheet programs (which we discuss next). Read the reviews in computer magazines and consult your computer dealer for advice on which data base management program to buy.

Spreadsheet Analysis

Spreadsheet programs are also available singly or as part of a package that also consists of data base-type programs. The premier stand-alone package is Lotus 1-2-3, which includes graphics along with some other capabilities.

A spreadsheet program literally creates a *spreadsheet* on your monitor, so that your computer screen looks like *ledger paper*. Anything you could do in a ledger can now be done in the computer.

One of the more remarkable uses of a spreadsheet program is in making cash flow projections. If you own your own business, for example, you can put all your income and expenditures on the computer spreadsheet. With just a few keystrokes you can factor in a 10% increase in costs (as an illustration) and see the ripple effect on your balance sheet 6 months or one year or more later.

Another use of the spreadsheet program is to assist you in keeping your tax records. The advantage is that all columns and rows can be instantly and accurately tallied and, if you wish, the results passed on to a tax preparation program. Remember, though, that setting up such a spreadsheet takes a lot of work. Every number must be entered from the keyboard. There is no other way to do it.

It's hard to imagine how the computer's spreadsheet capability could be helpful to salaried people who have one major source of income. The effort in setting up the program to do income taxes, for example, is many times the amount of work of doing taxes by hand as they've always been done. On the other hand, spreadsheet analysis programs can be extremely useful to businesses that do or would like to do cash flow projections or scenario analysis.

Programming

Traditionally, most people associate programming with computers. But programming is not the primary use of home computers. The most common home computer applications are already *pre-programmed* for you.

Of course, programming a home computer yourself is not only possible, but some people also find it challenging and very interesting. It allows them to "customize" their computer environment is a way that no pre-packaged program can do. And programming yourself has the added benefit of giving you more insight into how the computer actually "thinks."

You communicate with the computer through a programming language, such as BASIC, PASCAL or COBOL. Commands (instructions to the computer) are written in the syntax of the language with which you are working. These commands are then translated into the machine language (which consists of strings of zeros and ones) that the computer understands.

All home computers understand the language BASIC. If you want to work with another language, it is necessary to buy another program, called a *compiler*, which translates the program in this language into machine language. With BASIC, by contrast, the translation into machine language is done automatically.

Telecommunications

It's now possible for your computer to "talk" to other computers through the telephone lines by means of a device called a *modem*. Signals from your computer are transformed into sounds (beeps) which are then transmitted along phone lines by the modem and picked up by another modem at the host computer. The sounds are then transformed back into computer signals that the other computer understands. Different modems are designed for different computers.

Many banks now have a special service which, for a fee, lets you view your bank records and transfer money via your home computer. There are also services you can buy that allow you to access the latest stock market activity on your computer screen. You can even see the latest airline schedule and book flights through your home computer.

The telecommunications capability is probably not sufficient reason by itself to buy a computer unless, for example, you have a very large investment portfolio and want to be able to follow the market on your own computer. However, if you already have a PC or are going to buy one, it's surely worth looking into the telecommunications possibilities that now exist.

The single most important factor in deciding which personal computer to buy is determining what the primary use of the computer will be.

Here's how

BUYING A PC

First and foremost, it's terribly important to be realistic and honest with yourself. It might sound like a terrific idea to use the computer with a database management program so that you can organize all your files and retrieve information quickly and easily. But will you do it? If you're not a really organized person, it's unlikely that you would actually spend the 20 to 100 hours it would probably take to create a computer filing system.

The most popular PC application is word processing. So let's suppose you decide you need a computer for this purpose. Your first step should be to *explore word processing packages, not computers*. Start by reading the reviews of the different packages that regularly appear in computer magazines. Go back to older issues. Go to a computer store and ask for a demonstration of particular packages that you think are of interest. Talk to the salespeople in computer stores; they're often very knowledgeable. Ask friends for their recommendations. *Think long-term.* Features like indexing and the checking of spelling may seem desirable, but ask yourself if you'll actually make use of them.

Once you've decided which word processing package is best for your real needs, and for those you think you may really have in the future, it's time to find out which computer will run that package. Each word processing program has its own memory and disk drive requirements. Some require only one disk drive; others require 2 drives.

Memory requirements generally range from 64K to 256K. The figure 64K means 64 *kilobytes* of internal memory. That's 64,000 *bytes*. You can think of a byte as a single character of information, like a single letter, number or special character, such as a dollar sign ($) or a plus sign (+).

You're almost ready, but not quite, to begin your search for the right computer. Doing word processing also requires buying a printer so that you can produce typed documents. It also requires a computer display (monitor or screen) that gives you sharp, clear, easy-to-read letters.

Letter quality printers will give you type with the clean, sharp look of a good typewriter. *Dot matrix* printers, which are faster than letter quality printers of the same price, produce letters that are made up of very closely spaced dots. The print looks good, but you can tell it was printed by a computer.

All PC's support dot matrix printers, but not all computers support letter quality ones. If you expect that letter quality output will be important to you now or in the future, be sure the computer you select supports this type of equipment.

Some computers come with the display built in, while for others you must purchase a separate monitor. Color monitors are nice to look at, and are essential for graphics or games, but they do not provide the resolution you need for word processing. To save eye strain, a monochrome monitor is a must for extensive word processing. Different manufacturers offer different monochrome monitors; you can get screens that have green letters on a black background, amber letters on a black background or black letters on a light blue background. Only you and your eyes know what's best for you.

Now that you know the requirements of your word processing program, monitor and printer, you can begin looking for computers that meet those minimum requirements. Other factors like versatility, price, portability and manufacturer's reputation are also important considerations. On most, but not all, computers you can easily add more memory and special circuit boards that will increase your computer's versatility. Will you be moving the computer from room to room so that other family members can use it? Some computers are designed to be portable; others are not. Many computer manufacturers have gone out of business, leaving the owners of their equipment with no place to go in case problems develop. Buy a reputable computer from a reputable dealer.

Prices of computers vary widely but have decreased in recent years. For example, in the fall of 1983, an additional 64K of memory cost between $100 and $150. Two years later, it cost between $8 and $10! Reputable mail-order houses and discount stores offer computer products at considerable savings, but they don't necessarily offer the kind of help, support and service that a good computer store will. In shopping for a computer, like shopping for any other substantial appliance, you need to decide what you most need and be willing to make the necessary trade-offs.

It's best to "try before you buy." Try out several PC's that meet your requirements. See if you like the keyboard and the look of the equipment. All other things being equal, buy what you like best.

We used the example of buying a PC that was to be mainly used for word processing. Similar considerations are involved when purchasing a computer for other primary applications.

For example, Lotus 1-2-3 (a spreadsheet program) requires 256K, but works best with 512K or more. Furthermore, you must have a color monitor to take full advantage of Lotus' graphics capabilities. Setting up a large data base (file) on your PC may require 256K or more of internal memory (RAM— Random Access Memory) *and* the addition of a hard disk drive with 10 or 20 megabytes (a megabyte is one million bytes) of storage capability for all of your data. What this means is that your PC must be able to support all this hardware. Almost all moderately priced PC's allow you to add on the hardware you'll need to run a program like Lotus, but for some it is extremely costly because of the way the computer is designed.

In contrast, a relatively inexpensive computer with very little memory is all that is needed for video games. IBM and IBM-compatible computers all support a vast library of games (as do Apple and Apple-compatible computers) and perform the other applications as well. There are some less expensive computers which also do just fine with a very wide selection of games, but which can only support relatively small word processing and data base programs.

Don't let cost be the only determining factor. If you decide to buy a computer and you choose thoughtfully, you'll find it a worthwhile investment. Buy one that is capable of doing a little more than you now think you might realistically need so as to allow yourself some room in which to grow. Your increased confidence and expertise will surely warrant it.

INDEX

Absolute scale
(temperature), 121
Accumulation Factor
(multiplier), 41-42T
Achievement scores in
mathematics, xv
Acre(s), 210, 214
Addition, xiv, 23, 27, 28
Air conditioners, 245-48
Airplanes, 151, 153
Algebra, 107
Ampere, Andre Maria, 234
Amps (amperes), 234, 235
Annual effective interest
rate, 76-83, 84-86
Annual effective yield,
45-48, 50, 51-52, 53, 84
Annual return, 53-54
Apple computers, 256
Appreciation (investment),
50, 51, 53, 60
Approximations: air
conditioner size, 246-47;
centimeters to meters or
inches, 129; currency
conversion, 112, 113;
inches to centimeters,
130-31; kilograms to
pounds, 132; kilometers

to miles, 130; liters to
quarts and ounces, 134;
loan payments, 68-70;
miles to kilometers, 131;
pounds to kilograms, 132-
33; restaurant bills, 97;
salary, 13; sales tax,
101-2; temperature
conversion, 124-27; see
also Estimating
Area, xiii, xvii; of
circles, 213; computing,
210-18; of rectangles,
211; of squares, 211; of
triangles, 211-12
Area measure conversion,
214, 215
Association of Home
Appliance Manufacturers
(AHAM), 247
AT&T, 55-56, 243, 244-45;
consumer sales and
services, 240
Automatic teller machines,
20
Automobile loans. See Car
loans
Average, 188-94

257